J.W.Drinkswater.

KU-417-499

Caught in a Mirror

Caught in

LISA MARTINEAU

a Mirror

REFLECTIONS

OF

JAPAN

M
MACMILLAN LONDON

First published 1993 by Macmillan London Limited
a division of Pan Macmillan Publishers Limited
Cavaye Place London SW10 9PG
and Basingstoke

Associated companies throughout the world

ISBN 0-333-54937-6

Copyright © Lisa Martineau 1993

The right of Lisa Martineau to be identified as the
author of this work has been asserted by her in accordance
with the Copyright, Designs and Patents Act 1988.

All rights reserved. No reproduction, copy or transmission
of this publication may be made without written permission.
No paragraph of this publication may be reproduced, copied or
transmitted save with written permission or in accordance with
the provisions of the Copyright Act 1956 (as amended). Any
person who does any unauthorised act in relation to
this publication may be liable to criminal prosecution
and civil claims for damages.

9 8 7 6 5 4 3 2 1

A CIP catalogue record for this book is available from
the British Library

Illustrations by Debbie Lian Mason

Typeset by Cambridge Composing (UK) Limited, Cambridge
Printed by Mackays of Chatham PLC

For Paul

This world –
call it an image
caught in a mirror –
real it is not,
nor unreal either

**Minamoto no Sanetomo (1192–1219),
shogun and sometime poet**

Contents

Acknowledgements

NOTE TO THE TEXT

As is the style within Japan, names are rendered surname first, forename last. With the exception of public personalities, most names have been changed. The English rendering of Japanese words is given on the first usage only, as are the dates of periods and events. There is a chronology and glossary at the back of the book.

SOURCES FOR EPIGRAPHS

Black Rain by Ibuse Masuji, translated by John Bester (Kodansha International): pages 43 and 54

Contemporary Japanese Literature: An Anthology of Fiction, Film and Other Writing Since 1945, edited by Howard Hibbett (Alfred A. Knopf, New York): pages 92, 207, 214, 241

From the Country of Eight Islands: An Anthology of Japanese Poetry, edited and translated by Hiroaki Sato and Burton Watson (Columbia University Press, New York): pages 15, 31, 35, 68, 85, 106, 115, 121, 127, 134, 140, 151, 159

Monkey Brain Sushi: New Tastes in Japanese Fiction, edited by Alfred Birnbaum (Kodansha International): pages 201, 219, 250, 253

New Japanese Voices: The Best Contemporary Fiction from Japan, edited by Helen Mitsios (Atlantic Monthly Press, New York): page 265

Quest for Prosperity: The Life of a Japanese Industrialist by Matsushita Konosuke (PHP Institute Inc, Tokyo): page 227

PROLOGUE

Behind my face
I can hide myself

Japan has always held an attraction for foreign misfits, which is odd since for many years it has been regarded as an intensely conformist country. These travellers, and sometimes settlers, seem to revel in the subterfuge of Japanese life, the sense of being present at a perpetual masquerade. This is equally true today. In Japan there are cupboards and drawers full of masks to be worn, several for each social setting. You never have to be yourself. In Japan yourself is circumstantial. This, like much of a foreigner's experience in this extraordinary country, is at once disconcerting and liberating.

Within Japan the most famous foreign oddball of all was Lafcadio Hearn, the tiny, half-blind, chronically morbid Anglo-Irish Greek who is still the country's favourite explainer of itself to the West. Hearn first came to Japan in 1890. This was only twenty years after the country had reopened to the world after over two and a half centuries in self-imposed isolation. Much of what Hearn chronicled in his twelve books on the country was startlingly familiar to me, sitting, one hundred years later, in the glass heart of Tokyo, the most restless modern city on earth, in a Japan one might have been forgiven for supposing had changed beyond all recognition from his time.

What Hearn saw in 1890 was a Japan that, having rejected all things foreign for so long, was contentedly being reared by the West, adopting industrialization and Western garb with great felicity, eagerly readying itself to become an imperial nation in the full Victorian sense of the word. Like now, it was all dressing up: a Western *omote* (façade/surface) over a Japanese *ura* (back or reverse). The cracks soon poked through. *Sonno joi!* – Revere the Emperor and expel the Barbarian! – the revolutionary rallying cry against the shogun (military dictator) of the 1868–9 Boshin War, which restored the emperor as an absolute monarch, soon became a war cry against *kokusaika* (internationalization) and the ever dangerous outside world. So, in the thirties, when Japan strutted upon the world's stage decked out in Prussian costumes and the trappings of Western Fascism, it did so with an enthusiasm that found its inspiration and justification in the Japanese cult of the emperor, who, as a direct descendant of the Sun Goddess, is half man, half god; a divine being.

The end of this particular episode of national madness found the country destroyed, literally flattened. There was scarcely a building left standing in Tokyo and other major cities after the Second World War. Hiroshima and Nagasaki seethed with the half-dead, as the grotesque survivors of the atomic bombings picked their way through the rubble of the twentieth-century nightmare. This was the birthplace of post-war Japan, a Japan that would have a new future and a new past. Overnight this aggressively military nation could refashion, without the necessity of reconciling itself to the atrocities it had committed, into a 'peace-loving nation' proud of its 'peace constitution'.

Nearly fifty years on Japan is a feared nation once again, not for its fanatical military might, but for its apparent economic mastery. The masks Japan wears slip and slide; and the filter of latent orientalism through which we see the Japanese (without perhaps realizing that we do so) distorts. In the half century since the war the West's view of Japan and its people has undergone, like the beast in the fairy tale, metamorphic change. From the down-trodden defeated enemy, to a comic little country producing comic little goods that fall apart, to a place of artistic and spiritual refinement, to the home of the purveyors of economic miracles and hardworking producers of well-priced quality goods, to a devious and untrustworthy country that is out to destroy the West.

That this last feeling is increasing mutual, that many Japanese believe the United States, as proxy for the West, is out to destroy them – to such an extent that young people firmly expect they will have to fight a war with America – is almost completely unknown in the West. As it was in the 1890s it is in the 1990s: the Japanese know much more about us than we know about them.

So much of Japanese life is concealed behind a veil of form, shrouded by manners, tightly circumscribed codes of behaviour that have been constructed over the years to wall people in. To keep the (internal) peace, to keep the populace under control, has been the primary goal of Japan's leaders since the country was first unified by the shogun at the turn of the seventeenth century, finally bringing to a close centuries of civil wars. Social control was turned into an art in the Tokugawa period (1603–1868). Classes and castes were codified, their dress, language and food precisely controlled.

Today, so much effort is still expended on social control, perhaps because so much is needed. What is interesting in a country that sees its central attribute as *wa* (harmony), that sees itself as a society based on consensus, is the extent and profundity of conflict. Japanese society may be group-oriented, as opposed to individualistic, but it is a collection of *antagonistic* groups. Every era of Japanese history, including this one, has been one of intense internal strife. Even in the Tokugawa period of 'peace and unity', *ikki* (popular uprisings) continued apace. And during the Second World War there was serious rioting in Tokyo when the poor discovered through billeting that the rich were indeed different. After the war there was a clamour for social change and the removal of the 'emperor system', a lust for democracy. As in much of the West the unions grew strong and militant, and the young restless. In the sixties Tokyo burned just like Paris. But, unlike their French, British or American counterparts, Japanese rebels are born into a society in which the proverb 'Hammer down the nail that sticks out' is branded on to their DNA. What is remarkable in Japan is not, as is often thought, that it is a nation of conformists, but that anyone has the energy or wherewithal not to conform, so all enveloping are the mechanisms of social control.

Containment of unrest until the protest runs out of steam is one relatively benign method; containment that can continue for years, to the point of absurdity. Most visitors unknowingly ride past one of these hidden theme-parks of unrest when they enter Japan through its principal port of Narita airport, fifty miles out-side of Tokyo. The journey to the capital begins on a motorway much like any other, complete with the usual motorway country-side of bushes and a few trees, scenery that might as well have been airbrushed on so unnatural does it look. If you live in London or New York and have long since grown used to a generalized public squalor, you might be struck by the lack of litter everywhere and what appear to be recently scrubbed roads. Or perhaps, as the bus lurches out of the airport on to the expressway, you may notice, perched up on wide wooden plat-forms resembling oil rigs, tall steel grey watchtowers that envelop the airport and surrounding area. If you look carefully you will see that the towers are completely encased with barbed wire and guarded by what may be samurai (warriors), members of the old military caste who had a penchant for flamboyant armour.

Although it is not particularly obvious to the tired and disoriented, the efficient-looking airport is still only partly built, thirty years after the first bucket of concrete was poured, making the name of Narita synonymous with, and a catalyst for, violence and heroics that have continued unabated for a generation. For the left-wing protesters, stopping Narita's construction soon became imbued with amorphous symbolic meaning, like no other cause in Japan.

The gentlemen resembling samurai are Japan's riot police. They are shaped like triangles with heavy, densely padded long tunics covering most of their thick blue uniforms, a bulbous padded contraption tied around their necks to match, helmets with long leather flaps at the back and transparent visors that cover the whole face. Their hands, bloated with gloves as broad as baseball mitts, clutch broom-handle length wooden staves and elongated curved metal shields. They are dressed in these cumbersome uniforms all through the frigid winters and sweltering summers, ever ready to do battle again with their sworn enemies, the hotchpotch army of old farmers and young militants who are hidden behind the airport perimeter fence in the village of Sanrizuka, the proposed site for the completion of Narita airport. Perhaps concerned that Japan's promotion of itself as the land of *wa* will be belied, the government has ensured that you cannot see Sanrizuka from the motorway: the fence is egregiously high.

When I first went to Sanrizuka, about a year after I had come to Japan, and discovered what was going on behind that fence on the motorway, fifty miles outside of the capital of the second richest nation on earth, it at once became to me a metaphor for this country, a perfect illustration of the *sub rosa* mentality that permeates Japanese life, bleaching it to the roots: *tatemae* (face), the way things are said to be, behind which is hidden *honne* (real intention), the way things are; or *omote* and *ura*. Underneath the civilized *omote* of the smoothly run airport lurked the *ura* of violence and unfinished business that had delayed even its partial construction for seven years and continues to stop its completion.

For the tourist or the business person on the bus, the usual encounter with this dualism will be to discover that no matter how good your Japanese language skills, or how precise your translator, what is being said is not necessarily what is meant. As a former prime minister, Takeshita Noboru, said, 'I speak clearly but my meaning is obscure.' So do his countrymen. A phrase such as, 'I will do my utmost to ensure that the situation is satisfactorily resolved,' does not necessarily mean, 'Yes, I'll do it,' or even 'I'll do my best,' but rather, as often as not, 'I can't do it for some reason, but I expect you to respect my sincerity in wishing it was otherwise.' 'It's difficult', generally speaking, means 'no', especially when accompanied by a sharp prolonged intake of breath. Getting to 'no' can be as torturous as getting to 'yes'. This isn't to say that one's friends talk in this way for this is the language of public discourse between strangers, the language of *tatemae*. The Japanese can be frank to the point of rudeness when they know you. Like anyone they can say exactly what they mean and do exactly what they say they will. The function of *tatemae* and *honne* is essentially political, another method of control for the élite, a giant game of 'let's pretend' in which everyone is forced to take part. Those who will not play become extremists of one sort or another. For the ordinary person, however, the *tatemae/honne* dualism can be useful: as a place to hide from the madding crowd, from the rules and regulations, as an area of *puribashi* (privacy), a concept which is aggressively discouraged. 'Behind my face I can hide myself,' my friend Junko explained.

Much of the completed part of the airport stands on land once owned by the emperors, which has a certain irony. One of the things the farmers say they are 'fighting to the death' to protect by refusing to be 'bribed' into selling their homes and lands, is what the emperor is supposed to embody: the 'traditional Japanese way of life', which is to say rice cultivation and village society. As is often the case in Japan, the traditional way of life as exemplified here is actually of recent vintage: Sanrizuka was given to repatriates after the Second World War. The land was poor and the farmers poorer. They had to clear it themselves, often with their bare hands, and build their own houses if they wanted somewhere to sleep, which partly accounts for the depth of feeling the farmers have for this land.

When it can the Airport Corporation bulldozes the fields, destroying crops and soil, but the farmers do not give up and many of the fields in and around Sanrizuka not only bear crops but also makeshift wooden fortresses bristling with slogans and barbed wire. These shambolic abodes are occupied by members of small ultra left-wing cells, such as Chukuka ha, the Middle Core Faction, one of the most notorious and, by its own description, successful terrorist groups in Japan. At last count seventeen of Japan's radical groups had taken up the farmers' cause and are now resident in the area. There have been several disputes between the farmers and Chukuka ha, which has tried to wrest leadership from the old people, and some of the farmers have erected their own watchtowers abutting their houses. These are emblazoned with banners touting allegiance to one or the other factions of the Sanrizuka-Shibayama Rengo Kuko Hantai Domei (Sanrizuka-Shibayama Farmers' League Against the New Tokyo Airport), thankfully usually shortened to Hantai Domei. From the watchtowers farmers and/or radicals watch the riot police watching them. Any encroachment by airport officials or surveyors on to the farmers' side of the fence is invariably met with force.

Prior to the choice of their village for the airport, most of the farmers, as is usual here, were lukewarm supporters of the ruling Liberal Democratic Party (LDP), a coalition of centre-right factions which looks set to govern in perpetuity. Now the farmers of Sanrizuka have become radical extremists. Certainly their rhetoric is no less incendiary than that of the ultra left radicals. To the farmers, Sanrizuka has become 'a fortress of people's struggles in the whole of Japan,' from where they find themselves in 'diametrical violent confrontation with state power'. In a major land survey for the outer rim of the airport 1600 men from the Airport Corporation accompanied by 10,000 riot police fought pitched battles with hundreds of farmers who sprayed them with barrels of human faeces and urine. At other times the farmers have fought the police with hoes and sundry farm inplements, using martial arts techniques that were widely taught during the Second World War for defence of the homeland in case of invasion. Half a dozen people have been killed so far in these periodic clashes, hundreds injured and hundreds more imprisoned.

The farmers say that they mistrust the government because the Japanese people were 'misled and betrayed' during the Second World War. They are virulently anti-war and, at first, suspected that the airport would be used as a station for shipping American GIs to Vietnam. They still refer to it, twenty years after the end of Vietnam, as 'Sanrizuka military airport' because they think, or say they think, that the government wants the airport for military purposes. What they really seem to object to, however, is the overwhelming extent of government power in Japan; what they really seem to fear is that, as during the Second World War, there is no real check on this power.

The riot police have become used to dealing with the young women of the ultra left, some of whom, such as the leader of the Japanese Red Army, occupy positions of high command in these groups, and are, if anything, more violent and single-minded than their male colleagues. The police seem, however, to have been taken aback by the *obaasan* (the generic term for old women) of the Hantai Domei who have proved most irksome. One *obaasan*, close to ninety years old, allowed radical students to build a watchtower and fort on her farm. When the police attacked the fort she too showered them with faeces and urine – always in plentiful supply as, like millions of other Japanese throughout the country, the villagers are not on the mains. (Tokyo has unclosed ditch-like sewers running beneath its streets.) But the police, many from farm families themselves, seemed to have been most shocked by the obscenities which emitted from her mouth: 'She could have been my grandmother,' one said plaintively. Another *obaasan* shrieked at the police that if they wanted to remove her from her home they would have to put their staves up her vagina. With this she pulled up her kimono revealing said vagina and the brave young officers fled into the night.

To walk through the middle of Sanrizuka is to be followed by hundreds of faces bulging with binoculars. The police, the Hantai Domei and the militants all watch where you go and to whom you talk. As a matter of course, the police, in plain clothes but with those unmistakable ear-pieces, cruise up and down the village in unmarked jeeps. This amuses the farmers. Even with the militant groups, there are only four hundred households in the village. Everyone knows everyone else. At the centre of the village is a crossroads. One way is blocked by a chain-link electrified gate surrounded by barbed wire. In front of the gate are four lines of riot police. On either side are watchtowers and the sort of big barrel spotlights used in prisons. Attached to the gate is an electrified fence. Through the fence you can see Narita's main runway and terminals and the airport control tower that in 1978, just before the airport was due to be officially opened, the Hantai Domei managed to take over.

Although groups such as Chukuka ha regularly make largely ineffectual terrorist attacks on buildings, firing homemade pipe bombs at imperial and government sites, they have agreed with the farmers not to bomb airport targets or do anything that would endanger the public. If they did, the government would likely move into Sanrizuka with dreadful force; as it is, the government is in what it might term 'a delicate situation'. Throughout the country farmers are its traditional support base, and farmers are not best pleased at what they see as a too liberal food import policy. Moreover, to confront the farmers of Sanrizuka means to confront some of the hidden truths about the war, which in turn is to come face to face with the long murky shadow of the previous emperor, Hirohito, and his 'war guilt', something the government will do almost anything to avoid. For it is here that the flimsily constructed post-war *omote* that Japan was virtually an innocent bystander in the war hides the terrifying *ura* of the way Japanese society was and is controlled.

The Imperial Palace in Tokyo, like Sanrizuka, cannot be seen from the road, the rather plain wooden structures are secreted away from view. An emperor is not a king, he is not for gaudy display. He is the still centre to some, the apex of feudalism to others, yet even now an unequivocal god to millions. To most he symbolizes the continuity of the Japanese people, the vein through which their blood flows. The palace sits at the centre of the frantic sprawling capital, hidden within a tangle of thick, dark green silence, a seemingly dormant octopus's head. The emperors of Japan have, since the imperial restoration, occupied this site, on what was previously the shogun's castle. These 128 acres of palace grounds have been valued at more than the entire state of California. In Japan statistics dazzle like a window full of fake jewellery. But no matter how much the grounds are worth on the computer screen, the palace is still the place where the country begins and ends; the font of all its myths, ritual and form. It is here that our journey into Japan shall begin.

THE
EMPEROR'S
NAKED
ARMY
MARCHES
ON . . .

*As winter comes, the sound
from the valley stream stops,
   and a wind from the mountain
visits my window*

PRINCESS SHIKISHI (DIED 1201)

As Hirohito lay dying that last winter of the 1980s a new
Japan was struggling to be born, one that would be freed of the
'yoke and burden of 1945', freed from the 'era of shame' that
followed the ignominious defeat of the Second World War. This
meant wildly differing things to different people – from a more
democratic society in concert with the world, to the reinstatement
of the emperor's divinity and the return of Japan as a military
power. But for most people, X-Day, as the forthcoming unknown
date of the Emperor's death was officially referred to (with oblique
provisos such as 'X-Day – which we hope won't be for many
years yet' or 'X-Day – if it should ever come'), would nevertheless
be the last day of the Second World War, and the first day in the
life of a new Japan.

The Emperor's protracted death-bed scene lasted, almost
continuously, for over a year. His dying produced a sense of crisis
and confusion in the country, underlying which was the problem
of the Emperor's 'war guilt', or 'war responsibility' as it is more
usually called. While he was alive, the question of to what extent
he was responsible for Japan's Pacific misadventures could not be
asked. Although, in surveys that offered a measure of confiden-
tiality, a quarter of the population admitted they believed in the
Emperor's 'war responsibility', the government, and of course
right-wing thugs, ensured that the subject was taboo in public
discourse. Anyone, such as Motoshima Hitoshi, the Mayor of

Nagasaki, who said a month before Hirohito's death that 'the Emperor bore some responsibility for the war', was dealt with 'severely' – in Mayor Motoshima's case by being thrown out of the LDP and then shot and almost killed by a member of the *uyoku*, the violent ultra nationalist groups.

The police estimate that there are about 800 *uyoku* groups in the country with several hundred thousand activists. Some are financed by, or are part of, the *yakuza*, the Japanese gangster syndicate, the self-styled samurai of the underworld. The *yakuza* in turn have been known to finance and/or assist some of Japan's powerful right-wing politicians. The presence of the *uyoku*, who too often make good on their ubiquitous death threats, creates a climate of terrorized silence around controversial issues, loosely defined as any statement or position that these groups see as 'betraying the Japanese race'. Death threats by the *uyoku* groups are so routine that after a while I failed to take them seriously, failed to remember that they are sometimes carried out.

The slightest infraction can bring down the wrath of the *uyoku*, who have taken it upon themselves to issue the Shinto (the native religion) equivalent of a *fatwa* when any tenet of their faith is maligned. A journalist on the *Asahi Shimbun*, a broadsheet with a circulation of almost thirteen million, was killed for 'betraying the Japanese race' when he wrote a story about a Korean man who was roughed up by the police. And when Oshima Nagisa, the director of films such as *In the Realm of the Senses (Ai No Corrida)* and *Merry Christmas, Mr Lawrence*, did something as mild as calling Hirohito 'Tenno-chan' on television, using the familiar appellation of 'chan' customarily reserved for children or loved ones and dear friends, he too found himself under a death threat, for insulting the Emperor by humanizing him.

The 'new' *uyoku* groups, such as Nippon Seinensha, the Japan Youth Fellowship, eschew theatrical tactics favoured by the old guard, such as paramilitary uniforms and trucks blaring martial music and concentrate instead on recruiting young people, using the same wine-and-dine procedures as corporate Japan. They wear blue *sarariman* (salary man, Japan's term for its male white collar workers) suits with a rising sun flag-pin in their lapels. Nippon Seinensha, one of the most prominent of the new breed, claims to have sixty branches throughout Japan with three thousand hardcore activists. Like all *uyoku*, they believe that 'selective' terrorism against powerful 'anti-nationalists', such as Motoshima, is desirable. They also see the media as the main enemy of the 'Japanese race', and oppose with strong-arm tactics 'violence of the pen' and 'media terrorism', which is to say anyone who writes anything contrary to their beliefs. The group's leader, Nakagawa Seijo, admits that he is a 'consultant member' of the Tokyo-based *yakuza*, Sumiyoshi Rengo, one of the three most powerful *yakuza* organizations in the country.

For an ordinary person, depending upon his or her political perspective, the Second World War still tends to be seen as either unjust 'aggression by the military', or a just war because 'the white race had turned Asia into a colony'. Always, one way or another, it is the military marching alone, onward, without reference to, permission from, or approval of, the emperor, the people, or the government; a law and a country unto itself. In these scenarios, the Army and Navy are the collective Hitler, a severed head, blamed or acclaimed for the Fifteen Years War, as the Second World War, which began with the Sino-Japanese War in 1931, was for Japan. Everyone else, including Emperor Hirohito, are innocent, passive victims of circumstance: '*shikatta ga nai,*' there was nothing to be done.

The effort expended by the government to control what was said and thought about the dying Emperor bordered on the fantastic. Much of this effort was directed towards the unruly representatives of the foreign press, who were treated to constant debriefings by so-called imperial experts. The essential message was the same: the Emperor had no power to prevent the war from starting yet could use his powers to stop it but only at the late hour that he did so. When Edward Behr's BBC documentary *Hirohito: Behind the Myth* was due to air on American television, the Gaimusho, foreign ministry, hauled in the top American correspondents and went over it with them frame by frame, disputing Behr's claims that the Emperor knew and sanctioned what went on during the war, including of course the atrocities.

No opportunity was missed to convince the foreign press of Hirohito's innocence and what was written was carefully monitored and commented upon. I was rebuked for writing that the Emperor, who was in a coma at the time, was dying of cancer (which he was) on the grounds that (a) it wasn't true and (b) that it might get back to him. Patients in Japan are usually not told they have cancer, or any other serious illness, and no Japanese paper printed this fact until the Emperor had died, at which time the court doctor announced the cause of death. At one point, after an article I wrote about a prominent Japanist (a pre-war term still best used to describe the intellectual ultra nationalists who regard Japan as a religion and being Japanese its practice) was quoted from and commented upon in the Japanese press, my telephone showed every sign of having been tapped.

The Japanese press often reports on foreign coverage about Japan as a way of discussing subjects that are taboo. Japanese journalists, if they wish to keep their jobs, write the Party line. The slightest mistakes in imperial coverage are acts of *lèse-majesté*: a hapless editor on a national daily inadvertently pressed the wrong button and printed, before the event, an editorial entitled 'End of Showa' (Enlightened Peace), which was the name of Hirohito's era and by which the late Emperor is posthumously known in Japan. The editor was forced to resign, as were those responsible for printing a photograph of Hirohito in reverse on the cover of a popular woman's weekly magazine.

During Hirohito's illness the Japanese media mostly just chronicled his condition, and carefully itemized the respect shown by his subjects throughout the country. Graphs measuring his temperature, his blood pressure, his pulse and respiration rates, and the number and quantities of his blood transfusions appeared daily on the front pages of the newspapers and on the television screens. TV had the edge: the graphs, with their indecipherable blocks and squiggles, wavy and dotted lines, were, like the weather forecast, explained by a man with a long stick. '*Tenno heika . . .*' ('Celestial Emperor whom one regards from below . . .') the broadcasts and reports began, going on to detail the countrywide acts of *jisshuku* (self-restraint) being practised by the people in respect for their dying emperor.

Acts of *jisshuku* included the postponement of weddings, such as that of the pop star Itsuki Hiroshi, a £250,000 bash that was to have been televised live, and the routine cancellation of parties and concerts. Athletic meetings and sports events compromised, as one newspaper reported, by 'decreasing music volume, using whistles instead of pistols to start races, restricting firecracker use, removing decorative flags, withholding showy events, and restricting the *banzai*, may you live ten thousand years, cheer after the races or game.' *Banzai*, a salutation to the emperor, was the battle cry used by Japanese troops during the Second World War.

Weekly magazines such as *Gendai* and the *Weekly Post* stated that they 'will not carry the usual nude pictures of women on their front pages, but instead will feature more serious articles'. Bad taste was out too: a movie company scrapped its 'abusing contest' which was set to promote its film *You Idiot*. Showings of Hara Kazuo's documentary *The Emperor's Naked Army Marches On* were also cancelled. The film's subject was Okuzaki Kenzo, a former imperial foot soldier, who in the sixties had catapulted pinballs (which missed the target) at Hirohito as he was standing on the palace verandah giving his New Year's address, in order to make the Emperor 'take responsibility' for his wartime acts. Okuzaki also wanted his former troop leaders to 'take responsibility' for their wartime actions, and much of the film is taken up with his often hilarious confrontations with these men. The film was an art-house hit in Japan, but as one cinema owner put it, 'It is not appropriate to show this film when the nation is hoping for the Emperor's recovery.' Hara was furious. 'It makes me so angry to think that post-war democracy is meaningless if my film has to be cancelled,' he said.

Commercials were re-written: Nissan removed the phrase 'Are you feeling good?' from one of its TV ads, other companies erased the words 'new', 'congratulations' and 'birth' from their copy. And on days when Hirohito's vital readings were especially gloomy, some TV stations replaced comedy programmes with nature films. Even Tokyo Disneyland got in on the act, deciding, oddly, to 'refrain from holding fireworks displays on the weekends, but to go ahead with Mickey Mouse's birthday party'. Some companies asked their OLs (office ladies), the secretaries and clerks who are required to wear uniforms while in the office, not to wear bright colours to and from work. Other companies issued black armbands to all their staff in readiness for X-Day.

The government, which at first stated that it would not change its normal procedures, soon began cancelling overseas trips and 'discouraging' foreign dignitaries and delegations from visiting Tokyo. The ministries, and some of the companies, not wanting to be seen as violating the spirit of the constitution – which states that the emperor is the symbol of the people (not the head of state) – nor as behaving as they would have done in the thirties, denied that they were practising *jisshuku* and claimed their actions were just a 'coincidence', nothing at all to do with the Emperor's illness.

The government in Japan is many headed, a government of competing bureaucracies over which the elected officials, who are themselves members of competing political factions within their own parties, have limited influence. At times of crisis this becomes transparent. The Kunaicho, the Imperial Household Agency, an archaic and arcane bureaucracy of geriatric royal retainers, refused to allow the prime minister to enter Hirohito's bedroom to see for himself the condition of the Emperor. The Kunaicho eked out the information on the Emperor to the cabinet and the public, often belatedly, and frequently full of grotesque detail but little substance. In the last few months of Hirohito's life there were constant rumours, even in very top government circles, that the Emperor was already dead and that the Kunaicho was awaiting the most auspicious day for a person to die to announce the fact. Obuchi Keizo, the then cabinet secretary, complained that the cabinet was not receiving timely or complete information from the Kunaicho. Privately aides went further: 'We are being kept completely in the dark. We have no idea what is really going on across the moat,' one said.

The opposition parties became inarticulate with rage at all this, clinging on to the Church and State separation clause in the American-writ constitution, wrathful against the 'unconstitutional' get-well registers set up by the national and local governments; and accusing the media of manipulation by, as Doi Takako, the then leader of the Socialist Party, stated, 'creating an environment in which the Emperor is being treated like a living god again.' Doi was frightened by what she called the 'momentum of hysteria' surrounding the Emperor's death.

The streets were tense and full of riot police. Day after day hundreds and thousands of mourners waited on the parade grounds outside the palace gates to sign the get-well registers, a scene that was repeated daily in every city, town and hamlet in the land, despite the relentless pounding rain. As time passed, the government, which was embroiled in a parliamentary how-many-angels-can-dance-on-a-pinhead debate about Hirohito's status as a head of state who wasn't a head of state, arrived at a position on the Emperor's war guilt. The Gaimusho spokesman stated: 'Fundamentally, the issue is the same as the [censorship of] textbook cases, or the political comments made by some people in the past referring to the war. It is a matter of history and how we look at it – from what angle, on what basis, with what philosophy, and with what sort of sense of responsibility.' In other words, there is no truth, only changeable points of view.

Most official Japanese documents which would have helped clarify imperial and other 'responsibility' were destroyed in the two weeks between surrender and the arrival of the occupation forces. Arguments of Hirohito's culpability have to be based almost entirely on eye-witness accounts or private records that escaped the official bonfires and have subsequently made their way into print, such as *aide de camp* Kido Koichi's diaries, and documents and records belonging to the Allies. And, of course, on Hirohito's legal standing at the time.

The essence of the Meiji constitution, which was in force until the end of the war, was the inviolable sovereignty of the emperor, who held supreme political power. The cabinet and the parliament operated independently of each other; the cabinet was appointed by the emperor and was responsible to him. The emperor had legislative superiority over the Diet (parliament), and the sole right to some executive powers such as treaties. The Army and Navy were directly responsible to him, outside of the control of either the cabinet or parliament. Moreover the emperor was a living god. According to the government, however, despite this clearly delineated power structure, and the emperor's godliness, Hirohito was somehow hijacked by the military and had no control over events except, finally, to end the war.

It became clear as time passed that many eminent Japanese historians and intellectuals had always thought this official answer to be total nonsense, but had observed the 'imperial taboo' and would not have commented on it in the unlikely event they had been asked. A few months before Hirohito died I received a phone call from a historian representing, 'The Historical Science Society of Japan, the Japanese Society for Historical Studies, the History Educationalists Conference of Japan and the Association of Historical Scientists,' he said, reeling them off like a laundry list. They had, he told me, written a paper on Hirohito's wartime role, addressing the question of 'responsibility', and wanted to know if I would be interested in receiving a copy. However, he would not allow me to see the paper, even embargoed, until X-Day, nor would he indicate the paper's general position or direction. Moreover, he requested that I did not tell anyone of the existence of this document before X-Day, when he promised it would be biked round to me 'the very moment the death is announced'.

My contacts at the TV stations took the same line as the historians: 'hitherto unseen footage' about the war would be shown, but the stations refused to give any indication of what this footage might contain, stating that they had said too much in revealing this. It appeared to be as Kase Hideaki (adviser to prime ministers, political commentator, expert on the Imperial Family, rabid Japanist and Yoko Ono's cousin) had said: 'The Emperor exerts an almost occultist power over our nation.' This is what Doi and the others feared. It was a taste of the pre-war atmosphere. 'The starting point for democracy in Japan is being able to question the Emperor's wartime role while he is alive,' said the Reverend Tomura Masuhiro, head the United Church of Christ, a leading Protestant denomination in Japan, 'and we are nowhere near that.'

The newspapers continued to allude to X-Day scenarios, as did the government, which was concerned about uncontrollable outpourings of grief 'if X-Day occurs'. Contingency plans were underway to counteract outbreaks of mass hysteria resulting in the likelihood of hundreds, perhaps even thousands, of people committing *junshi* (suicide at the death of one's lord). Then, according to the government, there was the radical left, such as Chukuka ha, to contend with, whose members were likely to attempt to blow up Shinto shrines and government or imperial buildings in protest against the 'emperor system' as they had done in the past. Pitched battles in the streets between the extremes of left and right were predicted for X-Day, and so to thwart this expected mayhem the government arranged for the biggest security operation ever to come into full force.

Then Hirohito was finally dead. Helicopters swarmed over the dirty grey shell of the early morning sky, buzzing and circling like angry wasps. Teams of riot police searched cars coming into the city; others continued with the seemingly random house searches that had become a daily occurrence, as normal as lunch. The US government believed the Japanese predictions. The Far East Network, the US forces station, played funereal music interspersed with dire announcements warning service men and women not to go off base, under any circumstances, in their military uniforms, and to ensure that in any conversation they had with the native population they showed the proper respect for the dead Emperor.

That gloomy seventh day of January was an auspicious day to die, arousing further suspicions that the Emperor may have been dead for several days, perhaps longer, before the Kunaicho made it public. The proclamation was made live on television in the early hours of Saturday morning, first, naturally, by the Kunaicho and then by the cabinet, continuing their power battle in an unseemly scramble over who said what and when. The Kunaicho continued to refuse, for the most part, to speak to the foreign press, and maintained its hardline position that no foreigners, including royalty and other heads of state, should be invited to the funeral.

Hundreds of thousands of people milled about on the parade grounds outside of the palace waiting to sign their names in the book of last respects. Having listened for so many months to the grim prognosis on the state of the nation on this day, I was wary, watchful for outbreaks of violence that could so easily be directed at the few foreigners at hand as they had in times of crisis in the past. Instead faces turned towards me wreathed in smiles, many of them country faces full of curiosity and amusement at seeing their first *gaijin* (foreigner). There was almost a carnival atmosphere so contrary to that which had prevailed in the months leading up to X-Day. People were relaxed, chatting with each other, jostling and crowding around the TV cameras that had come in a futile search for their despair and rage.

Despite a televised request from the cabinet secretary for the public to don mourning, hardly anyone had done so: jeans and casual attire dominated. No one could properly understand what Heisei, the name of the new era, meant: 'Peace within and without at home and abroad' is how the Gaimusho explained it, later contracting it to a more elegant and manageable 'The achievement of universal peace'. 'The *kanji* [Chinese ideographs used predominately in the Japanese writing system] is too high,' a woman mourner said. 'Perhaps it is court language.' She was smiling broadly. 'It doesn't matter, Heisei is the new Japan!'

Japan is still on imperial time, or rather a pragmatic compromise of imperial years and Western months and days. Overnight the sixty-third year of Showa had ended and the first year of Heisei had begun. It was year one again. A great weight had been lifted from the country, as if Japan's equivalent of the Berlin Wall had fallen: something which had cruelly divided a people had gone. The press and photographers were everywhere, stampeding from one end of the parade grounds to the other, surrounding the one or two people who were trying to pray, searching for the story that was supposed to be happening. A group of photographers almost knocked over a lone ancient man garbed in full imperial military attire, who was standing in front of the palace moat, saluting the passing of his Emperor.

According to the advanced billing there should have been thousands of mourners like the old soldier and the couple I had seen earlier that morning, prostrate on the ground, their noses touching the gravel, bowing towards the palace. All day outside the palace there were no more than two dozen. Only a handful of old people up and down the country committed *junshi*; there was no great outpouring of grief; no mass hysteria and no violent clashes between the extremes of left and right on the country's streets. Instead there was open relief; relief, as one mourner said, to enthusiastic nods, 'that the Showa era is finally at a close'.

Over that weekend the television stations weighed in, mixing their anodyne eulogies with, as they had promised, footage of the war, hitherto unseen (in this country). The carnage was juxta-posed with pictures of Hirohito at his most generalissimo in military regalia astride his white horse (white being the Shinto colour of purity). The soundtrack was mostly silent, but the old advertising trick of associating one image with another was effective. The message was clear. 'Hirohito was the person with supreme responsibility in militaristic Japan,' the hitherto secretive historians now wrote, and therefore responsibile for it, including the final slaughter that befell the Japanese people at Okinawa, Hiroshima and Nagasaki.

The sun flags and official buildings were draped in black silk. The cabinet announced it would be in mourning for six days. But by early Saturday evening people were already queuing up at the video stores and the cinemas to get some relief from the constant Hirohito tableau which blanketed their television screens. The cabinet secretary had said that places of entertainment would close. They didn't. As night fell over Roppongi, Tokyo's young fashionable nightlife district, the boom, boom, boom of the discos could be heard. This was a very Japanese story. Up until X-Day the majority of people went along with *jisshuku* and enforced reverence. It was a question of *tatemae* hiding *honne*, the public face sheltering private feelings. After Hirohito was dead the mask, at least to a certain extent, could be lifted.

The Japanese had not always been as publicly deferential to Hirohito as they were in the months leading up to his death. Immediately following the war there was a popular movement to end the Showa era: over half a million demonstrators besieged the palace calling for democracy and the removal of Hirohito. Com-munist Party leaders, newly released from gaol, were heroes: they had stood resolute against the war machine while everyone else had faltered. The people seemed to want what the communists appeared to represent: a new democratic Japan, perhaps even without an 'emperor system'.

The unions called for a general strike. General Douglas

MacArthur, commander of the US occupation forces, and the supposed harbinger of democracy, ordered the cabinet to squash the strike by any means. It is said that during his eight-year sojourn in Japan, MacArthur, dubbed 'the moat-side emperor' by the locals, met only sixteen Japanese, one of whom, Hirohito, impressed him inordinately. The people's cries for democracy and a new beginning were like wind chimes in winter, as the colloquialism has it, a faint, barely noticeable irritation.

As the Cold War heated up, the left, which is to say anyone who opposed the occupation forces' plans for Japan as a sort of mountain of sandbags over which the red peril could not roll, was crushed. The occupation forces took over the censorship of films from the militarists they had defeated. Their main purpose was to keep the Japanese from discovering the extent of the atomic devastation at Hiroshima and Nagasaki. However they also confiscated films such as A Japanese Tragedy, Kamei Fumio's documentary which is highly critical of the imperial system. In 1948, the union at Toho, one of the biggest film companies, took over the studios during a labour dispute regarding the issue of dismissals. The union was one of the most powerful bases of the communists. The police and the Army drove them forcibly from the studio, the American forces arriving in tanks and aeroplanes. The public couldn't help but conclude from this show of might that the United States Army would forcibly crush all and any democracy movements in their country. When the Korean War began in 1950, the United States exported its communist blacklist from Hollywood, ordering the film companies to expel all communists and communist sympathizers from their studios. Kamei, a proponent of too much democracy for US-Japanese Cold War taste, lost his job as did hundreds of others in this red purge.

Union leaders wept openly that day, standing on the platform addressing the crowds with tears streaming down their faces. Worse was to come. Hirohito was to slip through their fingers like dishwater. The 'militarists', this vague amorphous group, were blamed by the government and the Americans alike: the war had been the militarists' war, a conspiracy, a manipulation of the poor little Emperor. The Americans had been convinced, as much by their own scholars as by Japanese imperialists, that Hirohito's rehabilitation rather than trial at the War Crimes Tribunal, which would no doubt have been followed by his execution, was the only way to keep control over the country. Two hundred thousand known militarists and sympathizers were purged from public office in those first heady days of the occupation, while the man in whose name they had acted remained untouched, now no longer portrayed as an inviolate god but as a gentle boffin. In this incarnation Hirohito was sent out in a raincoat to meet his people for the first time.

Forty-four years on and the Showa era was finally at an end. It was now time to revisit the scene of the crime. As promised, the historians had delivered their paper, 'the very moment the death [was] announced'. Someone must have tipped them off; the messenger arrived as the broadcast began. 'The obvious responsibility of Emperor Hirohito for the war should never be dissolved by his death,' they had written.

The paper went on: 'Hirohito eluded an indictment at the Far East Military Court after the war due to political considerations on the part of the Allied Forces led by the US. He has now died with no legal or political onus on him, although among the Japanese people there has been a demand to accuse him of responsibility for the war.' The paper included a quote from Hirohito given in a rare press interview which was conducted in the mid-seventies. When a Japanese journalist dared to ask him about his wartime responsibility, Hirohito replied, 'Since I am not an expert on literature I do not understand the nuance of the word responsibility.'

For the *uyoku* such questioning now as when he was alive was still 'betraying the Japanese race'. Organizations and individuals critical of Hirohito were threatened. 'Be prepared to pay for this with your life,' Morii Makoto, the president of Meiji Gakuin University, was told. Professor Morii had written an article condemning Hirohito and had refused to allow his university to send condolences, instead holding a week-long intensive course on the 'emperor system'. Politicians such as Ms Doi received death threats as did scores of intellectuals, historians, journalists and TV stations.

After three or four weeks, the articles naturally dried up. They had made little difference to what was going to happen. Hirohito was to be buried as a god with the full rites of Shinto, and his son, Akihito, was to be enthroned as one, both events to be paid for out of the public purse.

One Sunday, around the middle of the fifty days between Hirohito's death and his funeral, Mombusho, the Education Ministry, quietly announced that it was bringing in a new national curriculum that would 'teach understanding of, and veneration for, the emperor; require courses in patriotism and moral education; and instil a sense of Japanese identity and love of the nation by raising consciousness of being a Japanese and cultivating national identity in all course work.' *Sokoku keiai tenno keiai*, as the phrase has it: 'Love and revere the homeland and the emperor.'

Raising the sun flag and singing the Kimigayo, the *de facto* national anthem, which deifies the Emperor, were to become mandatory. Teachers who refused to comply would have their pay docked or promotion blocked. Togo Heihachiro, a hero of the Russo-Japanese war, and one of Hirohito's tutors, was to become the first military leader to be studied since the Second World War. The new curriculum came into force in 1990, two years ahead of schedule and several months before the historian Ienaga Saburo lost a thirty-year court battle against Mombusho's censorship of his history textbook *New History of Japan*.

Mombusho had cited 363 instances of 'inappropriate inclusions' in Professor Ienaga's book, which they said had to be removed before it could be used in schools. Mombusho routinely censors textbooks, something that Professor Ienaga claimed in the courts was unconstitutional and aimed solely at white-washing shameful episodes in the country's past, to conform, as he put, 'to the prevailing orthodox ideology that Japan was virtually an innocent bystander in the war.'

But Mombusho's patterns of censorship extend beyond the war. All statements in Ienaga's book which dismissed the tales of imperial origin (which claim that the emperors are direct descendants of Amaterasu, the Sun Goddess) and the stories of the 'Age of the Gods' as being not objective historical fact, had to be deleted. Statements that the Meiji constitution gave the emperor wide powers and parliament narrow powers had to be removed because it was 'a negative evaluation'. Mombusho said Professor Ienaga should instead emphasize that it was the first constitution in Asia. All examples showing that academic and political freedoms were not guaranteed under the Meiji constitution would also have to be deleted or 'modified'. In the chapter on the Pacific War, photographs captioned 'Air Raid on the Mainland', 'The Atomic Bomb and Hiroshima', 'Wartime Manners and Customs' and 'Damages of the War' were rejected on the grounds that they were 'too dark and depressing', that 'the whole impression is too dark'. In the same chapter, the word 'reckless', which Professor Ienaga used to describe the Pacific War, was ordered to be removed, as was a painting of a war widow with her children, crying over her dead soldier-husband's belongings, as this 'gave the wrong impression' of the war.

Pictures and prints showing scenes of ordinary people going about their daily lives during different periods of history would have to be removed, 'because Mombusho disagrees with the premise that people are the mainstay of history'. The eponymous title of the chapter also could not remain, nor could a photograph of demonstrators holding up placards reading 'Protect the Peace Constitution'. All references to the Rape of Nanking and other wartime atrocities perpetuated by the Japanese Army were ordered to be deleted or diluted until they were so opaque as to be unintelligible. And all references to Unit 731, the biological warfare unit that experimented on prisoners of war and segments of the Chinese civilian population among others, were ordered out as 'academically, the existence of 731 couldn't be sustained in detail'.

Occupation documents, freely available in the United States, confirm in detail the existence of 731. The US granted General Ishii Shiro, head of the 731 unit, immunity from the War Crimes Tribunal in exchange for information on Japanese biological warfare experiments, which the US wanted and were, at the same time, determined to stop the then Soviet Union from obtaining. 'This Japanese information is the only known source of data from scientifically controlled experiments showing the direct effects of BW [biological warfare] agents on man ...' a US discussion document notes. It concludes that Ishii should escape trial as 'information of Japanese BW experiments will be of great value to the United States' BW research programmes'.

Censorship is not just confined to children's textbooks. When Bernardo Bertolucci's film *The Last Emperor* was shown on general release in Japan, the scenes including actual war footage of the four-day massacre of Chinese civilians at Nanking by Japanese troops were cut by Shichiku Fuji Company, the film's distributor. (During the war around five million Chinese were killed by Japanese troops.) Serata Shinji, the spokesman for the company, said this decision was Bertolucci's: 'The director asked us for advice,' he said blithely. 'He felt that it might not be a good policy to leave in scenes which would only irritate and annoy the Japanese people.' This came as somewhat of a surprise to Bertolucci, who having learnt of 'his decision' insisted that the missing footage be reinstated. When the film had been shown uncut at its première at the Tokyo Festival it had done more than irritate and annoy the predominately young audience, it had horrified them. Some were in tears. Others gasped and cried out. One young woman sitting in my row said in a loud whisper, 'No, no, this can't be true!' as she watched footage of Imperial Army soldiers bayoneting Chinese babies and tossing them into a ditch.

In the cold winds, leaves are cleared from the trees night by night, baring the garden in the moonlight

PRINCESS SHIKISHI

On the day of Hirohito's funeral it rained again, unremittingly, turning Shinjuku Gyoen, the former imperial, now public, gardens in western Tokyo that were used to stage the event, into a hippopotamuses' bath. Hirohito had been dead for fifty days, the required time under Shinto doctrine for all the pre-burial rites to take place. Temperatures danced around freezing as the world's presidents, prime ministers, kings, queens, dukes and duchesses sat red-nosed, immobilized on their seats on the right-hand side of the *akusha*, the mourning marquee, waiting for what threatened to be for most, if not all, an incomprehensible and interminable ceremony. (It could have been worse. The funeral of Emperor Taisho, Hirohito's father, was, in keeping with strict traditional Shinto practices, held during the night.) Almost every country was represented at the highest level at Hirohito's funeral. It was a triumph of 'funeral diplomacy' for Japan, and a measure, if such a thing was still needed, of the country's overriding importance to the rest of the world. The Kunaicho had been defeated in its attempts to keep foreigners out of the funeral by the Gaimusho, who at the last minute had even managed to force the Kunaicho into providing 'tickets' to the event for the resident foreign press.

There were ten thousand guests at the funeral. At the front of the left-hand side of the *akusha*, the Japanese side as it were, sat the Imperial Family and the parliamentarians, all present and correct, except for MPs from the Japan Communist Party (JCP) who had boycotted the ceremonies in protest against the 'glorification and deification of Hirohito'. The most famous sumo wrestlers were seated at the back in full traditional kimono. Their wives, all as thin and small as the men were big and fat, interspersed them, draped in floor-length black mink coats over floor-length black dresses.

Hirohito was borne into the *akusha* in a three-level coffin hidden within a commodious one and a half-tonne palanquin. This was carried by fifty of the 149 funeral attendants, who were identically dressed in drab olive kimono and small pillbox black hats, each with what appeared to be a top knot attached. They tottered along on *geta*, traditional thronged wooden sandals with an oblong 'heel' at the front as well as the back. Other attendants carried gold and white banners representing the spirits of the gods, of which there are some eight million in Shinto. One of the chamberlains, wrapped in a white kimono, carried a wooden box inside of which were Hirohito's new shoes, special footwear to convey him to the next world.

The new, but as yet unconsecrated, Emperor Akihito, in full Western-style mourning attire and carrying a large black umbrella, walked alone, freed from the encumbrance of others. He drifted through the rain, a pleasant-looking middle-aged man in a black suit, followed several feet behind by the spectral figure of his wife, the Empress Michiko. Michiko, who took care to walk in her husband's footsteps, also walked alone and carried an expansive coal-black umbrella. Her floor-length black dress swirled over the wet grey gravel and her tent-like veil drifted around the top of her waist, hiding her bent elbows. She resembled the willowy stalk of a black mushroom. Her face, clouded by the veil, wore its usual aspect of profound sadness, for once more than suitable for the occasion.

The funeral was like a play, performed in two acts, full of chants and ceremonial procedures. In the second part there was a song of farewell accompanied by the doleful strain of the shamisen, an ancient stringed instrument now usually confined to shrines, geisha houses or the kabuki theatre. It is said that this song of farewell was first sung thousands of years ago to a dead prince who had resurrected himself as a crane and flown away.

The tragedy articulated in the song is for us wingless creatures left behind. By now, many of the Japanese left behind at the funeral were fast asleep, bundled up in overcoats and blankets. Offerings to Hirohito were made: cups of rice, a bottle of sake (rice wine), a pheasant, twenty quail, a wild duck, seven carrots, seven radishes – food he was said to have enjoyed in life, but no sign of the eggs and bacon which he was reputed to consume each morning in memory of the happy days spent as a visitor to Buckingham Palace in the twenties.

In the middle of these two acts was a sort of intermission during which the *mammon* (funeral curtain) was dropped down on to the stage. (The *mammon* also occasionally came down during the ceremony to hide the 'religious' Shinto rituals, i.e. those to do with Hirohito's standing as a god.) During the intermission most of the mourners stayed frozen to their seats or dashed in and out of the toilet. The foreign dignitaries talked quietly amongst themselves or, like the newly inaugurated President Bush and his wife Barbara, perhaps feeling it was disrespectful to do otherwise, stared silently straight ahead. But the Japanese parliamentarians rose *en masse* and headed in a great rush for the toilets. Five or so minutes passed and still not one had emerged. I went off and peered into the men's room where one solitary man leant against the urinals. The women's room was reasonably busy with sumo wives fixing their make-up. There was no other opening in the women's room, no back way out. I walked quickly through the men's room, passing the lone figure who was still nonchalantly fiddling around at the urinal. He seemed unimpressed by my presence. To the side of the urinal, behind the stalls, was an opening leading to yet another marquee, hidden and inaudible from the freezing, sombre *akusha*.

Here within this secret marquee were Japan's leaders, laughing, smoking, bellowing, and enjoying themselves as if it were a day at the races, much of their conversation firmly concentrated upon the shares-for-favours Recruit affair, an ever widening corruption scandal that implicated the present as well as the former prime minister, members of the cabinet, parliament and the bureaucracy. They seemed to know already that the scandal, which would force Prime Minister Takeshita out of office in a few months and threaten for the first time in thirty-four years the LDP'S tenacious grip on power, could do them no serious damage in the long run; that this, too, like the truncated excitable discussion of imperial war guilt, was a ritual of cleansing that would allow everything to go on exactly as it always had. The Recruit affair would oust ministers from office, aides, such as Takeshita's, would commit suicide to 'take responsibility' for their bosses' downfall, but the governance of Japan would go on as it always had, for as the proverb states, 'The party that gains the advantage is the Imperial Party.'

A short time after Hirohito's funeral, the government had worked out a new line on the war and responsibility. As a top-ranking official at the Gaimusho explained: 'The war could never be fully discussed or examined in Japan until everyone who was involved in it was dead,' in other words, until there was no one left either to care or to remember. Having reached the time, after Hirohito's death, when reconciliation and a full accounting on and about the war were supposed to take place, the goal posts had quickly been moved. Reconciliation and accounting had been postponed indefinitely.

Later that year, those already dead came back to haunt. Workmen unearthed thirty-five skulls and an assortment of bones from underneath what had been General Ishii's 731 Biological Warfare Unit headquarters in Shinjuku. For over twelve months the bones of what were, in all probability, POW victims of biological experimentation did the rounds like the proverbial hot potato. Starting with the National Museum of Science, one scientific institution after another refused to date or pass any comment on the find. Finally, the Ministry of Health and Welfare stepped in. It wrote a terse letter to Shinjuku council stating, in words that were a perfect metaphor for Japan's attitude towards the unfortunate facts of its past: 'The Ministry wishes that Shinjuku Ward will cremate and bury these remains without delay.'

The withered summer grass is truly all that remains of the dreams of the warriors

BASHO (1644–94)

August is the haunted month, the month of Obon, the festival of the dead, when you welcome the souls of your ancestors back home, a time of feasting and gifts. Afterwards the dead souls are gently shown the way back to that other world so that life in this world can continue as it must. Some spirits cannot go home: those who died violently, tragically, or were wronged in this life must haunt. August is the time of ghost stories, tales of these unhappy souls who walk the earth, restless with vengeance. Into this month of death and haunting came the bombs, one after the other, creating the inferno of the walking dead that haunts us all. The souls of the war dead possess the living – they have too many terrible tales to tell, too many stories that cannot be told. The past has been buried alive; it rumbles like an incipient earthquake, full of loathing and menace, awaiting its time to come again.

Nagasaki in August is still and clammy. A deadening watery heat drowns the city, muffling speech and movement. The sun hangs low and big, a quivering white emptiness in the middle of the scrubbed sky. On the ninth day of August, in 1945, the temperature was a reasonably temperate, albeit humid, 84 degrees Fahrenheit, about the same as it is today. When 'Fat Man' exploded at 11.02 a.m., the temperature of the earth around ground zero rose to 848 degrees Fahrenheit, four times hotter than the boiling point of water; a heat so ravaging that people's eyes melted and their skin liquefied down to the bone.

Over 65 per cent of those killed by 'Fat Man' were women and children. This, then, was the last act of the 'holy war' Japan had waged in order to 'reunite' all nations under the rule of the sacred emperor: 'The divine mission Japan has been called to fulfil from time immemorial,' Professor Kujisawa Chikao wrote in the wartime propaganda booklet *The Great Shinto Purification Ritual and the Divine Mission of Japan.*

There are no survivors in Nagasaki or Hiroshima now, only victims: the *hibakusha*, victims of the A-bomb. The *hibakusha* are often called upon as living testaments to the 'unique' suffering that befell this nation, that which must never be repeated. The *hibakusha* are Japan's moral edge, and the country hides much of its terrible wartime history behind their scars.

There are so many words for victim – *gisei-sha*, *higai-sha*, *so-nan-sha* – and further mutations of the words into ever more precise categories such as *hibakusha*. I am often told that as a nation, 'We Japanese suffer from *higai-sha ishiki* [victim consciousness].' Hiroshima and Nagasaki are intertwined in the heart of this consciousness. In the minds of many the atomic bombings are the point at which the war began and ended. 'At the time there was a great deal of unpleasantness and social unrest in the world,' the guide at Hiroshima's A-bomb museum said, by way of describing the Second World War.

Nagasaki, the second and, so far, the last city to be incinerated by an atomic bomb, was also a second choice. The US Air Force had intended to bomb Kokura, a port town diagonally opposite Nagasaki, on the northernmost tip of Kyushu, the third largest of the four main Japanese islands and the most southerly of this group. Fortuitously for Kokura, it was covered by cloud that day. An hour later 'Fat Man' was let loose on this stand-in city, a place the locals like to boast of as the 'San Francisco of the East'.

Nagasaki was once Japan's principal port for foreign trade and its most international city. To here had come the Portuguese, the first Europeans to arrive in Japan, followed by St Francis Xavier, who brought Christianity to the country. Other Europeans soon followed. Up until the time of the expulsion these foreigners were allowed to mix freely with the local population. From the mid-seventeenth century, when Japan was closed to the rest of the world, it was Nagasaki's port that remained open for limited trade with the Chinese and Dutch (who no longer were allowed to mingle with the natives). Today, this is sometimes told in a way that suggests the Allies were not sufficiently mindful of their shared history with this place. The Japanese, much more than Westerners, tend to see events with double vision: the thing itself and what it symbolizes. The reality of the event lies in its metaphor more often than in its fact.

I arrived in Nagasaki earlier than expected, nauseous with a belly full of sweet orange soda which I had mistakenly chosen over the faint green tea, the beverages most commonly offered on domestic flights. The plane, antiquated, noisy, bumpy and slow, as all domestic planes seem to be, somehow managed to arrive ahead of schedule. As soon as it taxied to the gate the wearisome crush for the exit began. People pushed and shoved, clambering over each other to be the first down the ramp only to idle at the luggage carousel. When getting on in Tokyo, despite the existence of preassigned seats, it had been the same story. There is always this air of panic in a Japanese crowd, always the need to get on or off a vehicle first. Perhaps it is a function of overcrowding, or a collective memory of shortages. Certainly the old people are the worst offenders, the most brazen, knocking everyone out of the way to reach their seats, like famine victims running after the food truck. But it is true of the young too. In the cinema, which never seems to be visited by anyone over twenty-five, the crowd thunders down the aisles as the previous show ends, sometimes before the credits are rolling, standing by the still occupied seats, diving at them as soon as they are vacated. In a country which loves order and safety and deafens you with continuous public pronouncements over loud speakers to 'Watch where you are going and be sure to take your belongings,' there is no attempt at all to control these hysterical crushes, none of the cries of 'Be careful!' or 'Dangerous!' which usually litter the air.

I had come at the invitation of Mayor Motoshima – this before he had been shot and almost killed for his comments on Hirohito's war guilt. At this time he was simply known here as a leader of Japan's peace movement. The peace movement is not a movement in the sense of, say, the British Campaign for Nuclear Disarmament, but rather an ambience radiating out from the cities of Nagasaki and Hiroshima. When I first met the Mayor he was propping up a wall at the cocktail party being held for us 'communicators'. He rocked back and forth on his heels, cradling a *mizuwari*, whisky and water, a favourite drink for men. He supported his drinking arm with the other, twirled the glass around in his fingers and hurumphed, hauling his shoulders up and down as he mumbled something unintelligible to no one in particular. He was listening to a former GI, once an occupier of this city, make a rambling speech. The speech was being translated by a nervous young woman who was doing her best to wrestle the former soldier's *non sequiturs* into Japanese. The Mayor appeared to be following the GI's thoughts intently, nodding and shaking his head by turns, humming and hawing as if it was the most interesting thing he had ever heard.

Later the GI committed the solecism of trying to return a lovely wooden ship that had been given to him by the mayor of Nagasaki during the occupation. Motoshima called the former GI an idiot, an appellation the nervous translator chose not to repeat. The Mayor was furious at the gross insult of giving back a gift, and would not be appeased by my attempts to explain to him that the American probably thought the ship had been given to him under duress and that it should therefore be returned. With dramatic shakes of the head, he steadfastly refused to receive the ship, which after an embarrassing few minutes was accepted by the translator on behalf of the 'mayor and the people of Nagasaki'.

This performance was vintage Motoshima, a man who revelled in confrontation. Before he was shot he was stocky, and still showed signs of the good looks that had been his as a young man. His rather melodramatic face was framed by thick untidy black hair; he had a wide sensual mouth and the confidence and easy charm of handsome men. But he didn't smile very much, not even back then. After he had been shot he never seemed to smile. He came out of the hospital wasted and pale, having shed the residue of his looks with his weight, and having visibly aged twenty years.

He had almost died, but it wasn't only that that had done for him. Slightly over a year had passed between his remarks and the assassination attempt. During this time he had been forced to live a circumscribed life totally alien to his nature, with a twenty-four-hour guard and constant death threats. He continued to try to run Nagasaki, a city now under siege: no sooner had the words on Hirohito left his mouth than sixty-two different *uyoku* gangs arrived in the city in a convoy of eighty-five paramilitary vehicles that cruised the streets every day, screaming death threats at the Mayor and his supporters. Motoshima knew he was done for but refused to apologize, back down or dilute what he had said. Now he is tired, preoccupied with his own death, with, in a very Japanese way, learning how to die, voraciously reading anything and everything on the subject.

Motoshima was always a bit of a natural outsider in Japan. His ancestors were Hidden Christians. On first encountering St Francis Xavier and the Jesuits in 1549, Nagasakians enthusiastically embraced Christianity. By the time Japan's first national shogun, Hideyoshi Toyotomi (who actually could not bear this hereditary title dating back to the tenth century, but is known by it because he unified the country after the Age of the Country at War (1467–1588)), had recognized the potential political power of the Jesuits as rivals to shogun rule, the Jesuits were virtually running Nagasaki and Nagasakians were overwhelmingly *kirishitans*, as Christians are called. In a little over twenty-five years Nagasakians had overwhelmingly been converted to Christianity and the Jesuit missionaries were spreading it further afield. Consequently, in 1587, thirty-eight years after it had arrived here, Hideyoshi outlawed the alien creed. Those who continued to practise after the decree, the so-called Hidden Christians, did so on penalty of death. As a warning to the people of Nagasaki, Hideyoshi had twenty-six martyrs, including six foreign missionaries and three children, brought from Kyoto and Osaka and crucified on a hill above the city. Even now 10 per cent of Nagasakians are *kirishitans*, a high percentage when compared to the 1 per cent of *kirishitans* in the general population.

During the early years of the Meiji era (1868–1912), Motoshima's grandfather was actively persecuted for his Christianity. When he was ten he was tortured by a method known as 'stone hugging', in which the victim was forced to sit on a stone slab while bits of wood were shoved between his legs and huge stones piled on top of his lap until his bones were smashed and splinters were deeply embedded into his flesh. Motoshima's grandfather never walked properly again. The Mayor remembers him as always walking with a very apparent, painful limp.

This was on the Goto islands off the Nagasaki coast, where Motoshima was born to a 'not yet married mother', as the euphemism has it, into a village of thirty households, all descendants of Hidden Christians. He was christened after St Ignatius of Loyola – soldier, founder of the Jesuits, and leader of the Catholic Reformation – a name he does not use. Motoshima is in many ways a politically astute Jesuit, a natural outsider who up until the point he chose to try for a Japanese Reformation – to do for the imperial institution what Loyola and the Jesuits had done for the Catholic Church – had been a natural insider too, a member of the LDP and the head of the nationalist organization Rising Sun Association. Not surprisingly the Association also denounced and dismissed him after his remarks about Hirohito.

Motoshima is consumed with an obsession that people will not understand the true horror of nuclear war. 'My great regret is that all these years after we cannot provide much in the way of evidence of the devastation of this city,' he says. 'Even the survivors cannot tell you exactly what those terrible conditions were. Both the Nagasaki and the Hiroshima museums have collected as many artefacts as possible, but it's just a ten-thousandth of what was done. I am afraid that some people will visit us and think the damages and the effects caused by the bombings were insignificant.'

But Motoshima's pacifism is not just retrospective. He wants Japan to sign the Pacific Nuclear Free Zone Treaty. 'The Government has reduced the three non-nuclear principles to less than even form,' he says, referring to an amendment to the constitution which stated that Japan would not manufacture nor possess nor allow nuclear weapons to be brought into its territories. Almost before the ink was dry, the government nullified the amendment in a secret agreement with the US which allowed that country to bring nuclear weapons into Japanese territorial waters aboard US ships, something Motoshima never misses an opportunity to attack.

Like most Japanese, Motoshima believes that the Americans

felt able to drop the atomic bomb on Japan, but not on Germany, because it meant exterminating Asians not Caucasians. But he doesn't hide behind this or use it to portray Japan as a victim. 'In Nagasaki schools the children are taught about the war, they are taught that the A-bomb wasn't just dropped on us for no particular reason. We teach about Japanese history, the rise of militarism, the events leading up to August 1945. We teach them not to hate Americans. What is necessary is for all of us to unite on just one point: the abolition of nuclear weapons.'

Perhaps in part because of Motoshima, Nagasaki unlike Hiroshima, has an existence and an identity that is far more than just a city that was destroyed by an atomic bomb. 'Hiroshima is no longer merely a Japanese city. It has become recognized throughout the world as the mecca of world peace,' states the Hiroshima Peace Reader, articulating the city's image of itself, a place where peace is the main industry. Hiroshima is festooned with monuments, memorials, fountains, parks, eternal flames, statues, tombs, peace bells and peace rocks, all commemorating August the sixth. Its centre is the Peace Park where the inscription on the Cenotaph reads: 'Let all the souls here rest in peace; for we shall not repeat the evil.' Lest anyone should be under the impression that the 'evil' in this elliptical statement was Japanese militarism, or the government, or the Emperor, the local *uyoku* forced a small monument to be erected nearby explaining that the 'evil' was war in general.

As the first city to be destroyed by a nuclear bomb, Hiroshima, not Nagasaki, has gripped the imagination of Japanese writers and film directors. There is a stock Hiroshima story. In the cinematic version the opening scenes are of a city soaked in everydayness. There is no war apparent in this city. Nothing could be more normal: children walk to school, women cook rice, and men work at civilian occupations. After Tokyo, Hiroshima was the main military centre, yet no one is working in a munitions factory, there are no scenes of the military preparing to conquer the world, no sightings of soldiers marching around Hiroshima Castle, no sailors on battleships, no veterans resting between campaigns, nothing which might suggest there was a war going on. The centre of the story is almost always a pretty young woman, the epitome of innocence, whose life, in one way or another, is destroyed by 'the explosion', as the atomic bombings are often called, a *deus ex machina* that fell from the sky.

*Once, when my shoe caught
on a body half consumed by fire
and the bones of the legs and
thighs scattered in all
directions, I shrieked despite
myself and halted, petrified
with horror*

**IBUSE MASUJI, *KUROI AME*
(*BLACK RAIN*)**

Mr Fukamaki was standing looking out of the window when I went into the city hall. He clutched a rolled up document behind his back that was inevitably my schedule. He spun round on his heels, smiled, bowed and came towards me, a small frail man in a light blue short-sleeved shirt and dark blue polyester trousers. If you are an official guest you are always assigned a minder in Japan, a shadow whose job it is both to control your movements and ensure you get to where you are supposed to be on time, and to make certain that you don't get lost, imprisoned or embroiled in any other mishap likely to befall the luckless foreigner.

Mr Fukamaki and I sat down opposite each other on plastic tan chairs that looked, as all bureaucratic furniture seems to look here, as if they had been made in the fifties. The plastic red coffee table completed the period set, with the large brown ashtrays adding the detail. He handed me a copy of my highly detailed schedule and then we went over it, minute by minute, Japanese style. There was nothing I particularly objected to. They had set up the interviews I had asked for. I was willing to go along with the rest. There was no problem, which is not always the case. Mr Fukamaki smiled and sighed, his face showing visible relief. These schedules tend to be cast in stone; they are 'difficult' to change. 'If there is time we will go and see the Glover House,' said Mr Fukamaki happily. There won't be time. It is just polite conversation, the Japanese equivalent of 'Let's have lunch some time' or 'You must come over.'

Thomas Glover was a British merchant who married a Japanese woman in the 1860s and spent his life in Nagasaki. His claim to fame is threefold: he brought the first steam train to Japan, established the first mint, and is supposed to have inspired Puccini's *Madame Butterfly*. *Madame Butterfly* is out of favour in official Japan now, for its perceived racism. News of this seems to have bypassed Nagasaki, however, where the Glover House is a major tourist attraction.

Every August, for 'many years', Mr Fukamaki has given a few days of his time to look after the Mayor's guests, journalists mostly, but also teachers and others with supposed influence, all invited to attend Nagasaki's commemoration ceremony, to bear witness to the legacy of August the ninth: Japan still believes in the efficacy of the endlessly repeated message. 'It is vital that the world knows what happened here,' says Mr Fukamaki, explaining why he does this year after year, 'so that it will never happen again.'

Mr Fukamaki is a secondary school teacher. He was twelve years old at the end of the war, and like all schoolchildren saw his own teachers make a volte-face after the country surrendered: one day they were teaching their pupils to prepare for 'glorious self-destruction', beating those who could not perfectly recite the imperial edicts; the next day they were instructing the class to paint black ink over those passages in the history, geography and natural science textbooks that explained the 'divine mission' of the Japanese. Then they began teaching the children the 'scientific truths', as they were called by the occupation forces. With as much vehemence and enthusiasm as the teachers had taught Mr Fukamaki the Emperor's Will, they now taught him the

American Way. The Japanese have a word for this type of behaviour – *tenko*, a seemingly real conversion that takes place under the pressure of state power.

The boy that was Mr Fukamaki found his teachers' *tenko* untenable. Everything he had been taught to believe he was now being told was untrue. This, coupled with the devastation of his homeland, made Mr Fukamaki's pacifism, like that of so many here, corporeal, bred in the bone, so far immovable – as popular opposition to the 1991 Gulf War and the sending of Japanese troops abroad as part of a UN peace-keeping mission demonstrates. Like Mr Fukamaki, many of today's teachers are pacifists, just as the slogan of Nikkyoso, their left-wing union, would suggest: 'Never send our students to the battlefield again.' Yet, like him, they teach a censored history in which Japan was an innocent victim in the war. Like him, they have to require from their students a mind-numbing conformity and a blind acquiescence to authority which makes *tenko* on a mass scale potentially so easy to bring about again. This is a habit of mind in Japan. Often you do not act in the way you think or feel. Things are lined up side by side. There is no need to connect.

Mr Fukamaki is as relaxed as a sack of bones; tucked up in the corner of the sleek black Nissan Princess, he appears to have collapsed inside of his small body. He gazes out of the window, watching the reconstructed Nagasaki drift past us, surreal, like a disembodied movie backdrop, wavering and shimmering in the heat. Geographically Nagasaki is closer to South Korea than to Tokyo, a southern city both in atmosphere and looks. Because of its fortunate geography of mountains and water, Nagasaki, a hilly city on a bay, is much prettier than Hiroshima, and most other Japanese cities, but is not the 'San Francisco of the East', as Mr Fukamaki and the brochures would have it. The post-war ugly commercial buildings, which do not vary from one end of the country to the other, detract from its promise. But Mr Fukamaki gazes out at it and smiles with the air of a man pleased with what he sees.

The car, its engine growling, twists and turns up the mountain.

Mr Fukamaki folds one leg over the other and jiggles his foot. He has a kind face, open and curious; behind his glasses his small dark eyes are alert and watchful. The mountain road is narrow, the surroundings verdant. Warm perfumed air tumbles in the window, sweet and heavy, suffusing the car. It is here, to Mitsuyama, that the *hibakusha* came after the 'explosion' to escape the fires, and where some now live in the Hill of Grace nursing home. The home is run by the Sisters of the Immaculate Heart of Mary, an improbably named order founded in the thirties by Hayasaka Januarius, Japan's first native Christian bishop.

Below us is the city and the sea – one of the bays perhaps, Omura or Chijiwa, or the Pacific Ocean at the intersection with the Sea of Japan through the Tsushima Strait. Mr Fukamaki is unsure. It is lovely up here, hot and lush, washed in a harsh sunlight that exaggerates and breeds colour. 'Everything grew back,' Mr Fukamaki says. 'They said nothing would grow for five hundred years. But even down there, even at the epicentre, the grass grew back after some time.' He smiled proudly as if he feels somehow responsible for this.

The nursing home sits on the summit of this table-top mountain, a jumble of pastel-coloured buildings, yellow, pink and blue, surrounded by small formal arrangements of bushes floating on islands of preternaturally green grass. To one side is an artificial pond with a large and vibrantly coloured statue of Mary in the centre. She wears a sky-blue cape with gold trim. In her arms she holds the infant Jesus, clothed in a long red gown and gold trim. Mary stares at the water, her head bowed, a pose of sadness bordering on despair. At her feet, rather incongruously, is an oversized sculpture of a mother frog with her baby on her back.

Mitsuyama is cowed by the other mountains, a great chain of them, hump-backed and clad in violent shades of green, surrounding the neck of the bay. It is easy to forget when you are in the cities that almost 70 per cent of the Japanese archipelago, a land mass the size of Italy, is mountainous, that its 125 million people live on just 20 per cent of the land.

Inside the nursing home it smells of disinfectant, the over-powering stench of fake pine smothering the musty aroma of enclosed airless rooms and decaying flesh. We sit in the staff room with a few of the nurses, doctors and the Sister, drinking O-cha (honourable tea, the bitter green tea drunk in Japan) and eating sickly bean-paste sweets, which are actually more like miniature cakes, the traditional accompaniment to green tea to offset its bitterness. Taking tea together before getting down to business is traditional, but is often now truncated to a cup of tea during the business itself.

We begin to discuss suffering. 'Once patients enter the home they will never leave,' the Sister says. 'Other than the cancers they suffer or have suffered, all of them lack physical strength. They have no resistance. They catch cold easily and generally speaking they are weaklings. There are many who produce nuclear bombs today without knowing the horrible face of the bombings.' She sits bolt upright, alarmingly glacial, composed with religious certainties. Doubts and questions could have little place in her life; she would wave them away like flies. She tells us that there are 335 patients here, one hundred of whom are bedridden, ranging in age between their late forties to late nineties. The youngest were exposed to radiation *in vitro* or shortly after birth.

We are led down a corridor to a large room, an institutional sitting room with too many chairs and not enough focus. About three dozen of the patients are here, waiting for us, eager to tell their story. It's like being in an orphanage full of imploring faces: 'Pick me, pick me,' each seems to be urging. I apologize for disturbing them, for probing into what must be painful memories. 'It's all right, that is what we are here for,' one of the *obaasan* says, to a chorus of emphatic agreement. It is as if they have given up their right just to be people; it's as if they are career *hibakusha*, and this is their assigned place on the dance floor.

'I was ten years old and about one and half miles from the epicentre,' Fukuda Eiko says. As she speaks, she shrinks down into herself, sinking into her story, luxuriating in its familiarity. I think she will never come back. I think that she has no idea that either Mr Fukamaki or I are here. Occasionally she looks at me, her eyes skating over my face. 'This is where our house was,' she says, pointing at the map of Nagasaki drawn so that ground zero is at the centre. 'I was standing outside with one of my brothers who was twelve. He worked in the munitions factory and had come home for an early lunch. My mother was standing talking to the next door neighbour. We were to have rice and pickles for lunch. I had to give my brother money to buy sake. Suddenly we were blown into the ditch. I didn't feel any pain. I wasn't afraid. Almost every day we had an air raid. My mother dug us out. I looked at the house. It was in flames. There was fire everywhere. My mother's dress had torn. Her breast was bright red. There was a lump of wood stuck in my head. Everything was on fire. Everything had been flattened. It was so hot, you cannot imagine such heat.

'We went off to find my other brothers,' Ms Fukuda says. 'My eldest brother was a primary school teacher. We found him first. His fingers, hands and arms were charred black. There were thousands of people on the road just wandering around. Some of them were screaming. Others were dazed, their hair was all frizzled, their bodies burnt like charcoal. We went off towards the mountains. There were officials on the road shouting at us to cover ourselves with leaves and crawl along the ground so that we could not be seen from the air. My mother tore part of her dress off and tied it around my head. Suddenly she pushed me into a pond. I didn't know why she did that and I hated her for doing it.'

Ms Fukuda looks down at the table, her face still and cold as stone. 'Later,' she continues, 'my mother told me that she had done it because she couldn't stand looking at her child covered in blood and she thought the shock of cold water would stop the bleeding. Everyone who could walk or crawl had hurried towards the mountain in order to escape the raging fire. By the time we had got halfway up the mountain my eldest brother had died. Almost two-thirds of his body had been burnt. My mother told us to get some leaves and cover him up. We took turns in keeping a vigil.'

I finger the local government brochure. It is stuffy in here. This is the way Japanese people tell you stories: by relating everything they can remember, or think they remember. There is little emphasis on events, nothing seems more important than anything else and it takes such a long time to get it all said. It is not so much a question of not getting to the point, often there isn't any point to get to. The idea of the story is to create a feeling rather than to impart facts or drama. Here, I am beginning to see that when these people speak, the monotone often employed in the speech is accompanied equally often by a monotone of expression: the immovable blank mask of the *hibakusha*.

I doubt whether the other residents have listened to much of what Ms Fukuda has said, they would have heard it many times before. Their heads are bowed respectfully; some of them stare at the middle of the table; others keep their eyes closed. A few snore softly. A television chatters away inanely in a corner. It is tuned to some sort of tabloid TV programme in which a woman is standing outside a house, talking through the intercom in high-pitched, ultra polite tones to another woman whose child has just been murdered.

The Nagasaki brochure lists the first major event in Nagasaki's history as the destruction of the invading Mongol fleet by a typhoon, the original kamikaze (divine wind), which saved Japan from invasion. In 1281 Kublai Khan, who had successfully invaded China and made himself its ruler, was preparing to invade and conquer Japan. The Mongols had already made one invasion attempt a few years earlier. They had, miraculously, been seen off of Kyushu's beaches by the samurai, who had never fought foreigners before and had arrived in full elaborate warrior garb. The samurai, as usual, followed *bushido* (the way of the warrior), their code of ethics that among other things required them to strut up and down the battlefield issuing lengthy challenges and boasting of their fighting prowess. This was somewhat over the heads of the non-Japanese-speaking Mongol army, who began to attack the startled samurai before they had had chance to finish their soliloquies. Despite this, the samurai managed to force the Mongol army from Japanese shores.

At news that a second larger armada was underway, the Japanese prayed continuously. Bells and gongs sounded from every temple and shrine in the country. The then emperor, Go-Uda, wrote to his ancestors beseeching their help, but to no avail. Around 150,000 Mongols landed off the coast of Nagasaki in 4500 ships. For seven weeks, in what was increasingly a losing battle, the samurai held them at bay. It was time to call upon the help of Japan's most powerful gods and the shogun sent a messenger to plead with the dragon god of Haguro. That night the sky blackened and a furious typhoon, which was immediately dubbed the kamikaze, swept over the sea where the Mongol fleet was anchored, rampaging for two days until the entire armada was utterly destroyed. The defeat of Kublai Khan by what was thought of as supernatural means gave the Japanese a feeling of invincibility. This was successfully exploited during the Second World War when it was constantly claimed that the 'Japanese spirit' would always triumph over Allied might.

The connection between the first kamikaze and its wartime namesake is not noted in Nagasaki's brochure: the words 'kamikaze' or 'divine wind' are omitted and 'a storm' is substituted. Admiral Onishi Takijiro, the founder of the modern kamikaze, who was also one of the architects of Japan's attack on Pearl Harbor, wrote in the last months of the war: 'The Japanese people have not suffered enough yet ... They must suffer more and become complete, full Japanese.'

'Until I was twenty-seven I suffered from terrible pains in my head,' Ms Fukuda continues. 'Pains so severe that I never went to a hairdresser, except for once when I was twenty-five, the very latest age for marriage, when my mother forced me to go. There were rumours that the effects of radiation would be handed down through the generations. I was driven with such anger and such sadness. All of us who were exposed, especially the young women, got angry at the rumours, but we all abandoned the idea of getting married. My mother said that marriage was the only way to make a woman happy. Later on I did get married and even had a child. But when she was two years old I fell ill and was taken to the medical school in Nagasaki.'

She sighs and looks at me steadily. 'The cause of my paralysis is not clear,' she says. 'The doctors do not know whether it was caused by radiation. After many years I was brought here where I have been for many years. The doctors do not know why I am paralysed but it is advancing rapidly and they think that in three or four years I will be dead. Once in a while I see my husband and daughter. Once or twice in the summer holidays I see them.

'I had three brothers. The eldest died on that day. The second died ten days after the explosion. The third, whose body was rotting off of him, touched the side of his head and his finger went through it. He died twenty days after the explosion. We burnt them, my mother and I, burnt them on makeshift funeral pyres of leaves. I cannot ever forget that inexpressible odour of burning flesh.' Ms Fukuda looks out from deep inside her tragedy, an animal licking its leg in a trap; she cannot get outside of herself, her suffering is all that she can taste. Later, I ask the doctors whether her paralysis is psychological, a delayed result of the trauma perhaps. They evade the question, no matter how many times or in how many ways I ask; it's as if they think that this would make her case less real, less deserving of sympathy. I ask Ms Fukuda whether she thinks the bombing was in any way justified, whether she thinks that it brought a swifter end to the war. 'Nothing,' she says vehemently, 'could ever *ever* justify such an evil thing.'

Sister walks quickly, stiffly, holding her empty hands together in front of her breasts as if she is praying. She encourages me to take photos of the bedridden, a ward full of them lolling barely *compos mentis* in cots. Some of them know I am there and try to smile. They are used to visitors, used to being stared at, used to being catalogued and photographed. They keep their dignity locked up somewhere for safe keeping. Once they were daughters, lovers, wives, mothers. Once they worked in factories, shops and offices. Once they read and laughed. Once they were women, not bodies. The lack of privacy appals me, but perhaps that's a Western thing. Perhaps when Sister and I look at this ward we are looking at two different places. No doubt these bedridden patients, those who are aware of anything, believe too that this is what they are here for, but I cannot photograph them. I cannot treat them like exhibits in a museum.

'They would rather be here so as not to bring shame on their families,' Sister explains of her patients. 'Many have keloid scarring on their faces. They are marked and their families would be marked by their presence: despite the evidence to the contrary, people still believe that the effects of radiation are passed down through the generations.' She gives a tight little smile. She is alluding to the considerable prejudice the descendants of the *hibakusha* still find in a Japan in which 'purity' of blood is of almost mystical importance. There is something accusatory about the way Sister says this, as if she thinks I might be one of these atavistic believers.

An *obaasan* shuffles by and tries to bow. The left side of her face is a mass of the distinctive, thick keloid scarring that marks many *hibakusha*. It was formed when the melted skin fused back together and solidified into grossly distorted clumps and ridges. The place where her left eye was is covered with a screwed up piece of flesh. Our party walks along the corridor in silence. I am surprised that many of these people are quite old, that they have survived for almost fifty years after suffering from radiation sickness. I had imagined that the effects of radiation were always quick and lethal. Mr Fukamaki walks with his hands behind his back, still clutching on to my schedule. He has been here many times before, and some of the patients greet him like a long-lost friend as they shuffle along beside us as we walk towards the hall.

The rest of the patients who can walk, or who are capable of remaining upright in a wheelchair, are already in the hall waiting. Some stand up and all of them clap as we walk down the aisle. Once we are on the stage Mr Fukamaki tells me that the patients are going to 'sing their little song for us'. It's like school: the slightly out-of-tune piano, the smell of wooden floorboards and rubber soles. It is intensely uncomfortable standing up on the stage with this little party of officials. I listen to these thin, creaky old voices singing out of tune, quite unselfconsciously, about peace and hope and love. I look at their faces: the incongruity of their childlike expressions covered with scars, crevices, lines, folds, imbued with the sorrow of old age. They have finished singing. Two women, who must have been *in vitro* or tiny babies at the time of bombing, come up on to the stage to present me with gifts, things they have made: a collage representing the day of the bombing and hope for the future, and an origami doll. They giggle when I thank them, hiding their teeth behind their hands. Almost all Japanese women cover their mouths in this way when they laugh. It is from the ancient dictate that an inferior must never pollute a superior with his or her breath.

Mr Fukamaki nods at the microphone. 'You don't have to say

much,' he had earlier implored, 'just a little something, but please, Lisa san, you must say something!' I had told him that I couldn't do it, that, unlike the Japanese, Westerners weren't brought up to it. In Japan everyone makes speeches all of the time. Children are taught to do so in school and almost anyone can do it, quite unselfconsciously. The thing is never to say anything of consequence. 'The sky is blue and the Emperor is in his palace' will suffice. 'You're not American; you don't have to apologize,' Mr Fukamaki whispers now, thinking, perhaps, that this is the reason I am so reluctant to make a complete fool of myself. Many American visitors do apologize. I have seen them on the television leaning over one exhibit or another, usually at the Hiroshima A-bomb museum, blurting out regrets to the camera; but whether this is prompted by collective guilt or suggestions that such a gesture would be appreciated is unclear. Historical apologies are important in Asia: it is 'accepting responsibility' for one's acts and it is supposed to put everything to rights again. I stand at the microphone, looking out across this desert of expectant faces. I must have said something because they are clapping and smiling now. Mr Fukamaki squeezes my arm: '*Gambatte!* [persevere/hold on/stand firm],' he says, bristling with emotion. He lifts up his glasses and dabs at his cheeks.

Yet who could have foreseen that its end would be of such horror as this?

IBUSE MASUJI, *KUROI AME*

'Between the ages of ten and sixteen, every child in Nagasaki is brought to the Atomic Bomb Museum,' Mr Fukamaki says. He walks in front of me, peering at each exhibit as if he is looking at it for the first time. I watch a group of chubby, spotty teenagers being led around the cases, their faces as solemn as professional mourners. A few of the girls catch sight of me and start to point, whispering and giggling behind their hands, their sorrow pleasantly diverted by the sight of a *gaijin*.

What can they find in this minutiae of devastation? What could it all possibly mean to them? Everything recoverable has been kept: every last shard of melted glass, every scrap of discoloured and distorted brick, every smashed and scorched roof tile. There is a warped metal girder from the Mitsubishi Iron and Steel Factory. The factory did, and still does, make armaments. One of the more ironic facts of life for this staunchly pacifist, aggressively anti-nuclear city is that it is the company town of one of Japan's major weapon makers. What went or goes on in the Mitsubishi factory is not mentioned beneath the photograph of the devastated plant, a plant operated then almost entirely by women and children, like Ms Fukuda's brother.

A half-melted metal lunch box is displayed, along with a woman's kimono, the pattern seared off the back. A clock stopped at 11.02 a.m., the time of the Nagasaki bombing, is hung on the wall; record books listing the dead are displayed alongside some of the leaflets dropped by the US Air Force. The leaflets call for a renouncement of war and detail what had already taken place in Hiroshima. Although rumours that something terrible had happened at Hiroshima had already spread as far as Tokyo, these leaflets were dismissed at the time as propaganda, and often, according to Mr Fukamaki, turned in unread. Today, they are the museum's only mention of the war: the chart entitled 'The Events Leading up to the Atomic Bombing of Nagasaki' begins on 16 July 1945, with the successful test of a plutonium bomb in the New Mexico desert. The museum, like its bigger sister in Hiroshima, is literal to the extreme, an ahistorical portrait of an event that appears to have happened, like a natural calamity without context or circumstance.

The mayor of Hiroshima once agreed with a coalition of anti-nuclear groups to have what was dubbed by the press as 'a Japanese aggression corner' installed in that city's A-bomb museum. Immediately members of the local *uyoku* threatened his life and the mayor, perhaps mindful of what had happened to Motoshima, withdrew his consent, saying, 'The museum must focus on what actually happened that day in 1945,' a sentiment that has become the motto for both the Nagasaki and Hiroshima museums.

The photographs of the aftermath, both here and at Hiroshima, are the most powerful of the artefacts. Both museums include the picture taken in Hiroshima of the most famous shadow of all – the soldier and the ladder. The younger soldier was halfway up the ladder on his way to the watchtower the split second the bomb exploded. The tar was burnt off the tower except for where he and his ladder stood, leaving his form in black outline on what remained of the building. The clock stopped at 8.15 a.m. and changed the world. Every August the sixth, in every major city in the Western world, some artist or another gets out of bed and stencils black figures on the pavements; reminders of the shadows that were scorched into buildings, the ones we see in these pictures, the shadows of men, women and children who were incinerated where they stood.

The majority of the Nagasaki photos were taken by Yamabata Yosuke the morning following the bombing. They show a decimated landscape of smouldering rubble. In one overview of the city, nothing except the remains of its three most important symbols – a wooden *tori* (the sacred gate of a Shinto shrine), the walls of the Urakami Catholic Cathedral, and the iron frame of the Mitsubishi factory – are left standing. There are a few trees, stripped of their leaves and branches, black and frigid like a life-form on a distant planet. Within these scenes of desolation are the corpses of people who were incinerated on impact and flung from one place to another, bodies charred black, transmuted into slabs of burnt meat.

When I first looked at some of these photos I didn't see the bodies, they were so rigid, so discoloured and oddly positioned, their arms and legs stuck in the air above them, frozen in poses of walking or reaching like grotesque mimes. Of Nagasaki's population of around 210,000, at least 74,000 died instantly, some 75,000 were badly injured and 120,000 were rendered homeless. The photos of the half dead are the stuff of nightmares: children, women, old people, their faces mad with grief and incomprehension, their bodies caked with blood and grime, sitting among the corpses, unable to get up and leave, or sometimes, according to Yamabata Yosuke's record, even to drink the water which would have helped quieten the fire in their bodies. Later the rain fell on them, poisonous with radiation, black and glutinous. Atomic rain. *Kuroi Ame.*

I stare at a photograph on the wall: a skinny boy lies face down, motionless, on a camp bed. His eyes are closed, his arms twisted to the side of him, bent like pincers; it looks as if he is trying to hold his stomach up from the bed, or as if rigor mortis has set in. There is no skin on his back or on his left arm, just a neon-red lava-like gelatinous mess.

'When I see that picture of me,' Taniguchi Sumiteru says, 'I always feel such uncontrollable anger about the war and the bomb. It brings it all back to me, all the pain and the hardship, all the agony.' There is no emotion in his voice, nor in his face; he stands beside me blank and shrivelled. He too wears the still mask of the *hibakusha*, but I can smell his bitterness. The photograph, of the young Mr Taniguchi, was taken by the US Army as part of the record of the after-effects of the bombing. The caption says that the boy had to lie in bed on his stomach for twenty-one months, but had miraculously escaped death.

Mr Taniguchi was a boy on a bicycle delivering the mail when the 'fierce hot wind' came and blew him away. The children whom he had seen playing at the side of the road were all dead, 'One of them was smoking.' He remembers lifting up his own arm and looking at the skin that hung down from it 'like an old tattered rag,' believing it to be his shirt at first until someone cut it off him. There were moaning bodies all around: 'Somewhere I remember somebody – perhaps it was more than one person – whispering to me, "My name is so and so, I come from such and such, and I'm going to die. Please inform my family about me."'

After 'some time' he was taken to the Naval Hospital where he would have to lie face down for nearly two years. 'I was in blinding pain now and I had a high fever. I remember I kept shouting, Kill me! Kill me!' When finally he could stand up he saw that his chest was potmarked by cavernous bedsores that had chewed up his flesh. It took another two years of convalescence before he was allowed to leave the hospital. The burns on his back and arms did not heal for fifteen years. He has had skin cancer 'of course' and in the last four years has had eight operations. The skin, 'or rather the scars on my back and arms,' still gets ulcers which have to be continually removed. 'All these years later, there is still something wrong with my body that causes me great pain. It will never end. Only death can end it.'

We walk over to the table so that he can sit down. He looks like a grey old dishcloth: thin, worn and frayed. His skin is stretched tightly over his bones; only the keloid has any substance to it. He works for the A-Bomb Survivors Consultation Council now, a body which seeks reparations from the government. Those certified as *hibakusha* are entitled to free medical treatment and a disability payment of around £150 a month, which the Council feels is an insult. He says that some people think the Council has the right to, and indeed *should*, pursue the US government to 'take responsibility' for the *hibakusha*. But Mr Taniguchi feels that although 'obviously it's true that the United States dropped the bombs on us,' the Japanese government signed away the right for reparations from the US when it signed the San Francisco Peace Treaty. Moreover, he says, 'If the Japanese government hadn't pursued a militaristic policy then the United States government could not have dropped the A-bomb on Japan, so our government should assume responsibility for us.

'The government uses us, it parades our scars in front of the world but it will not help us. It wasn't until 1968 that any aid was given to *hibakusha*. Every year on August the fifteenth the government holds a service of remembrance for the dead souls who died in the war. Each year there are more *hibakusha* to pray for. We shall all be dead souls soon. How can we be satisfied with this when the government started that war and sacrificed too many of the Japanese people?'

The war situation has developed not necessarily to our advantage

EMPEROR HIROHITO

Mr Fukamaki is talking about the Americans, describing them in terms you might hear in a B-movie about the occupation. They were 'very kind'. They gave 'us children Hershey Bars'. That was the first time he had tasted chocolate, which he thought delicious. He was impressed by the GIs' size, their bulk. Their bigness made them glamorous to him, like super heroes. Here were the conquerors that no amount of 'Japanese spirit' could keep out. 'We felt very small,' he says, 'these people were giants.'

The GIs walked around Nagasaki as if they owned the joint, determined to teach the Japs – 'a nation of twelve year olds' – some manners. 'A GI got on the bus and ordered all the men to get up and give their seats to the women,' Mr Fukamaki says smiling. 'We were very surprised: as you know, Japan is a man's country. Men are not expected to give up seats for women.' The embarrassed men did get up and give the equally embarrassed women seats, but as soon as the GI got off the bus the women got up and gave the seats back to them. Mr Fukamaki chuckles at this exemplary illustration of the occupation and its aftermath.

Some of the GIs were apparently lacking in chivalrous behaviour, however. According to Mr Fukamaki, it was mostly the Australians and the black American soldiers who raped the women. This is a popular view, despite the lack of evidence to suggest that rapes were disproportionately committed by the Australian soldiers or the black GIs. The supposed outrages by the Australians have faded with time, but the folklore about black GIs has become a cliché of pornographic and sometimes non-pornographic films about the occupation. In these films, when a GI is shown raping a Japanese woman, that GI is invariably black. Japan had never been occupied before. Perhaps the Japanese found it easier to divide its occupiers into the good, white, powerful Americans, with whom they tried to identify, and the relatively powerless bad blacks and non-Americans. In this way they could displace their fears and resentment, not to mention feelings of sexual inadequacy.

Japanese soldiers were no strangers to rape as a by-product of war and occupation. During the 1910–45 Japanese occupation of Korea, Imperial soldiers rounded up some 200,000 Korean women and forced them into prostitution, taking the majority to Japanese-occupied China and Southeast Asia to staff 'comfort stations' for the troops. Many of these *inanfu* (comfort women), were eventually killed and most were regularly and brutally beaten during their captivity. After the war Japan constantly denied that this had happened, finally admitting what it had done in 1992 when Prime Minister Miyazawa Kiichi formally apologized to the president of South Korea. However, Japan continues to refuse to pay compensation to the Korean women who survived this ordeal.

To Mr Fukamaki, who was a child at the time, the occupation seemed not unpleasantly endless. He isn't really sure whether the adults feared that it would never end, but he remembers, 'Most people were so relieved that the war was finally over, that at last someone had come and brought peace and order back to the country, that, in the beginning anyway, they didn't care who it was.' I have been told this, in one way or another, many times before. That the occupation was a welcome respite is genuinely believed now, and to a certain extent it may have been true. At the time, the defeat and the occupation were suffused with unreality. Right up until the end the newspapers, which were controlled by the military, maintained a constant barrage of propaganda. America was 'condemned to destruction' by the Japanese spirit. The one hundred million inhabitants of the Japanese archipelago were told by the government to turn themselves into a fireball, to prepare for *hondo kessen* ('the last and decisive battle on the main islands,' the term used by the military to describe a 'glorious ending'). The planners of *hondo kessen* thought it best that the children, the old and the sick be killed before this final battle in defence of the homeland, lest they should get in the way.

From the Battle of Midway in 1942, it became increasingly inevitable that Japan would be defeated, sooner or later, and this was privately acknowledged by the military, the government and Hirohito. A faction within the military wanted to end the war, but those who believed in *hondo kessen* as the right path for Japan prevailed, even though they too admitted among themselves that defeat was inevitable. The last year of the war took a terrible toll on the homeland: since March 1945 all the major cities, especially Tokyo, had been firebombed by the Americans. Approximately 200,000 had perished in the air raids and as many again would die in the bombings of Nagasaki and Hiroshima. By April the Americans had invaded Okinawa and were engaged in one of the bloodiest campaigns of the Pacific War.

Okinawa, the biggest of a group of islands once known as the Ryukyu Kingdom, is so far south from the main Japanese islands that Shanghai is the nearest major city. Throughout its history, the Ryukya Kingdom has been contested between China and Japan. During the Tokugawa period, the kingdom was a tributary state of China, but Satsuma, a semi-autonomous district in southern Kyushu, claimed suzerainty over the 'autonomous king-dom' in the conquest of 1609. In 1879 Japan, over the objections of China and the Ryukyus, established Okinawa.

The Battle of Okinawa claimed the lives of some 100,000 Japanese troops and 50,000 American troops. But the real horror lay in the terrible deaths endured by the 100,000 Okinawan civilians who were deliberately slaughtered or forced to commit suicide (by such methods as blowing themselves up with hand grenades) by the Imperial Japanese Army. The Japanese were supposed to be protecting the Okinawan people from the 'foreign barbarian', but as well as forcing them to commit suicide, the Imperial troops chased the citizens – mostly women, children and old people – out of the caves where they had hidden, straight into the line of enemy fire. Okinawans were ordered to speak Japanese without a dialect by the troops – if they did not or could not they were executed as subversives. Although some Okinawans did voluntarily commit suicide to avoid their fate at the hands of the 'foreign barbarians', the Japanese myth of heroic sacrifice for the war effort by the Okinawans is just that. The Okinawans have never forgiven the Japanese (to whom anyway the Okinawans are not 'proper Japanese') for what they did to them during the Battle of Okinawa, or for the way they were treated afterwards.

The US was allowed to keep Okinawa as a troop base for twenty years after the occupation had ended on the mainland and the island was an important base and rest camp during the Korean and Vietnam wars. Although Okinawa was 'returned' to Japan in 1972, 75 per cent of all US troops in the country are based there, occupying 20 per cent of the land, so the island still feels like occupied territory.

Finally, on 15 August, a week after the bombing of Nagasaki, Hirohito put a stop to the war. For the first time the populace heard his high-strung discordant voice squeaking in elaborate and indecipherable court language over the radio: 'The war situation has developed not necessarily to our advantage,' he said, in the now legendary understatement. It had become necessary to 'accept the unacceptable'.

'We are painfully conscious of your sentiments today, you Our subjects. Therefore, We have decided, in accordance with the dictates of fate and of the present time, to pave the road towards a great peace for generations to come by enduring the unendurable and supporting the insupportable.' Afterwards an announcer broke in to explain in ordinary Japanese that the Emperor had just announced that the war was over. The word *shusen*, the end of the war, was used by officials and citizens alike to describe this momentous event, never *haisen*, defeat in war. Nevertheless the people were in a state of profound shock: a defeat, whatever it was called, simply could not be true.

Robert Guillain, a French journalist who had been held under house arrest in Karuizawa, a resort near Fuji-san, as Mount Fuji is reverentially called in Japan, reported that the villagers, who had listened to the recording on a collective radio with their heads respectfully bowed, retreated to their houses, sobbing in a subdued way. Once everyone was indoors, the village became absolutely silent. The next day the villagers emerged from their houses smiling cheerfully and greeting him and other foreigners (who as a group had been beaten up and killed by the populace or arrested and sometimes tortured or killed by the police) like long-lost friends. The villagers may have been smiling to hide their feelings, which is encouraged in Japan, but Mr Guillain appears not to have thought so. Some Japanese social anthropologists claim that the relatively peaceful acceptance of the occupation by a people who had up until that very moment been prepared to fight to the death was based on two cultural traits which are seen throughout Japanese history: mass denial (the war had *ended*, it had not been *lost*) and identification with 'superior' peoples (who then later always become inferior, in this instance white Americans).

The occupation forces were called *shinchugun* (advance forces), almost never *senryogun* (occupation forces), following on from Hirohito's rescript ending the war, in which he claimed, 'We declared war on America and Britain out of Our sincere desire to ensure Japan's self-preservation and the stabilization of East Asia. It was not Our intention . . . to infringe upon the sovereignty of other nations or to seek territorial aggrandisement.' Editorials and analysis in newspapers took up this theme. Thus, on the very day of defeat, the *Yomiuri Hochi* could write in an editorial, 'The Great East Asian War has been a war of justice as well as a war of self-defence and self-preservation. The objective of the war has been the liberation of East Asia and the peace and the welfare of a billion people. It was intended to contribute to peace in the world and progress of mankind by establishing eternal peace in East Asia. There was no intention to seek monopoly or the acquisition of territories.' This view of the war and Japan's role in East Asia (not one shared by the Asian victims of Japanese imperialism) is still the official version in Japan.

As Mr Guillain had observed in Karuizawa, the most immediate effect of the imperial announcement was, not surprisingly, weeping. Scenes of mass desolation took place throughout the country. Inconsolable crowds gathered on the parade grounds outside the palace in Tokyo, weeping and apologizing to Hirohito because they had not won the war for him. Cries of 'Forgive us, your Majesty!' rang out above the eerie sounds of the sobbing multitude. Particularly towards the end, the feeling that the war was being lost because the 'populace were inadequate to the task' had been consistently engendered by the government and there had been numerous pep rallies during which military officials had chanted slogans such as 'Haven't we been lacking in dedication?' The correct response from the assembled masses was 'We haven't tried enough. We must be more loyal.' However, after the surrender the citizens showed anger as well as shame – General Tojo, the wartime prime minister, was told by the crowds that he should commit suicide (he tried but failed and later took the rap for the Emperor at the War Crimes Tribunal) and soldiers were beaten up by civilians on the streets of the capital.

Although the Japanese were supposed to submit to 'glorious death' should they be overwhelmed by the enemy, suicides were less in number than expected. Before the occupation began on 28 August, 527 military personnel and thirty-nine members of various *uyoku* gangs had committed suicide. Many Japanese retreated into mysticism in order to distance themselves from their defeat. As they read in the *Asahi Shimbun* of 16 August, 'Japan has been based on the interrelationships between man, nature and god. This is based on harmony, and power of this harmony has been the driving force to overcome many national difficulties . . .', so they believed.

For many soldiers there was great shame attached to losing the war. Mr Fukamaki remembers his soldier-father weeping when he came home, 'apologizing to us for bringing shame on Japan'. Afterwards, as Mr Fukamaki recalls it, when the initial shock subsided the country was possessed with the need to rebuild. 'It was as if we were trying to concrete over the past.' Mr Fukamaki knows that one cannot say that war or even a military government will never happen again: 'I don't think we can ever say that, can we? But I do think the Japanese are a very peace-loving people.' This is how the majority of Japanese see themselves now, a 'peace-loving people', proud of their American-writ 'peace constitution'. Both phrases are repeated like mantras, as if saying it will make it so.

Actually Article 9 – the war-renouncing provision in the 'peace constitution' in which the Americans wrote, 'The Japanese people forever renounce war as a sovereign right of the nation . . . land, sea and air forces, as well as other war potential, will never be maintained' – was eroded in 1954 when the so-called Self Defence Forces were organized under the Defence Agency. Japan indeed maintains a land, sea and air force and spends more money, in dollar terms, on defence (currently about $33 billion a year) than any other country except the US and the former Soviet Union.

This social presentation of a 'peace-loving people' observing a 'peace constitution' is part of the *wa* myth that, as we have seen, could even be articulated in the *Asahi* at the close of a bloody war. *Wa*, one is constantly told, infuses Japanese society from the boardroom to the ball game and (except for when the militarists took control) has supposedly been this country's permanent state: harmony with nature; harmony between people; harmony with the gods. However, with regard to the people part of this equation nothing could be further from the truth. Its citizens may like to be part of a group, but Japanese society, more than most others, is a collection of antagonistic groups.

Every period of Japanese history, including ours, has been one of intense internal conflict. Even in the Golden Age of Heian-kyo (794–1185) revolts and rebellions occurred in the provinces – and government by warriors was about to come into being. In the following centuries feudal wars proceeded apace, culminating in the Age of the Country at War, which began with the Onin Wars in 1467 and embroiled the whole country. The Tokugawa period, 'the two hundred and fifty years of peace and unity' which followed as the seventeenth century began, was marked by constant rebellions: from one end of this period to the other there was an average of 113 documented peasant uprisings and/or protests every decade, probably more, as many village and fief records were destroyed. In the second half of the Tokugawa period the peasant revolts became more numerous still, averaging fifteen a year. They were bigger and more violent, destroying much of the property in their way. This despite both the shogun and the *daimyo*, the provincial warlords, keeping large standing armies of highly disciplined samurai, whose loyalty was unquestioned and who could always be called upon to squelch a rebellious, unarmed populous.

It took a civil war in 1868 to restore the emperor to power and end shogunate rule. The Meiji era saw Japan rejoin the world but within twenty-six years it was at war again, this time externally, in the first Sino-Japanese war of 1894–5. The Russo-Japanese war, 1904–5, followed; then came the violent annexation of Korea in 1910. The Fifteen Years War, which began with the 'Manchurian incident' in China in 1931, and whose inglorious ending Mr Fukamaki and I am now commemorating, put a stop to Japan's exterior wars for the time being, quieting its drive for military conquest and replacing it, as is often pointed out, with a hitherto more successful drive for *economic* conquest.

Resistance and rebellion in one form or another have always been a part of Japanese life, something the powers-that-have-been spent much of their rule trying to squash. Pacifism isn't just the 'post-war phenomenon' it is often decried to be – there was opposition to the Russo-Japanese war, mainly from the 'people's movements' which had formed in the 1870s. The movement for 'Popular Rights and Freedom' had been started as a grass-roots opposition to the oligarchy being established by the Meiji era leadership and was expanded to embrace all people, including feminists.

The feminists were apparently seen by the government as the biggest threat to the social order. By 1882 women had been banned from making political speeches and by the turn of the century it was illegal for women to form any political organization whatsoever, or to participate in any political activity, including listening to speeches. Women, such as the founders of Sekirankai, the Red Wave Society, which was active in the early twenties, ignored this law and were arrested. Some, like Ito Noe, the young editor of the influential feminist magazine *Seito*, were assassinated.

The government took a dim view of all these early pacifists, not just the feminists, and aggressively clamped down on their activities, closing magazines and arresting leaders. This repression turned many reformers and pacifists into anarchists and bolshevists. The First World War, in which Japan was Britain's ally, created even more radicals: wartime inflation caused housewives to lead rice riots, which lasted for six months at a time and involved around a million people. This in turn led to further crackdowns by the government on the press and critics, and inexorably to more militancy. The next year there were five hundred strikes nationwide. In the late twenties the government began arresting anyone suspected of being a communist or social-ist: over a thousand 'leaders' were taken into custody. Those who escaped went underground.

By the beginning of the thirties many of the unrepentant feminist reformers and radicals were in prison, including the communists, the only organized group in Japan not to submit to *tenko en masse* and suddenly find the war necessary. The govern-ment absorbed all of the remaining women's groups into the Greater Japan Women's Organization, a militarist umbrella group. And these women, like the majority of the previous radicals and reformers, were turned into a patriotic front for the war effort.

According to public opinion polls, the majority of today's Japanese women were opposed to the Gulf War, which they saw as being both morally wrong and 'fire on the other side of the river' (that is, of having nothing to do with Japan). NHK, the state broadcasting network, took a poll the day after the air war began when many Western opponents of a military solution had put their misgivings aside. It found that only 20 per cent of women supported the action of the United States-led coalition forces compared to 58 per cent of men. Only 27 per cent of women supported Japan's stance of verbally and financially supporting the coalition, compared to 53 per cent of men – strikingly divergent opinions that bare the truth of where the heart of Japanese pacifism lies.

Today 77 per cent of Mr Fukamaki's compatriots think that Japan 'observes pacifism', the same percentage as those who do not want any further increase in defence spending. The only way the government could extract from parliament the £4½ billion 'donation' to the coalition's war chest was to accede to the demand of a small opposition party to shave the defence budget. The donation was finally approved on 6 March 1991, one week after the Gulf War ended; the *tatemae* was that the money was not to be used by the United States to pay for anything of a military nature.

So do not speak with too much
love, divine prince of eight
 thousand spears. This is the
way the story is told

**FROM THE SONGS OF THE
KOJIKI, THE FIRST BOOK OF
LEGENDS, SET DOWN IN THE
EIGHTH CENTURY**

When Hirohito died, at the age of eighty-seven, his only son, Akihito, had waited to ascend the Chrysanthemum Throne longer than any other Japanese crown prince. Hirohito was beginning his sixty-third year on the throne and was the world's longest reigning living monarch. He had reigned for over half of the 121 years since Japan had emerged from its self-imposed isolation, an isolation that was abruptly ended in the mid-nineteenth century by the arrival of American gunboats.

On the morning of Hirohito's death, a private ceremony took place within the palace in Tokyo, in which Akihito received from the chamberlains the sacred sword and necklace, two of the three talismanic treasures of office. The sacred mirror, the most consecrated and the most magical of the treasures, is kept at Ise, the central Shinto shrine dedicated to Amaterasu, the Sun Goddess, the pre-eminent Shinto deity. It is to Ise that the emperors go to worship their ancestors, of which the venerated Amaterasu is the first and most illustrious; and it was here that Akihito went after Hirohito's death to inform Amaterasu of what had taken place.

According to the legends laid down in Shinto's sacred books, the Kojiki (Record of Ancient Matters) and the Nihongi (Chronicles of Japan), the eight islands of Japan were created by the coupling of two *kami* (divine spirits/deities) who were brother and sister: Izanagi (he who courts) and Izanami (she who courts). The Kojiki and the Nihongi were written down from the spoken memory of one Hiyeda no Are, an old court woman who was commanded by the Empress Gemmio (708–15) to tell the stories of which she alone was the hereditary custodian. The Kojiki was completed in 712, the Nihongi in 720, but both manuscripts appeared during the subsequent reign of the Empress Gensho (715–53).

Once women could and did become empresses in their own right but, although there were two empresses as late as the Tokugawa period, as a matter of course women could no longer inherit the throne after the eighth century. The spread of Buddhism and Confucian, both misogynistic belief systems imported from China, made female rule untenable. However, perhaps because Buddha did not have a mother in quite the same way as Christ did (so there was no Mary to supplant the female goddesses) the Japanese – one of the only peoples to see the sun as female – maintained Amaterasu as their most venerable deity.

In the Japanese story of the creation, after Izanami gives birth to the god of fire she dies and goes down to the Underworld. Creation is then a male pursuit and Izanagi gives birth through his nose to Susano-o, the impetuous male, and to the Moon Goddess and Amaterasu from, respectively, his right and left eyes. Amaterasu sends her grandson Ninigi to rule over earth, equipping him with the sword, the necklace and the sacred mirror. Ninigi descends upon Kyushu and meets a mountain spirit who offers his help and the hand of his eldest daughter, a repulsive winter spirit but one who can grant immortality to the now half-man half-god that Ninigi has become on contact with the earth. He refuses her hand and the immortality that goes with it, choosing instead her beautiful younger sister, which is why the half-god half-human emperors of Japan must die. Ninigi was the great-grandfather of the first legendary emperor Jimmu who founded the Japanese state on 11 February 660 BC, an amazingly precise date in a country with a penchant for precision, even in its myths. Emperor Jimmu's enthronement is still celebrated annually every February on National Foundation Day. The sacred treasures, the legend says, were handed down the line from Ninigi to Jimmu; and in the legend of the unbroken imperial line, the sacred treasures of office have been passed on in this way from emperor to emperor.

For an emperor one birth is not enough. In Shinto, before an emperor is truly – which is to say spiritually – so, he must be reborn from the womb of Amaterasu, reborn as half-man, half-god. This is achieved through the most sacred of the Shinto ceremonies, the *daijo sai*, the Great New Food Festival, a re-enactment of part of the Japanese creation myth. Every year the people and the emperor celebrate a Niinamesai, Festival of New Food, a type of Harvest Festival primarily in thanks for the rice harvest. Amaterasu first performed this festival in the Plain of High Heaven, and when she sent Ninigi down to rule the world, his wife performed the same ritual. The *daijo sai* is the first time the emperor offers the new food to the Sun Goddess. Following one full year of mourning for the previous emperor, after the new rice has been harvested the subsequent year, the ceremony must then take place on an evening around 22–25 November.

Upon Hirohito's death, arrangements for Akihito's *daijo sai* got underway. The priests were summoned and instructed to choose the two rice paddies, one to the east of the capital and one to the west, where the sacred rice for the ceremony would be grown. They built a fire in the palace grounds and sat around it wearing white flowing gowns and black hats, resembling cottage loaves with double antennae. Burning on the fire was the shell from a tortoise. When the priests heard it crack, one of their number, a ritualist said to be a descendant of the Urabe family (who first brought this ancient practice of divination back from China a thousand years before), removed it from the flames. From the way the shell had cracked, the location of the two paddies was divined.

Time immemorial: Akihito is Japan's 125th emperor, an official head-count that includes his mythical as well as actual predecessors. Myth and fact have a way of disappearing into each other here, of becoming indivisible. As Mombusho had refused to allow Professor Ienaga to write that the tale of imperial origin and the Age of the Gods were myth, not objective historical fact, so there are hundreds of tombs of great historical importance in this country, some dating as far back as the fourth century, that have never been unearthed because they are thought to belong to a different imperial lineage and would, therefore, destroy the mystique of the broken imperial line.

In 1972 when the Takamatasuzuka tomb was opened it revealed a brilliant, almost pristine wall painting which displayed the unmistakably immense Sino-Korean influence on the Imperial Family. Scholars have stated that the earliest and largest of the imperial tombs, such as Nintoku near Osaka, may belong to a different, probably Korean, royal lineage that preceded the current imperial dynasty. This suggestion is far too heretical for antiquarians and the government to contemplate and permission to excavate these tombs continues to be denied. Archaeological digs that have accidentally come upon finds that contradict the myth of the unbroken imperial line have immediately been closed down, the evidence resealed, and the site closed off (often accompanied by an official explanation that funds for the project have dried up). Scholarship must serve the orthodoxy. Myth must be preserved as objective historical fact at any cost; it is the *kokoro* (heart/soul/mind) of the country.

This orthodoxy is the legacy of fundamentalist state Shinto, the official pre-war religion, codified in the Meiji era. State Shinto portrayed an imperial dynasty far from the Kojiki's bawdy tales of divine folly and greed. Shinto means the Way of the Gods, and that Way, outlined in the sacred books, is of nature and ancestor worship. Everything in Shinto has a *kami*: a tree, a bird, a stone, a twig, a mountain. The life of the human spirit after death is an accepted tenet of Shinto. Before Buddhism came to Japan, the concept of reward or punishment after death had no place in Shintoism, which does not have moral teachings. Although the cornerstone of Shinto is the veneration of the Sun Goddess and her relations and imperial descendants, the concept of the *infallible* emperor was one invoked by Meiji politics. The restoration of the emperor as divine head of state was an expedient vehicle to overthrow temporal shogunate rule. The last of the Tokugawa shogun had shown himself to be impotent to resist the 'foreign barbarian' in the shape of Commodore Perry of the US Navy who forced Japan to reopen to the world. Confronted by the superior technology and military might of the West, Japan turned to its 'unique' divine emperor to hang on to its sense of itself as a superior culture. The country returned to a system of *osei fukko*, imperial rule as it was in ancient times. Gradually, the Meiji concept of the emperor, which was put away by the occupation after the war, returned latterly, and most clearly, with Akihito's *daijo sai*.

Tsugu no Miya Akihito was born on 23 December 1933, the fifth child but the first son of greatly relieved parents, Hirohito and the Empress Nagako. The chamberlains had become so distressed at what they assumed (incorrectly in the light of modern knowledge about sex selection) to be Nagako's inability to produce a son and heir, that they offered Hirohito a concubine. The Emperor is said to have declined.

Akihito is packaged as the embodiment of a modern mikado, as the newspapers of the twenties show Hirohito to have been. In Akihito's case he is portrayed as dapper, tennis playing, and English speaking. And, unlike Hirohito, he has friends outside the court whom he consults about public policy, international affairs, politics, or whatever else on which he is not supposed publicly to express an opinion. However, as befitting an emperor, he is also portrayed as unworldly. In the early nineties it was reported that he expressed shock, surprise and dismay at having just discovered the poor state of Japanese-American relations, something that had been constantly in the headlines for a decade.

People who know Akihito personally describe him as being, like Mr Fukamaki and many other Japanese who were children during the war, a liberal-leaning pacifist. He is said to be pleasant but quite humourless. Akihito has indicated that he wishes to be a modern monarch (as if any monarch or monarchy can be modern). His gestures towards modernity, in a country which loves these parlour games, have been carefully laid out and picked over: he has fired some of his food tasters; he has instructed his cavalcade to stop at some traffic lights; and he has bowed his head deeply at the shrine of the Nagasaki *hibakusha*. No emperor has ever bowed towards his people, even those who died sacrificially in the emperor's name. Such an action took the country's breath away. This supposed modernist tendency worries the Japanists. They fear the worst: 'loss of national polity' and the 'barbarism' of a British-style monarchy, fodder for the tabloids, their chief priest and his entourage turned into items of salacious gossip.

Akihito has said that he attaches 'great importance' to his religious practices. As the chief priest of Shinto he performs twenty of its fundamental rites annually: rites of passage in which he may or may not believe. The Japanists fear Akihito to be 'tainted' by Christianity, because of his exposure to Elizabeth Vining, an American Quaker who taught him English after the war. She found him a poor little boy, lonely and painfully shy. As was the imperial tradition, Akihito had been exiled from his parents when he was three and sent to the chamberlains to be reared and given the requisite imperial training. Akihito broke with this tradition and allowed his three children to remain with their family. Later, much against the will of the Kunaicho, he sent the two princes (but not the princess) to Oxford.

As a child, Akihito was kept from the natural company of children – such children he did see were brought in specially for supervised 'play'. Later he was sent to the Peers School, a sort of Japanese Eton. A god-in-waiting in a rough woollen blazer. A god-in-waiting who played tennis. It was on the tennis court that he was introduced to his future empress: Shoda Michiko, the English-speaking daughter of an industrialist, a commoner, and worse, one who was educated at the Sacred Heart, an élite Catholic girls' school. 'Our modern history is a history of reaction to the Christian threat which endangers our polity and independence,' says Kase Hideaki. Michiko, 'the Cinderella princess', who gives form to the expression painfully thin, was set upon in the palace. It was the typical tale of the outsider, the person from a 'lower class' background being introduced into the socially superior household. Michiko fell victim to a whispering campaign: she was indoctrinating the children with bible stories; she carried her baby son openly in public; more, she admitted to breast-feeding, something princesses should not do. She wore the wrong dresses and gloves, the wrong hats and shoes. It was said that Michiko was too glamorous by half, too Western by far. After several years of this torment, Michiko cracked up. The Kunaicho issued a terse statement to the effect that the Crown Princess was suffering 'great mental strain' and was being hospitalized for an abortion. She disappeared for four months, a long time for an abortion, but the agency vigorously denied a mental breakdown. Abortion is acceptable in Japan; mental illness is not.

You don't have to do much to be considered too Western. The present prime minister, Miyazawa, an eloquent English speaker, was once criticized for being too Western because he read the English language edition of *Newsweek* in public. His presumed Westernness, not his involvement in the Recruit scandal, was said to have kept him from the premiership he sought for so many years. Now, having finally attained it, he is barred by press and government hysteria from speaking in English to English-speaking heads of government, as 'he could give too much away' in negotiations (English being a language less suited to amorphous circumlocutions than Japanese). As a result, in theory at least, he is in the absurd position of having to conduct these negotiations with President Bush et al through an interpreter.

On the night before he underwent the *daijo sai*, Akihito was spiritually aligned through a *Mi tama shizume no matsuri* (Pacification of the Soul ceremony), which took place in the palace grounds. The four spirits that Shintoists believe dwell in all people – a gentle spirit, a rough spirit, a luck spirit and a wondrous spirit – were harmonized to ensure that they did not wander from his body. The ceremony is believed to afford the emperor inner tranquillity and to lengthen his life. A *miko*, Shinto shamaness, holding a spear and bells, would have danced on a contraption which looked like an upside-down tub. She would then have banged the spear on the tub ten times, while a priest tied ten knots in a thick silk cord.

The dance the *miko* performed was first enacted in front of the heavenly cave in which Amaterasu had hidden herself, furious at the behaviour of Susano-o, her boorish brother. Susano-o had come to Amaterasu's domain on the pretext of apologizing for a previous misdemeanour but had proceeded to desecrate her property and destroy her rice paddies by letting loose wild horses upon them. Amaterasu retaliated by withdrawing into a cave, rolling a boulder in front of it, casting the world that was Japan into darkness. The gods and goddesses gathered to entice her from the cave, one making a mirror, another a necklace – the mirror and jewel. These gifts were not enough to bring Amaterasu from her cave, so the goddess Ame no uzume performed a strip-tease dance. The assembled gods whooped and guffawed, prompting the curious Sun Goddess to roll away the boulder whereupon she saw her reflection caught in the mirror the deity had fashioned; the first mirror in the world and the first reflection. With this she removed herself from the cave, releasing her light once again upon the eight islands of Japan.

The Yuki den and Suki den, the sacred halls where the *daijo sai* would take place, were specially erected in the palace grounds. These halls were identical wooden structures suggesting, with their triangular thatched roofs, traditional farmhouses. They were built on a platform and separated from each other by an interior brushwood fence, with a similar fence surrounding and enclosing the compound. The trees from which they were made had been grown specially. It took, as it must, less than a week to construct these halls, and, as it must, construction was begun seven days prior to the date of the *daijo sai*, a few days after Akihito's public enthronement, an event, like his father's funeral, attended by a high-level representative from almost every country on earth. The government decided that the guests should not be asked to shout 'Banzai!' however, because of its unfortunate association as an imperial war cry.

I imagine Akihito that cool November evening in 1990, the night of his *daijo sai*, walking through the palace grounds, heading towards his unquestioned destiny. He enters a pavilion where his priest-attendants purify him, dressing him in a white raw silk gown that billows about his five-foot-five-inch frame, an unwieldly parachute that snags in the bushes as he walks further into the woods. On top of his tarnished silver hair sits the incongruous black hat of the Shinto chief priest, with its pillbox base and a long flapping antenna, hare's ears to connect him to the eight million gods and goddesses of the pantheon.

Inside the grounds it would have been as deeply dark as unrealized thought. At the edge of the woods where the palace ends and Tokyo begins, there is a diffuse glow; the tops of the trees are yellow at the tips from the glare of the capital. Akihito and two dozen attendants, the priests and the *miko*, enter through the gate in the brushwood fence to the Yuki den and the Suki den. The priests and the *miko* are dressed as the Emperor in white raw silk gowns. The priests wear similar hats to his; their faces beneath them impassive as stone. The *miko* wear their hair loose, hanging long and straight over their backs, a shiny charcoal blanket. Everything has been purified, blessed, readied for the Emperor and the Sun Goddess. One of the priests rubs two sticks together, making a flame with which he lights the lamps in the halls. The strains of atonal music trickle through the night, a lonely wail of something lost or forsaken. The Song of the Rice Pounding is played as the *miko* mime this action, their bodies swaying. Akihito enters the outer room of the Yuki den followed by his courtiers. The court musicians sing the folk songs native to the district east of the capital, where the rice that will be eaten in the Yuki den was grown. The ritualists and *miko* proceed into the outer chamber carrying bowls of food. When everyone is inside, Akihito, flanked by only two of the *miko* now, withdraws to the inner sanctum where no one else may tread.

Inside is a vast couch of three levels composed of *tatami* (compacted rice straw mats). This is the *shinza*, the *kami* seat. The base of the couch is made of six *tatami* mats: six mats, the size of a room in a typical Japanese house or flat. (Traditionally floors in Japan are covered with *tatami* mats two or three inches deep.) By the side of the bed is a *tatami* night table, on which has been placed a comb carefully wrapped in paper and a fan. On the floor are a pair of purple slippers, with turned up toes, Chinese style. The two *miko* bring in Amaterasu's food first, placing it on the food mat. Then the Emperor's food is put on his mat beside the Goddess'. He sits facing the Great Shrine at Ise.

Akihito lies down on the bed and pulls the white silk eider-down over him. Behind the screen the *miko* are on their knees, completely prostrate, their noses on the floor. The *daijo sai* is a secret ceremony. In the past, Japanese scholars and Shinto ritualists who told of what they knew transpired were imprisoned. Only the emperor knows all of what manifests during his rebirth, but this is the way the story is told. The emperor is transmutable.

Now he too is a *miko*, ready to receive the rice god, the spirit made flesh, the body of his country. Now he is himself again. Amaterasu descends. She looks like an idealized woman of the Heian court with luxuriant pitch-black hair down to her calves and a plump white moon-shaped face, tiny bow-shaped mouth and slivers for eyes, the Heian-kyo epitome of female beauty. And male beauty too. She personifies the attributes of the period. Akihito is becoming the embodiment of Japan, mingling his blood with the goddess, entering her body, making love with her spirit, being born again through her womb. The emperor is now the emperor in fact as well as name, his *kokoro* is the same as the Goddess' *kokoro*. Their mind-hearts have fused.

By 6 a.m. the ceremony has been completed twice, once in each of the sacred halls. I imagine Akihito making his way back through the grey winter dawn, hurrying through the palace woods, feeling the rising sun whispering over his face. He has been reborn as himself, half-man, half-god, an emperor of Japan, the latest incarnation of the heavenly sun dynasty.

Akihito, like Hirohito before him, is now Shinto's chief priest on earth and a divinity in its pantheon, a living god – despite the fact that after the war, as part of the surrender agreement, Hirohito renounced his divinity and, to Western thinking, the divinity of the subsequent emperors. To the Japanists, 'The poor Emperor was forced at gunpoint to renounce his divinity,' and as such the act had no meaning either to Hirohito or to his people. The left agrees, pooh-poohing the Americans 'degoding' as 'trying to cut through the Japanese mist with Western scissors,' as the Reverend Tomura puts it. In other words, the renunciation was the necessary *tatemae* to enable the *honne* of imperial divinity to continue unabated. The government either denied that Akihito became a god during his *daijo sai* or hedged its bets: 'Some scholars think the *daijo sai* turns the emperor into a god,' a po-faced deputy cabinet secretary told parliament, 'but it is not for the government to say.'

IN
THE
COUNTRY
OF
EIGHT
ISLANDS

Shikoku, the smallest of Japan's main four islands, floats in the Seto naikai, the Inland Sea, between Kyushu to the southwest and the island of Honshu curled up around its eastern and northern flanks. Although it is now linked to the mainland by the 'longest double-decker car and train suspension bridge in the world', and to the world by a new 'international airport' (joining the four domestic airports already in existence on the island), Shikoku, population five million, still feels remote, quaint, almost of a Japan long past, a Japan once known in antiquity as the Country of Eight Islands.

Shikoku is still predominately rural. Only segments of its northwestern coast around Matsuyama, the largest city, are over-industrialized like the rest of the country. The island, which was linked to Honshu in only 1988 by the Seto Ohashi Bridge, has been saved by its relative inaccessibility. Most Japanese have never been to Shikoku, perceiving it to be too out-of-the-way and uninteresting. Perhaps because of its perceived dearth of tourist attractions, or the fact that it is not written about much, few foreign visitors find their way here either. This is a shame as you have to go to the far reaches of Hokkaido, Japan's most northerly island, to find countryside as unspoiled as that which exists in much of Shikoku.

The Japanese who do visit Shikoku are usually the elderly on a pilgrimage of the eighty-eight Buddhist temples that are strung haphazardly around the island. The pilgrimage is in honour of the temples' founder, Kobo Daishi, a Buddhist saint who was born here in 774 as Kukai. Kobo is his posthumous name and Daishi, Great Master, his title. Those who successfully complete the eighty-eight-temple circuit in honour of Kobo Daishi are said to be released from the doom of the Buddhist cycle of rebirth. It takes at least two months on foot to complete the peregrination, although these days most pilgrims, dressed for the part in smocks and matching cloth hats and carrying staffs, opt for the bus tour which takes only thirteen days.

According to legend Kukai emerged from the womb with his hands held together in an attitude of prayer. There are many stories and legends associated with him. He was renowned in his life as an excellent sculptor and perpetual traveller, as well as a priest and miracle worker. As befitting an important religious figure, he was plagued by visitations from evil spirits during his training for the priesthood – dragons and sea monsters came upon him while he was meditating, but he repelled them with incantations and spit. And not ordinary spit according to the legend – light from the Evening Star filled his mouth and he frightened the devils away with its rays. As St Francis drove the snakes from Ireland, Kobo Daishi drove the foxes (one of whom tried to deceive him) from Shikoku. Kukai constantly travelled around Japan, usually incognito, dressed as a beggar, dispensing favours or punishments as he went: he created an everlasting fountain for one poor old woman who had given him water, but turned an old man's potatoes hard for eternity when the peasant refused to give him anything to eat.

When Kukai was thirty he set sail for China where he studied the Indian Tantric 'true word' school of Buddhism, which uses the mantra to achieve enlightenment. He returned to Japan and founded the Japanese version of this Buddhist Tantric tradition, known as the Shingon sect. Kukai is also said to have brought the practice of homosexuality back from China, up until then apparently unknown in Japan, another example of a precise beginning. This love, which very much dared to speak its name, soon became popular among the monks, and then later the samurai and others of noble birth, before spreading into the population as a whole. Kukai died aged sixty, but to true believers his spirit lingers on in his tomb, waiting for the coming of Miroku, the Buddhist Messiah.

The word Shikoku means four countries, and reflecting these early divisions it is divided into four counties today: Kagawa, Tokushima, Ehime and Kochi. Running east to west through the centre of the island is a rugged mountain range that both temperamentally and geographically splits Shikoku in half. The northern side, the Seto naikai half of the island, has a dry climate, with little rain even in the typhoon season, whereas the southern flank, the Pacific side, is often sodden from the oceanic storms, but is warmer and experiences very mild winters. The people of Shikoku are said to mirror these meteorological conditions: colder and more formal in the north; warmer and laid back in the south.

Shikoku's mountains can be vast and dramatic; rugged and chipped they soar up to 6500 feet. The mountains are separated by tree-stuffed ravines and lush plump valleys which seem to have sprung from the earth whole to shove the mountains apart. Japan's natural world, which was formed and reformed by constant volcanic activity and earthquakes, often looks simultaneously tumultuous and ethereal. Here in the valleys are small farming communities, scattered villages which have been sequestered away within these mountains for hundreds of years. When I first saw these settlements, from high on a mountain ridge, I felt as if I were gazing at the past, miniaturized and frozen, through the wrong end of a telescope, looking at a different country, one as far away as a long-dead star. Even in the countryside the Japanese build their houses close together, cheek by jowl, herded as one for warmth and protection against marauders. The farmhouses here were huddled side by side, each with a small vegetable plot at the front and a rice paddy at the rear.

The time warp continued. I was welcomed like an emissary from the outside world, a traveller from Eikoku (England, literally 'civilized country') *circa* 1868. No one had ever met anyone from England before and to a man and a woman they expressed great admiration for Tatcher san. Tatcher san, who was generally much admired in Japan, a country where it would be impossible to be either a woman prime minister or an autocratic prime minister, was where their vision of modern England (never Britain) began and ended. For the villagers to whom Eikoku existed at all, the idea of it wandered through their minds in a pastoral vacuum, forming itself in a bucolic haze of white crêpe dresses and picture-box hats. There were roses around the doors and teacups in Eikoku, a country that seemed to have sprung to life bright and fully formed from those vividly painted Victorian prints so beloved by the old biscuit-tin and chocolate-box manufacturers.

As an example from this otherwise delicate race, I could only disappoint. Later I discovered, with some relief, that England was often confused with Italy or France, or even Germany and Sweden, by most people, the majority of whom had never left Shikoku. 'And she has blonde hair, and blue eyes,' they would gush down the phone to friends and family on other parts of the island, as if it were by way of a *coup de grâce*. I began to feel like some rare breed of animal or a seldom sighted bird.

I look around: humans like green stalks at this rice planting time!

BUSON (1716–83)

I slurp through the rice paddy wearing a spare pair of Mrs Shibata's wellington boots. She nods encouragingly, but I really can't get the hang of it. The boots are continually fighting with the mud and the mud usually wins. It wrestles them down, drowning them in water and silt, a cold, cloying mixture that gropes insistently between my toes, sucking and spitting as I lurch along. Mr and Mrs Shibata are planting the rice by hand, bent over double, twisting their arms under the water. You can get machines to do this, but the Shibatas feel that it isn't worth it for their quarter of an acre of paddy; more, that it would be lazy to employ a machine for such little work. They prefer to use the old ways to plant this perfectly square field.

Their oldest son, Tenshi, and their daughter-in-law, Kume, work beside them. Planting rice, and harvesting it, is traditionally a family affair. Even Tenshi and Kume's small children are here, solemn-faced, up to their elbows in chilled silt. Fumio, the boy, is five, Keiko, the girl, is nearly three. Kume teaches them a morning song from the nineteenth-century rice planting songs. Small children are taught to remember long poems and songs as a matter of course. At around the age of three many mothers start to teach their children to read and write one or both of the Japanese syllabries, *hiragana* and *katakana*. Fumi chan (most children are called by the diminutive of their name, plus 'chan') can count to one hundred and do simple addition and subtraction involving numbers under ten, skills Kume has taught him, strengthening his memory which will be his most important asset throughout his school life. I listen to them singing with their mother, their voices reed thin but clear; their faces are smooth with happiness. Mrs Shibata beams in Kume's direction. Kume is what the tenth-century writer Sei Shonagon categorized in the *Pillow Book* under the heading of 'A Rare Thing': a daughter-in-law who is loved by her mother-in-law.

Japanese paddies always look like machine-perfect squares or rectangles, slotted into a landscape that is itself uniformly angular, either flat or pointed. Nowhere does the Japanese countryside undulate like that of England. It is never gentle. At the point where the flinty, sharp-toothed mountains begin the severed edge of the valley is as sure as the end of a table. The light is bruised, a faint blue singed purple at the edges. Flat, soft-edged plates of white mist float through the misshapen mountains. As it crawls up the early morning sky, the sun does little to heat the thin air. We work on farmers' time here. Even in midsummer the sun sets around seven in the evening and rises at 4 a.m. Like the price of rice, the daylight is arranged around the fewer and fewer farmers.

The children in their T-shirts and shorts must be cold. They are being taught to endure. *Kuro saseta hoo ga ii* – it is good/ better to have (the child) endure difficulties, the maxim has it, physically and mentally, it is how you become a proper person. It is quite common to see small children wearing skimpy shorts or skirts in the cold weather, even in the cities. Some schools practise what is called Naked Education, a system in which three- to six-year-olds wear nothing but gym shorts and gym shoes all year round outside in the playground as well as inside in the unheated classrooms. Much is expected from young children, and much is given in return in lavish amounts of care and attention, especially from their mothers. It is a truism in Japan that the central emotional relationship is between mother and child, not between husband and wife. Up until seven a child lives with the gods, as the proverb says, in a love affair with its mother. Early childhood is always remembered as a paradise by most Japanese, a state of bliss from which many, especially men, feel themselves to have been roughly ejected.

Everyone is silent now, folded over in the paddy like origami figures, the tops of their round heads facing the mountain. Shafts of wind come and go, tousling hair. The rest of the villagers are also in their paddies, bending and stretching, line upon line of them, just like their ancestors before them. This is my Victorian print, my picture-perfect Japan; a Japan as yet uncovered in concrete, whose dreams have not been paved over.

The local news station wanted pictures of the *gaijin* in the field, the envoy from the outside world, whom it hoped would explain to this outside world Japan's position over rice – its intractability, its steadfast refusal to accept rice imports – explain the troublesome grain's religious and cultural significance. Explain, I thought as I listened in horror to what they believed I was doing here, how this country manages to be at once an advanced industrial nation within an agrarian fantasy; in short, a hi-tech feudal state.

I saw myself on the television, standing in the rice paddy, Mr and Mrs Shibata fastened one on either side of me like guardian angels. He was smiling, showing the viewers his paucity of teeth. His hair looked startlingly white against his nut brown face. We stood head to head he and I, which contrived to make me look tall, as I never do in the city standing close to the well-nourished urban specimens of my generation. Mrs Shibata floated around my shoulder, dark and rotund as a laughing Buddha. She laughed without covering her mouth, also exposing the gaps between her teeth. The Shibatas looked amazingly poor, like peasants in a third-world country, though in fact they are far from poor. The camera is a terrible liar, a fast dissembler of the facts. It wasn't only the lack of teeth that accounted for this verisimilitude of poverty, but also their cheap-looking polyester clothes, each item of which seemed designed to jar against the next. We stood the three of us like victims of a home movie, still and solitary, putting on a brave face, the mountains stark and brooding behind us.

At a couple of acres the Shibatas' farm is small, but not peculiarly so as the average Japanese farm is merely three acres. The Shibatas are part of the only expanding group of farmers: those who are over sixty-five. Before they retired from their 'outside work' – as a waitress in an *udon* (wheat noodles) restaurant and a factory worker at a crane manufacturer – they tended to the rice farm part-time, as do around 70 per cent of all farmers. Over half of all farms grow rice – the importation of even small quantities of the stuff is illegal. In order to subsidize domestic production, the price of rice is set artificially high by the government. As a result the consumer pays between five and eight times the world price for its staple food.

Many farming households keep up the rice paddy, or the solitary peach tree that passes for an orchard, solely for tax reasons and to ensure for their parents, and later themselves and their children, a supplementary retirement income. The Japanese say their complicated tax system is based on the nine-six-four premise: *sarariman*, who can claim few deductions, pay 90 per cent of their taxes; doctors pay 60 per cent and farmers 40 per cent. There are approximately four million farming households in Japan, home to twenty million people, of whom six million are classified as full- or part-time farmers. Because of tax incentives and state control of crop price, farmers have an annual income one-third higher than ordinary mortals. Even in densely populated Tokyo there is approximately 90,000 acres of defined 'farmland', sometimes containing little more than a couple of apple trees, tended by 125,000 registered farmers.

Nevertheless, you hear little real complaint about the farmers, and most people seem willing to pay outrageous sums of money for their harvest, perhaps in order to keep the concept of rural Japan alive. This is especially true of Japanese rice, which people have been taught to believe has mystical qualities, akin to the Communion wafer – the Emperor has a paddy field within his palace grounds, which he farms, or at least stands by for photographs during spring planting and the harvest. The central role of rice in Shinto fertility rites is seen over and over from the *daijo sai* to the guardian foxes with the very long phallic tails that are found around the thirty thousand shrines of the rice goddess Inari, the patron of agriculture and commerce. That rice is the symbol of fertility is not, of course, just a Japanese or Asian custom. Even in Eikoku, where rice is not grown, we still throw it over the bride and groom to shower them with fertility. The Shibatas were surprised when I told them this; surprised, as Japanese people inevitably are, that foreign practices can be similar to those in Japan. In the Japanese way, the couple had lifted their voices to the sky and said simultaneously, '*Honto desu ne?*' Is that really true?

Increasingly, the language of the trade dispute over rice is couched in egregious terms: as Kamei Shizuka, the acting head of the Basic Issues group, a collection of fifty or so Japanist LDP MPs, puts it, 'We should never give in over the issue of rice, it cannot be used to redress the trade imbalance. It is the basis of Japan's culture, our civilization, the basis of our history. Our agriculture, our lifestyle is based on the cultivation of rice. It is the backbone of our spiritual life. The countryside is Japan's spiritual life. If California rice is allowed in, rural areas will collapse, then we Japanese will not be able to return to our spiritual home. We will be deprived of a place where the soul can go back to . . .' However, this mystical Japanist reverence for native rice cultivation hasn't always been so: 'Japan is the fountain source of the Yamato race, Manchuko [Manchuria] is its reservoir, and East Asia its paddy field,' explained *The Way of Subjects*, the wartime ethical code published in 1941. In those heady days of Empire, Japan imported most of its rice from its domains in East Asia.

Moreover, feelings about the countryside are decidedly mixed. The Japanese carry the spiritual aspects of the country life to which Kamei refers on their backs. Most Tokyoites are only two generations from the land and they continue to observe its rhythms in the city during the Shinto festivals and observances. The country lives on in all the cities in plainly observable ways. Almost everyone in Tokyo can speak two dialects: that of the big city and that of their *furusato* (hometown). During Obon, the capital becomes a ghost town as sophisticated Tokyoites don their country speech and return to the *furusato* of their ancestors. It sometimes seems that every *enka* (popular ballad) is a cry of nostalgia for *furusato*. Yet most middle-class Japanese do not covert a country cottage in the way their Western counterparts do, they are too soon off the farm for that. However this may be changing – most of the bigger companies have country places that their employees can rent for short holidays, and the rich are increasingly buying country homes. The concept of a weekend in the woods may yet become fashionable. At the moment, however, it is probably not much of an exaggeration to say that almost everyone would rather live, and remain, in Tokyo if they could – ski and golfing trips excepted. The very word for countryside, *inaka*, more properly means anywhere that is not the capital and the word carries within it feelings of disdain and an attitude of dismissal towards the country bumpkins and their deeply unfashionable antiquated habitat.

Resistance to rice imports is more political than mystical. The farmers, and especially the rice farmers, enjoy the patronage of the ruling party which benefits from constituency boundaries that have been gerrymandered in such a way as to ignore demographic change. The urban constituencies, which are often and always potentially more sympathetic to the opposition, have proportionally fewer MPs than the rural constituencies. Only 37 per cent of parliamentary seats are allotted to urban areas, where the majority of the population lives; the remaining 63 per cent are assigned to rural areas. Some urban voters regularly, and so far ineffectually, take the government to court over this. The LDP takes care of the farmers and the farmers take care of the LDP.

The relationship between the two is based on *giri* (obligation), a system that weaves through Japanese society, sticking each member to the other like the grains in a bowl of glutinous rice. All farmers are organized in *nokyo*, farm co-operatives, which are unofficial tentacles of the Agriculture Ministry. The farmers are obligated to buy their fertilizers and farm equipment from the *nokyo*, at what even a government report found to be 'exorbitant prices'. The *nokyo* has even managed to get into marital business by organizing lucrative wedding bashes for the farmers' children; and the *nokyo* bank, Norin Chukin, which takes care of all the farmers' banking and insurance needs, is the world's largest institutional investor.

The farmers, as is true in most countries, are perceived to be socially and politically conservative, which indeed they are on subjects such as food imports. Zenchu, the farmers' union, has shown itself capable of almost anything in order to scare restless consumers away from the lures of cheap foreign food. It has produced vitriolic anti-food-imports films that claim, among other things, that Siamese twins were deformed thus because their mothers ate 'foreign food'. One of the films, backed by Zenchu money, was produced by two of the biggest mainstream consumer associations, which, in the topsy-turvy world often prevailing in the Eight Islands, in reality represent the interests of the producers.

Are You Still Going to Eat Imported Food? was widely shown to labour and civic groups throughout Japan in the late eighties. In it wards of howling children suffering from skin diseases and physical deformities were shown with a menacing voice-over informing viewers, 'Diseases in children are increasing in proportion to the percentage of imported food . . .' Customs officers, wearing gas masks and space-age protective suits, traipsed in slow motion through Yokohama's quayside, peering into oil drums of rotting foreign fruit while the voice intoned, 'Foreign fruit spends at least two years here, sometimes five . . .'

The Shibatas, who saw this film, believed it, as did the average viewer. Not surprisingly, like the majority of farmers, the Shibatas are conservative on food imports and the Zenchu–Nokyo–Agriculture Ministry axis has exploited this successfully as part of its control over the countryside. Like the majority of farmers, the Shibatas come from a district which up until the war was self-governing and they have never taken kindly to rule 'from the government in Tokyo'. The Japanese as a whole have never taken comfortably to central control. In effect there still is no central control in Japan.

No distinctions among us.
All taught to die

KANEKO MITSUHARU
(1895–1975),
SONG OF LONELINESS

For 250 years the Tokugawa shogunate tried to enforce centralized control over Japan. The shogunate regulated everything it could and codified people into a six-tier feudal caste system of samurai–farmer–artisan–merchant–*eta*–*hinin*, each with its own dress code. The *hinin* (non-humans) were those who had taken part in a treasonous plot against the emperor. And the *eta* (the filth) are what are now called *burakumin* (hamlet people), a euphemistic name for the three million or so strong caste akin to India's untouchables. The *burakumin* first came about during Heian-kyo, when the precept of Buddhism that condemns the killing of animals merged with Shinto's association of death with pollution. These people were and are a Shinto taboo, ritually unclean, polluted by death and confined to the unclean professions: butchers, leather workers, grave diggers. Up until the last century the hamlets in which *burakumin* were forced to dwell were nameless places, quite literally off the map.

Although discrimination against *burakumin*, who are ethnically indistinguishable from other Japanese, is now illegal, Japanese people who will talk honestly about this admit to feeling a physical revulsion around people they know to be *burakumin*. Companies and the families of prospective spouses routinely employ private detectives to search into a person's background to ensure he or she is not *burakumin*. Access to the *koseki*, the household register of families, without permission is now technically illegal, but it is still relatively easy for a private eye to uncover someone's background. There is reputedly an unofficial directory of *burakumin* names to make the job even simpler. With both the *koseki*, in which everything is recorded, and the illegality of changing your name, there are few corners in which to hide in Japan, few opportunities to reinvent yourself.

During the Tokugawa period, only the samurai, who were in the service of the *daimyo*, were allowed to be armed. Their function during this time of relative internal peace was largely to put down the ubiquitous peasant uprisings that continued apace. Samurai in some form or another go back to the tenth century, where the word was used in the sense of military retainer. But the samurai as a *warrior* class came into existence as Heian-kyo fell in 1185. The highly stylized Heian court in what is now Kyoto, one that was dominated by literature, love and intrigue and considerably created and maintained by women as a sort of cult of femininity, was destroyed by a warrior cult, personified by the samurai. The dandified court lost its worldly power because it was peopled by aesthetes, whose exaggerated concern for beauty, both physical and artistic, became stylized empty formalism, ossified and meaningless. The dwellers in Heian-kyo paid no attention to what went on outside their immediate world. They were in love with the romance of love, the idea of it, its poetic consequences, as well as its physical manifestations. The courtly arts extended to the bedroom and *sei*, the Japanese word for sex (combined from two *kanji*, one meaning heart and the other life), could have been the court's motif.

As members of the permanent standing armies of the myriad *daimyo* during the endemic feudal wars that followed Heian-kyo, the samurai developed a strict ethical code known as *bushido*, evolved homosexuality into a cult of the 'purest love', and glorified death. In the sixteenth-century *Code of the Samurai*, the author's first words to the novice are: 'One who is a samurai must before all things keep constantly in mind, by day and by night, from the morning when he takes up his chopsticks to eat his New Year's breakfast to Old Year's night when he pays his yearly bills, the fact that he has to die.' This was echoed in pithier style by the eighteenth-century tome known as the *Hagakure* (A Life Hidden Behind the Leaves) in the phrase, 'The Way of the samurai is found in death.' Inevitability was made a virtue. 'Glorious death', so necessary to maintain fanatical loyalty and a permanent state of civil war, was now in vogue. Failing death on the battlefield, the samurai were instructed on *seppuku* (suicide by ritual disembowelment with a sword), which became an integral part of their discipline, something to be carried out to avoid the shame of defeat and 'awarded' to a transgressor as an honourable punishment, a form of suicide that could not be undertaken by mere commoners.

The acceptance and even glorification of suicide is one of the better known facets of Japanese culture. But this is a samurai legacy, it was most certainly not always the case. In the books of the legends, death is the supreme defilement. In Shinto, as we see from the attitude towards the *eta* and now the *burakumin*, even to look at a dead person or animal was to be in need of purification. Suicide was an ungodly and dishonourable act. Ritual suicide did not begin to occur until the Kamakura period, the beginning of the warrior culture, which followed the collapse of the Heian court. By the Tokugawa period, death, and especially suicide, had come to be thought of as purifying through the blood it shed. This cult of death, now for the glory of the god-emperor, permeated the Second World War: 'The purity of youth [who die on kamikaze missions] will usher in the Divine Wind,' Admiral Onishi wrote. The kamikaze were boys in their late teens to early twenties, constantly likened, and indeed who likened themselves, to the exquisite *sakura* (cherry blossom), cut down in the acme of their radiance.

> If only we might fall
> Like *sakura* in the spring –
> So pure and radiant

is typical of the obligatory poems penned just before a suicide mission, and often printed in newspapers after the 'success' of a kamikaze attack.

Nothing so much personifies the way the modern Japanese define their concept of beauty as *sakura*. The trees bloom in the spring, an explosion of vibrant pink glory lasting barely a week. Like a consumptive poet of another age, *sakura* dies at its zenith; often it neither fades nor withers but falls from the trees in a rainstorm of pink. The romance of death, the beauty of death, the cult of death. Japanese culture, to paraphrase, defines beauty as dying of its own despair. The kamikaze were always dressed so nicely for death; their white scarves so white; their Rising Sun *hajimaki* (cloth headbands) tied so precisely. In the photos of them toasting the Emperor in sake they looked calmer than a wooden floor. But those who never got to fly their final mission tell it differently. As they dive-bombed the target, the pilots were often drunk and popped uppers like Polo mints. They were supposed to scream *banzai* as they headed towards their death but as often as not they cried out for their mothers.

The samurai codes dwelt upon the minutiae of etiquette. The smallest detail of behaviour and style were prescribed and described, perhaps to detract from the foregone conclusion of imminent, probably nasty, death. There were some compensations. Like the Spartans and the Prussians, the samurai were armies of lovers. They specialized in *shudo* (the way of adolescents), in practice 'the way of young men' usually in their late teens to early twenties. These young recruits became the lovers of the older samurai. Women, whom they married later in life and used 'as holes to be borrowed' for producing heirs, were often despised as weak inferior creatures, so contrary to their exalted position in Heian-kyo. By the eighteenth century, the robust aspects of homosexual love had given way to a platonic ideal. As it is written in the *Hagakure*: 'The ultimate ideal love is the unknown love hidden in the depths of the heart. This is because once it comes to the light of day, our love can become less pure and less passionate, and thus less noble. To die having all our life kept our passion secret, this is the true essence of love.'

As the Tokugawa period progressed the samurai, like the dwellers of Heian-kyo, became dandified. There was little for them to do save put down the unarmed peasant rebellions and look after the estates of their *daimyo*. The shogunate required all *daimyo* to spend one year in every two in Edo, as Tokyo was then called, thereby keeping them away from the source of their power. (Kyoto, where the emperors were ensconced, was still the capital, but the power lay now in Edo.) Meanwhile the samurai-retainer, who did not own any land of his own, received from the *daimyo* a small stipend about the size of what the farmers were earning, an amount barely above subsistence level. All a samurai was left with, therefore, was his codes of conduct, his honour, his class status, and his right to bear a sword and use it as he saw fit on any passing commoner. (There are numerous stories of samurai testing the sharpness of their blades on an unfortunate commoner's neck.)

The Tokugawa shogunate expended a great deal of energy keeping the unruly populace under control. Except for through the tiny island of Deijima off Nagasaki, the country was completely closed to foreign influence and foreign trade, which kept the merchants (the fourth tier on the six-tier caste system, above only the outcast groups), as they were: poor and powerless. The Tokugawa regime seems to have understood that a prosperous merchant class often has a tendency to bring about an end to feudalism. The shogunate ruled that all social castes were required to post on their door their hereditary status. There was, in theory, no social mobility whatsoever. Not only were the clothes each group could wear prescribed, so was the food they could buy, and the kind of house they could live in. Naturally, the censor was an important man in Tokugawa society, in which every art form was censored. (The *ukiyo-e* artists developed elaborate and changing visual codes to get their political and satirical messages across to the public.)

The shogunate tried, unsuccessfully, to impose a 'joint control system' on the villages. At the end of the Tokugawa period, this system existed as it had in the beginning – only on paper. The majority of villages still managed their own affairs. To further control both incipient and active unrest by the peasants, as well as potential anti-shogunate alliances between the *daimyo*, the shogunate strictly limited travel within Japan as well as without. As foreigners were banned from entering the country, the Japanese were now forbidden to leave it. Those who did and were foolish enough to return were executed. Exceptions to the internal travel restrictions were made for pilgrimages, which, like Shikoku's eighty-eight temple circuit, became extremely popular as a result.

Just when it might have seemed that the immovable shogunate in Edo was just that, the American 'Blackships' arrived, determined to blow the country open if necessary. Unfortunately for the shogunate they had given insufficient thought to controlling an educated standing army that was kept in near poverty. The samurai saw their chance in the personage of Commodore Perry, and in 1868 rose up and formed an anti-Tokugawa movement, which in three years completely overthrew the shogunate: *sonno joi!* was the samurai rallying cry. The Meiji government that followed, with the emperor restored as head of state, was a government of samurai, Japan's educated as well as warrior class. Those samurai who did not go directly to the government became journalists and other keepers of the culture, as well as leaders of the new burgeoning industries. Japan had exchanged one oligarchy for another.

The samurai Meiji leadership also tried, unsuccessfully, to rein in the villagers, as did the later pre-war Showa government which attempted to use the first *nokyo* organization to arrange the farmers into manageable entities. It wasn't until 1943 however, when the Nogyokai, the Imperial Agricultural Association, was formed as part of the war effort that the villagers were brought under Tokyo's control. Membership in the Nogyokai was mandatory, as is, for all intents and purposes, membership in the postwar organization of the *nokyo*, which directly descends from the Nogyokai. Many farmers, like the Shibatas, resent having to be part of the *nokyo* system which they believe, quite rightly, rips them off. Feelings of separateness and rebellion against the modern immovable shogunate run deep in the countryside.

A man far from home knows no shame

PROVERB

We sit eating an early lunch of rice, pickles, fish and miso soup. (The Japanese eat at least one bowl of miso soup a day, but it can be served at every meal. Basic miso is made from soya beans but tofu and seaweed are commonly added.) Now we are alone, without the other villagers popping in and out like extras in a particularly lively farce, the Shibatas ply me with questions, beginning with the one everyone asks you if you travel alone in Japan: 'Aren't you lonely?' It is usually a two-part question, with 'Are you alone?' asked in wide-eyed amazement at the onset. Having been brought up to find solitude abhorrent, the average Japanese finds it impossible to believe that at times it could be freely and gladly chosen, never mind luxuriated in. Contrary to what you might expect, people, perhaps especially in the countryside, ask personal questions of complete strangers: 'Are you married?' Or rather, to a woman alone, 'Why didn't you get married?' – because if you were married your husband would not stand for you to be wandering around on your own. If marriage is established then the next question, asked with an intonation of incredulity, is: 'Your husband doesn't mind?' As the existence of children is a given for any married person of a certain age, the following enquiry is usually, 'What did you do with your children?' The knowledge that their father is looking after them provokes shaken heads and gasps of 'whaaa . . .' accompanied by looks of complete wonderment, as if the peculiarities of foreigners surpass all understanding.

Mrs Shibata congratulates me on my skills with the chopsticks. This is a standard comment to any Westerner who manages not to drop them on the floor. Fumio and Keiko giggle. They are using children's training chopsticks, which are clipped on to the correct fingers with ring-type contraptions. Kume makes sure they eat properly, constantly altering the position of their hands and bodies. She does it as she talks to me, as unselfconsciously as if she were clearing the table. The children take this rearranging as a matter of course. They are expected to do things properly, as is everyone else: it is part of belonging. How you behave in Japan depends on where you belong. In a very real sense a Japanese alone does not exist. The meaning of his or her life and his or her behaviour is derived from others in a way that is short of incomprehensible to most Westerners (although not to most other Asians). A man far from home knows no shame, he is no longer in dread of what others think of him. He does not belong. He has no one to answer to. The Japanese fear that the stranger/foreigner will at once become unstable or be a destabilizing influence.

Mr Shibata is the headman of the village, because, I gather, his father was and his father before him, *ad infinitum*. There are several families within this village called Shibata, all unrelated to Toshiko and Daisuke and their family. This is not an uncommon circumstance for until the mid-nineteenth century only noble and samurai families were allowed to have surnames. After this commoners were given surnames by the shogun or *daimyo*, who bestowed the same name upon everyone in a village so that they could keep check on who was who and were where they should be.

The interior of the Shibata house is dark and dank, like the inside of a cave. The *shoji* (wooden screens covered in white paper) are tight against the window, closing off the outside world of the paddy and the mountains, a dead white eye. In the corner, a three-legged paraffin stove gives off its acrid smell. The older Shibatas feel the cold and keep their legs stuck under the *kotatsu*, the multi-coloured electrically heated quilt. The children have contrived to keep most of their bodies under the quilt. Their faces, which earlier in the paddy had become pinched and shrunken, are now damp and pinkish from the welcome warmth. The unheated part of the *kotatsu* covers the table like a regular table cloth, but it is thick with heating paraphernalia on the bottom, curled like a stylized wave. I keep its pulsating heat away from my legs, pushed to the side of me over the *tatami*.

The room is crowded with knick-knacks, china animals and the like, so typical of the décor in ordinary homes. It often seems that the average person goes out of their way to display the opposite of the much-vaunted Japanese aesthetic of minimalism. A big television sits in the corner, encased like a tortoise in a brown cracked shell; its ungainly plastic knobs leer off its side. The televisions in private homes, or even in the hotels, always look as if they were made on the cheap in the sixties. It's as if no one actually buys the sleek flat black sets that fill up the shops. In an unwieldy heap by the side of the television are a stack of sumo wrestling magazines. Above it is the family shrine, opened slightly to reveal photographs of the Emperor and Empress on one side, and the Shibata family and ancestors on the other. The Shibatas have three children, who collectively produced six issue. Mr Shibata can gaze languidly forward into eternity now; his family's continuance is assured at least into the second generation. Mrs Shibata, having joined his house on marriage, can vicariously do likewise.

We talked about sumo for a while, Mr Shibata's all-consuming interest. Sumo is the national sport, the sport of the emperors. Although in Japan *besuboru* (baseball) is now as popular as sumo, and has been made (like Makudonarudo, as McDonald's hamburger establishments are called) quintessentially Japanese, it has none of the native sumo mystique. Once these stylized wrestling matches were performed as Shinto rituals at popular shrines. The building of a *dohyo* (wrestling ring) still involves elaborate Shinto rituals conducted and overseen by priests. The *dohyo* is constructed of specially prepared clay with twenty small rice-straw bales sunk into it. On the day before each tournament a *dohyo matsuri* (ring ceremony) is undertaken by the Shinto priests and sumo referees, who forsaking their elaborate green and gold court costumes which they wear during bouts, don the same white gowns and black hats as the priests. On each corner of the *dohyo* is placed a consecrated stick with white paper tassels, said to be attractive to the gods of creation. Buried in the centre of the ring is an unglazed earthenware pot containing food for the gods, such as dried chestnuts and seaweed. As part of the ritual of purification, salt and sake are poured on to the *dohyo*. Suspended from the ceiling above the ring is a wooden shrine canopy, with coloured silk ribbons representing the four seasons: green in the east corner for spring, red in the south corner for summer, white in the west corner for autumn and black in the north corner for winter. The sacred *dohyo* can never be trodden upon with shoes, nor, of course, by a woman. Between the bouts the *dohyo* is purified with salt by the *rikishi* (sumo wrestlers).

Sometimes sumo is still practised in its original Shinto form and setting, such as at the Kamo Shrine in Kyoto, where every September the Ceremony of Crows takes place. The ceremony, officiated by the priest, is a series of ritual sumo matches enacted by young boys. And at Oyamazumi Shrine on Omishima, one of the hundreds of islands crowded into the Seto naikai, a priest single-handedly wrestles with a deity in a sumo ritual. Naturally, he is always defeated by his invisible godly opponent. Sumo did not become part of *bujutsu* (martial arts) until the middle ages, when it was employed by the samurai in hand-to-hand combat during battles. Once adopted by the samurai it became the forerunner of judo and kendo.

Although in the West we tend to think of *bujutsu* exclusively as unarmed combat such as judo and karate, in Japan the canon includes all of the armed arts that were employed on the battlefield and learnt as a discipline of physical skill, technique and inner control: archery, spear fighting and swordsmanship are the three major armed *bujutsu*. Off the battlefield, as a form of self-defence (or attack), say by a lone peasant against a lone samurai, the canon of armed *bujutsu* extended to using the fan and the pipe. Such devices were wielded with great technical accuracy and skill, even against swords. Wooden implements such as the staff were also employed by non-military folk, as were the various forms of unarmed combat – Japan's most famous poet, Basho, for example, was also a whizz with the staff.

Many women were taught armed and unarmed *bujutsu*. By their eighteenth birthday girls of samurai families were expected to know how to wield, with great dexterity, the *naginata*, a long part-sword part-spear contraption, and were trained to use all traditional weapons to fight off invaders. Some even fought alongside their menfolk on the battlefield. Today women are still active practitioners of *naginatado*, which nowadays is executed with wooden staves. Samurai women always carried a short sword in the sleeve of their kimono in case they should be attacked by an intruder. If they lost this battle they used the sword to commit *jigai*, the female equivalent of *seppuku*. Unlike her husband or father, the samurai woman did not slit her abdomen, a 'privilege' retained for the men, but tied her ankles together in the prescribed ritualistic manner before slitting her throat so that she would be found in a dignified position after her agonizing death.

The mystique of *bujutsu* lies less in the physical prowess and technical skill displayed by its adherents than in the *haragei*, a condition of being 'centred', in control mentally of your own powers and energy, and by extension the mind of your opponent. When sumo *rikishi* stare each other out at the onset of a bout they are engaged in mental combat, said to give *bujutsu* its edge: the strongest mind, not necessarily the strongest body, is thought to be the one capable of victory. A *rikishi* promoted to *yokozuna* (grand champion) needs to possess *hinkaku*, the noble Japanese spirit and detached style that the samurai first observed in the Buddhist monks they were sent to quell and found quite unconcerned about meeting their deaths.

A bigger than usual Japanese body does not go amiss either. Sumo wrestlers appear to have always been on the tall side, but they were never as copiously fat as they are today. The minimum height and weight now for a *rikishi* under eighteen is 5 feet 7 inches and just over 11 stone (155 pounds); for those over eighteen it is an inch taller and 10 pounds heavier. By the time they reach the upper ranks of *ozeki* (champion) and *yokozuna* (grand champion) the average *rikishi* weighs over 21 stone (300 pounds) and is 6 feet tall. Some are much heavier, such as Konishiki, the legendary 6 foot 2 heavyweight Samoan-Hawaiian *rikishi*, whose weight fluctuates between 35½ stone (500 pounds) to just over 41 stone (576 pounds).

When Konishiki, whose real name is Salevaa Atisnoe, arrived in Japan from Hawaii he had two languages to learn: Japanese and Sumo, which has an entire vocabulary of its own, one that extends to quite ordinary words. He also had to learn the way of the apprentice in Japan: 'When they hit you over the head you just say thank you,' he said, 'and when they hit you again you say thank you even more.' He was describing life in the accurately named stables where the *rikishi* live. The juniors cook and serve the champions their meals, clean up the place, and are beaten regularly like gongs. They are humiliated, their personalities peeled away until there is nothing but the spirit of the *rikishi*. It is so gruelling that six out of ten of all sumo recruits run away from the stables.

Konishiki survived this training but there was worse to come: his success at the national sport was deeply resented and there was much official talk of banning foreigners from sumo altogether, accompanied by anonymous death threats that only increased with his mounting success. There have been foreign *rikishi* before Konishiki, but none as successful. He was surprised, at first, by the intensity of hatred that poured forth from callers and letter-writers who believed that sumo was a pure Japanese martial art which could, and should, only ever be performed by a pure Japanese. It was more than 'Go home, Yankee' – and anyway in Japanese eyes Hawaii is more a Japanese holiday resort than American (in terms of financial ownership it is actually increasingly Japanese) – we were back to blood and race again, the Japanist spirit: the barbarian was polluting the *dohyo*, so he should be killed.

Although the death threats have now tapered off to a trickle, Konishiki's position in sumo became controversial once again in March 1992 when he won the coveted Emperor's Cup for the third time, making him a potential *yokozuna*. Like much else in this country, the rules for obtaining the status of *yokozuna* are vague, and wrestlers are promoted on a 'case-by-case' basis. There have been only sixty *yokozuna* in the three hundred years of the sport's modern history, and since the retirement of the legendary Chiyonofuji there is only one active *yokozuna* wrestling today. Needless to say no *yokozuna* have been foreigners and if the country's old guard continues to have its way, none will be. Writing in *Bungei Shunju*, one of Japan's widely read magazines, Kojima Noboru, a member of the sumo committee which decides who is promoted and who is not, summed up their feelings: 'To become a *yokozuna*, a wrestler needs not only strength but *hinkaku* and an aura of dignity, a unique notion of sumo that does not exist in any other country. Foreign wrestlers trying to emulate this might be confused and embarrassed.'

Konishiki may have become confused and embarrassed by the debate swirling around him and found the pressures outside the *dohyo* detrimentally affected his *haragei*, for he subsequently lost a tournament that the Japan Sumo Association said he must win in order to be considered (even though wrestlers of lesser stature have been promoted). He may or may not become a *yokozuna* later on, but he is unlikely to survive the damage done to his knees by his gargantuan girth. As if to 'show 'em', he became the heaviest *rikishi* ever, taking the idea to its logical conclusion. A man of cartoon proportions, his waist measures 6 feet. When I stood in front of him I felt tiny and frail, fascinated and appalled by this wobbling mountain of flesh, trying to imagine just how much you would have to eat to create so much fat. Waiters moved deftly before him, rearranging tables and chairs so that he could walk through without knocking anything over. Although, like all *rikishi*, he is surprisingly supple from the daily stretching exercises, you could see that it wasn't the easiest thing in the world for him to breathe or walk. As an *ozeki* he was allowed to wear his hair in an *o-icho-mage*, pulled back into a top-knot and doubled over into a fan shape, resembling the leaf of the sacred ginkgo tree. (The lower ranks are only allowed to wear the simple top-knot.) Incongruously, he smelt of a Camellia, that fragile bloom more associated with pale, thin, consumptive women. Later I found out that all *rikishi* smell this way: it comes from the specially prepared oil in which their hair is dressed.

Top division *rikishi* are national celebrities with formidable fan clubs. Every year they go on a progress around the country-side, performing, often in the open air, on specially built *dohyo*. Their six annual *basho*, sumo tournaments, are televised live from the stadiums in Tokyo, Osaka, Nagoya and Fukuoka. Almost everyone knows the top *rikishi* by both their fighting name and their nickname. The fighting name 'Konishiki' means 'little trophy' or 'banner', something that his size and his nickname 'Dump Truck' firmly contradict. Most Japanese *rikishi* are given more poetic fighting names and nicknames. Fighting names are often taken from places and nature, such as that given to the stylish former *yokozuna* Chiyonofuji, which means a thousand generations of Fuji. Chiyonofuji, who recently retired after one of the most successful careers in sumo history, is more often called by his nickname the Wolf, an animal he seemed to embody on the *dohyo*. Chiyonofuji hails from Hokkaido, as do several other top *rikishi*, all descendants of the despised Ainu, the 'northern barbarians', who are racially different from other Japanese: having both European and Asian antecedents, they tend to be taller, hairier and bigger.

Once I saw Konishiki from a distance at a concert in Tokyo, lumbering across the grounds of the Big Egg stadium (so called for its shape) to the VIP seats. *Rikishi* always wear kimono in public, and Konishiki's Astroturf-green example enveloped him like a cocoon, making him look even wider and larger than usual. Konishiki has a thriving fan club with his own magazine and is very popular with young people. The young women gasped, screamed, giggled and, along with the young men, applauded as he waddled across the stadium. Behind their hands they whispered: what would he be like to sleep with? The thought of sinking into those mounds of flesh made them shudder and laugh hysterically. Yet *rikishi* are never in want of a wife or a date: their prestige and glamour triumphs over their unprepossessing exaggerated bodies.

When Konishiki married his girlfriend, Sumika, a month before winning his third Emperor's Cup, the wedding was televised live and was attended by many of the nation's top politicians and businessmen. Sumika, a model, is a typical sumo bride: fashionable and thin. At a fifth of his weight she is narrower than either of his legs. Unlike in the West, the Japanese regard marriage, which is to say sex, as a source of strength for sportsmen, something that is energizing rather than enervating, and the headlines telling of Konishiki's post-nuptial victories always included the phrase 'Marriage Power!' as an explanation of his continuing success.

They've cut down the willow – the kingfishers don't come any more

MASAOKA SHIKI (1867–1902)

An armada of six dark cars flits over the Seto naikai, graceful as a line of cormorants in an empty sky. The bridge is flung out in front and behind us, a wide yawn of pale grey metal. Below us the smooth and wistful sea is a rich cobalt blue. It looks deep, unfathomable. It is full of ships, tiny and tremulous, dragging their white tails after them. Every so often, the sea is interrupted by splotches of bottle-green coloured spills that are canopies of tree-tops smuggling compact islands beneath them. The islands look weightless from here, ragged bits of flotsam caught up in the tide. The sky above the horizon is three-coloured; lavender blue at the bottom, a flimsy grubby white in the frayed centre, and a sharp, ice-blue on top.

This was Mrs Shibata's idea. She insisted that I see the Seto Ohashi Bridge, 'now that it is really finished', even though, as I explained, it had been quite finished when I had seen it before. The truth is she has never been on it; at some thirty-two pounds a trip it costs too much for most people to use regularly. If she has any business in Honshu she takes the hour-long ferry journey. The six miles of six bridges, anchored by three small islands, took ten years to build at a cost of five billion pounds, adding the Seto Ohashi to the lengthy list of Japan's biggest feather-bedding projects.

The Country of Eight Islands has long since become one. The archipelago has been connected, reconnected and doubly connected by new bridges, tunnels, railways, airports, and to a lesser extent roads, muffling the bruised countryside in a surfeit of concrete, iron and steel: hard money to keep the regions afloat. Hard money, of which a healthy percentage finds its way back into the coffers of the LDP in the form of contributions and kickbacks from the *yakuza*-sodden construction industry.

We whirl down a ramp on to one of the bridge's connecting islands where a cavernous restaurant with sea views has been thrown up to feed weary travellers. The local government hopes the bridge will become a tourist attraction, that thousands will flock to marvel at this feat of engineering. A pleasure steamer has been inaugurated as an added attraction. This is an old trick here: first build your railway and then put something at the end of it to give the public a reason to ride.

We dutifully stand outside the restaurant and gawk at the bridge. Where it crosses the small islands, on which people live, the lower level railway bridge has been masked in 'sound proof-ing'. The noise of the train is muted, but the vibrations are not. The aerials on the little houses shiver. The steamship comes in. It has gone under the bridge and around it in a big loop. The disembarking passengers are middle-aged and elderly, country people laden down with cameras. Perhaps they saw enough of the bridge out at sea: they snap more pictures of me than they do of it, taking it in turns to nonchalantly sidle up close enough to get the *gaijin* into the frame.

Having been connected to the mainland by the underused bridge, Shikoku proceeded, with considerable financial assistance from 'the government in Tokyo', to build an international airport capable of handling jumbo jets close to an existing airport just outside of Takamatsu, a small provincial city with a population of around 330,000. I had seen the airport during construction. Standing by the little portable Shinto shrine that resembled a card table, I had watched with a mixture of wonderment and consternation as the bulldozers ripped open the valley below, turning the lush greenness into brown sludge. The bulldozers charged back and forth like jousters spearing the earth. Battalions of men frantically tore about. No one was walking, and no one was sitting. This is how Japan builds, as if there isn't a second to spare. It is how it destroys too: buildings, streets, whole villages even, can be removed from the landscape, sometimes literally overnight. In a land of earthquakes, fires, volcanoes and typhoons, nothing is built to last and anything may be destroyed in an instant.

Japan's natural and commercial world is echoed by Shinto which decrees that, for reasons of purity, shrines such as its central shrine of Ise be torn down and rebuilt from scratch every generation, using exactly the same type of wood and building methods that have been used for the last seventeen hundred years. Other religious structures such as the emperor's sacred halls used for the *daijo sai* must be built specially for the event and destroyed afterwards. There are few actual physical manifestations of the past in Japan. More often than not when you see an old castle or other historical sites you are looking at a perfect reproduction. What is physically old is not valued as it is in the West: old is in need of replacement. In the countryside there are skeletal remains of ghost villages, places that were abandoned *en masse* as the inhabitants headed for the cities. With surprising speed, helped along by slow, wet, hot summers, these ghostly villages rot down and eventually disappear without trace.

For the local politicians the biggest disappointment about the Seto Ohashi Bridge is not so much its lack of use, but their failure to convince the 'government in Tokyo' to install on it the very expensive tracks for the *shinkansen*, Japan's high speed train, more commonly known as the bullet train. In Japan the feeling is that if the *shinkansen* does not reach you you cannot be reached. The tentacles of the efficient and comfortable bullet train stretch far into remote parts of the countryside, another measure of the power of a modern local *daimyo*. There are, relatively speaking, surprisingly few roads in Japan and those there are tend to be permanently clogged. For journeys of any distance people prefer the *shinkansen* over the roads and over domestic air travel. Unlike many of the new bridges and airports, the trains *are* used: over three billion passengers have travelled on the *shinkansen* routes since they began operating in 1964. Many of the routes are filled to 200 per cent capacity at the weekends and on holidays, with people standing like commuters for hours in the aisles. There are few arguments put forth against additional faster sleeker trains in Japan (except occasionally the cost to the taxpayer).

In the case of the newly proposed MagLev trains, the perceived health danger from living close to the enormous magnetic fields the lines could generate when the trains are operating has caused some concern. The MagLev, a superconductive magnetically levitated train, has repelling magnets which keep the train up on a cushion of air some four inches above the track. The MagLev, which Japan sees as the natural successor to the *shinkansen*, reaches speeds of 320 miles an hour, compared to top speeds of 145 miles an hour on the *shinkansen*.

A billion-pound, twenty-seven-mile MagLev test track is in the process of being hammered through the mountains around Sakaigawa, a charming country town some eighty miles west of Tokyo. Sakaigawa is known for its hi-tech golf course where automated golf carts follow the players, many of them LDP politicians, over the links: membership in this club costs around £80,000, not exorbitant by the standards of Japanese golf clubs. If the MagLev test is deemed successful, Sakaigawa will be a short commute away from Tokyo, and will become yet another suburb. The district just happens to be that of Kanemaru Shin, the LDP's most important fixer and the power behind successive prime ministers.

In the spring of 1992, a piece of political theatre that somehow could happen only in Japan took place: an ultra-nationalist fanatic tried to assassinate the seventy-seven-year-old Mr Kanemaru by firing a gun at him at point-blank range in a crowded meeting hall. Incredibly, the would-be assassin missed. Equally incredibly, Mr Kanemaru, who had stood rooted to the spot seemingly unperturbed as the bullets whisked past his ears, said that he hadn't realized he was being fired at but had 'thought that wind or an insect was passing by me'. Ultra nationalists in pursuit of 'the pure noble Japanese spirit' – or their protection money – are wont to attack corrupt politicians. Later that year what the bullets were alluding to became clear. Kanemaru was forced to resign after it was revealed that his coffers – in common with those of many of his colleagues – were stuffed with *yakuza* money. This is unlikely to have been exposed unless Kanemaru had failed to meet his obligations.

Months before Sakaigawa, a town of 4500, was chosen in mid-1990 as the experimental site, land prices doubled. The *shinkansen* had been built the same way – lining the pockets of the residents who had the good fortune to live in districts represented by powerful politicians, such as a former prime minister, Tanaka Kakuei, who managed to coat the far reaches of northern Honshu in *shinkansen* tracks, leading to his constituency of Niigata. As prime minister, Tanaka, whose background was in construction, had similar plans for the whole country. His book, *Remodelling the Japanese Archipelago*, which was published in 1972 to great excitement and sold over a million copies, called for grandiose construction schemes, including development of 'neglected' Shikoku, some of which went ahead with often depressing results. However, Tanaka is more often remembered in Japan for his role in the Lockheed bribery scandal of the seventies in which the American aeroplane manufacturer played the Japanese 'money politics' game by greasing the palms of the prime minister and others to convince them of the superiority of its Tri-Star planes over Boeing's DC 10s. Lockheed claimed, under immunity from prosecution, that it had paid Tanaka five hundred million yen in exchange for contracts. At least one high-reaching 'money politics' scandal, such as Lockheed, the Recruit shares-for-favours affair and the most recent *yakuza* money débâcle (which threatens other politicians in Kanemaru's wake), has happened at least once in every decade this century in Japan, except for the thirties when the government had more serious matters on its mind.

We drive through Takamatsu, a flat white city with a central wide avenue called Chuo dori on one side, as if it were a beach front. 'Chuo' means 'centre/middle/heart', and like the British high street or American main street, most cities and towns have a Chuo street. Mr Shibata is excited about the prospect of the up-coming anti-nuclear power demonstration. Mrs Shibata is anxious. She is worried that something may happen, that it will get out of hand. Mrs Shibata wants us to eat first, to 'build up our strength', and we go into Ritsurin Koen, a lovely classical Japanese garden located at the northern end of Chuo dori and the city's only real tourist attraction. As was the fate of many Japanese cities, much of what was attractive about Takamatsu was destroyed during the war.

It took a hundred years of landscaping to construct Ritsurin Koen and it was finally completed in the late seventeenth century as a summer retreat for the Matsudaira family, the head of which was the local *daimyo*. The north side of the garden has wide expanses of lawns, whereas the south side is laid out in the classical Japanese manner. There are ponds bulging with variegate carp that are traversed by humped-back wooden bridges; hills that resemble the local mountains; arrangements of rocks and pruned, honed trees and bushes. At every turn and pause on the south side is a carefully constructed painting as it were, where all these elements have been arranged with great artistry as a perfect rendition of the imperfect natural world.

On one of the ponds is a wooden teahouse, seemingly afloat. We sit inside on the *tatami* sipping O-cha. One side of the teahouse is open, overlooking the pond with its hedgerows and rocks and miniature mountains curved around its edges. Two *obasan* ('little mother' – like the more elongated *obaasan* for old women, it is the generic term for middle-aged women) stand in the centre of the severely bent wooden bridge. They are gazing down admiringly at the carp, ugly oversized goldfish to my eye, all gaping thick-lipped mouths and tilted back heads. Carp are sacred fish in Japan and specimens with unusual markings such as these cost thousands of pounds. Except for ourselves and the two women who charge admission and serve, the teahouse is empty. The tea is served in a most unceremonious fashion, from a flask that expresses it alarmingly with an angry hiss.

Mr and Mrs Shibata are as silent and still as two freshly laundered bed sheets. Their eyes float over the pond and the bridge. With the exception of a tea pavilion such as this or a room overlooking a contemplative garden, when you sit in a Japanese room you face inwards with your back to the covered windows. Japan is a country of interiors. Things are either *uchi* (inside) or *soto* (outside). *Soto* and *uchi* are distinct, separate and unreconcilable places. The idea of a view or a vista from an interior is alien.

Even when there *is* a view it is constrained like this, framed by the rocks, a beautifully culled landscape in which there is no sky. It is an anti-vista. Your vision is drawn to the particular, to the setting, to the smallness, the detail. Your eyes do not rise above the bushes or the tree-tops. From this aesthetic comes a way of seeing that is shared by most Japanese in which you do not see the totality but rather the particular. Japanese cities are often quite ugly when taken as a whole, but Japanese people will focus on a detail and seemingly not see this ugliness, focus on, say, the solitary plum tree that is growing alongside a soulless ferro-concrete structure. As might be imagined, it doesn't really matter what the outside of a building looks like so much as the inside, the detail of the interior. The Japanese are taught to see in a localized way, quite the opposite of how we are taught to view things. Grasping the big picture has little merit in a culture where connections are at best an irrelevance.

We walk over to one of the lawns to have lunch. Mrs Shibata has bought us *obento* (boxed lunches), beautifully wrapped in green paper. I open mine carefully, revealing the wooden box: 'made of tropical timber,' the words run through my head like an electronic ticker tape, bringing the bad tidings that there are fewer and fewer innocent pleasures. Inside is the beautifully arranged food: in this case the rice, the dried yellowish orange fish, the red and green pickles and the chopsticks, also wrapped in pale green paper and, like all disposable chopsticks here, also made of tropical timber. The excessive wrapping and packaging, which is such an attractive part of Japanese life, is extracting an awful toll on the world's forests. Company canteens, restaurants, hotels and catering operations get through twenty billion pairs of wooden chopsticks every year. A few companies have recently outlawed wooden chopsticks from their canteens, installing special chopstick-washing machines for plastic reusable ones. But chopsticks consume no more than 1 per cent of all the tropical timber, Japan, the number one importer, brings in.

There is a gradual awareness, mostly among young people, and especially among women, that in this land of prodigious consumption some of Japan's voracious appetites will have to be curbed; that the environment can no longer be despoiled for the momentary convenience of items such as disposable chopsticks; that there are consequences to uncontrolled growth. This isn't translating into membership of green organizations such as Friends of the Earth Japan, whose coordinator Kamei Naomi will not quote the membership 'because it is so low', or the Worldwide Fund for Nature, which has a pathetic 24,000 members in Japan, but all over the country, at the sites of proposed new dams, resorts and buildings of all descriptions, are protesters, uncontrolled, unorganized, but so far incorruptible and more than anything persistent.

In Zushi, near Kamakura just outside of Tokyo, the mayor, Tomino Kiichiro, in his words 'led by the women of the town', has been fighting for over a decade to stop the destruction of Ikego forest. The government wants to turn the forest into a housing site for United States Navy personnel, with 854 housing units, swimming pools and sports facilities, plus 'other accommodations typical of an American suburb,' Mr Tomino puts it. Over 80 per cent of Zushi citizens are against the development, which would destroy the forest, the habitat of over one hundred species of bird. So far, lawsuits have kept the first brick from being laid, as have frequent and, to the Japanese government, embarrassing trips to Washington by Mayor Tomino to lobby the United States Navy. But bulldozers have started to clear the forest and the citizens of Zushi have turned their efforts to appealing directly to the US, managing to get the Sierra Club, the Audubon Society and other American environmentalist groups publicly on their side. In the early nineties the group made an energetic push to get the support of ordinary Americans too, by taking out full-page ads in leading US newspapers, in a hands-across-the-sea save-the-forest plea.

However, outside of specific local issues, environmentalism is a new phenomenon in this relatively newly rich country. Awareness of wastage, of finite resources or irreplaceable nature has only really existed in any form since the beginning of the nineties, and can hardly be said to penetrate deeply or affect the day-to-day life of the majority, despite Japan's pitch to be the eco leader at the 1992 Earth Summit in Rio. Now, while you can go whale watching off of Hokkaido, or buy whale-shaped ashtrays,

T-shirts, etc, outside the exhibition on the beauties of this endangered species at Parco, a trendy department store in Tokyo's hip Shibuya, you can still go down the road and eat whale meat. A short walk from Parco is the Ganso Kujira-ya (Pioneer Whale House) that continues to do a brisk business in whale sashimi and whale anyway-you-like-it, courtesy of the Agriculture and Fisheries Agency's scientists who are killing minke whales for 'research purposes' (the loophole in the current international ban on whaling) and allowing the whale hunters to sell the whale meat after the contents of the animals stomachs have been 'scientifically examined'. Partly in response to international condemnation over whaling, and partly in reaction to the greening of its citizens, the Environment Agency announced that there had to be 'new social ethics of harmony with nature' and that 'an economy-first mentality' had to be abandoned, as did the idea that 'technology can cure environmental problems'. This is the message that former Prime Minister Takeshita took to Rio, statements cynics say are designed more to bolster the new environmentally safer products developed by Japanese companies. However Japan did pledge one trillion yen of foreign aid to be distributed over the next five years specifically for environmental purposes.

... *the things we have in front of us, the pan and the pot, and the burning fire*

ISHIGAKI RIN (1920—)

'Sayonara genpatsu,' the crowd chants, goodbye nuclear power. It's more like a street party than a demonstration. Mr Shibata works his way through the dancing, chanting, singing huddle, which ducks and snakes like the head of a lion dance. He holds on to my wrist tightly, as if I were an attaché case full of money bobbing precariously in his wake. His cronies are dancing with their arms flung around each other, wearing Rising Sun *hajimaki* and toothless smiles. They whoop when they see him and hop up and down, turning their skinny knees outwards like anthropomorphic frogs. They are all dressed in a similar fashion to Mr Shibata, like poor men – the farmer's uniform. The distaff half of the farming team cheers from the balcony, a line of chubby *obaasan*, including Mrs Shibata, leaning over the parapet of the fourth floor of a multi-storey car park, waving and clapping. They overlook the blank granite face of the Shikoku Electric Company, the focus of this particular protest. Other than Mr Shibata's friends, most of the demonstrators are youngish women: mothers and farmers, the core activists in Japan's grassroots anti-nuclear power movement.

The farmers are here simply 'because these plants are not safe,' they say, 'and if the food gets contaminated no one can eat it. What happens to Japan's food security then?' 'Food security' is an expression more commonly employed by government ministers and Zenchu officials to explain why they cannot and will not allow food imports. The farmers in the anti-nuclear movement, much to the government's chagrin, seem to have taken this to its logical conclusion. An anti-nuclear movement might seem natural in a country with first-hand experience of atomic radiation sickness, but it took the accident at Chernobyl to activate the underlying Japanese fear of all things nuclear.

The government, however, does not share its citizens' concerns about the safety of nuclear power. Currently this densely populated archipelago, at the centre of the 'ring of fire' earthquake zone, gets a little over a quarter of its electricity from forty nuclear stations; twelve more are under construction. Japan suffers more earthquakes than any other country in the world, but according to the Atomic Energy Commission, 'All of the nuclear power facilities are earthquake-proof.' It is true that the power stations are of 'seismic approved designs', even that Japanese anti-earthquake design is very good, but past a point, as any seismic engineer will tell you, nothing can be fully earthquakeproof. Or fire proof; fire causes most of the destruction during and after an earthquake, and is as feared in Japan as the event itself.

When Japan's worst nuclear-power accident, at the Mihama nuclear station some two hundred miles west of Tokyo, occurred early in 1991, the anti-nuclear movement, which had undergone setbacks during the Gulf War, gathered momentum again. The campaign to halt the government's plans to double the country's nuclear capacity in the next twenty years swung back into action. The Mihama débâcle could have resulted in a meltdown of the core, as the operators had spent fifty minutes trying to decide whether the meter showing a sudden jump in radioactivity was incorrect. Apparently this meter often reads radioactivity levels wrongly, but this time it was correct. There is a reluctance to shut down nuclear plants unless it is proven to be absolutely necessary as it ruins Japan's safety record. Japan's nuclear industry is very proud of its low record of reactor shutdowns.

Six weeks after the Mihama incident, the Takahama reactor not far from Kyoto was shut down when a similar sudden increase in radioactivity was uncovered. Takahama is one of a cluster of half a dozen nuclear plants on the Sea of Japan coast due north of Kyoto. Tokyo has a similar cluster close to it on the Pacific coast. Given the density of the population in both areas, and indeed in most of Japan, evacuation in the event of an accident would be impossible.

The potential for such near accidents to result in full-blown disasters like Chernobyl is what had brought Ohara Yoshiko 'to the brink,' as she puts it, brought her to balancing precariously on the roof of this white mini-van: 'We can show Shikoku Electric what we think of it, and its Ikata nuclear plant,' she says through the bull-horn. 'Die-in, die-in, die-in,' the crowd chants, falling prostrate in the road. At the edges of the crowd riot police are gathering, hundreds of them, like a flock of starlings at dusk, filling the air with their noise and presence. They jump off buses and jog around the protesters, bristling their white nightsticks and giving clenched fist salutes. They pull down the facemasks from the top of their blue helmets, rattling them in place in a synchronized display of might. Beside them the ordinary white-helmeted police look docile and ineffective, cut-out paper dollies. Ms Ohara turns her bull-horn towards the police. 'It's your lives as well,' she says. 'Everyone in this region is at risk right now!'

Before Ms Ohara, who is in her mid-thirties, became involved with the anti-nuclear movement, she was, she says, 'completely apolitical, a typical Japanese housewife'. Like many of the women here, she became aware of the nuclear power issue through her Mothers' Group. Following the Chernobyl disaster the dangers of nuclear power was all anyone talked about. 'After Chernobyl I felt as if I had to find out everything I could about nuclear power,' she says. This is a Japanese point of view: knowledge may not be power, but without it you are impotent. This is Mayor Motoshima reading everything he can get his hands on about death in order to learn how to die. This is a friend's co-worker, who having been squarely beaten at a game of English-language Trivial Pursuit learnt all the answers to every question by heart and is now invincible. This is Ms Ohara feverishly memorizing every fact on nuclear power ever recorded. These are the products of the much-maligned rote-learning system, people trained from infancy in feats of memory. What moved Ms Ohara emotionally into action, however, was a lecture she attended: 'Up until then I hadn't known what was going on in Japan. I realized then that I hadn't been thinking for myself.'

The lecture had been given by Hirose Takashi, an author and Japan's most famous anti-nuclear activist. Among his other projects, Mr Hirose sues electric companies over the safety of their nuclear reactors. Ms Ohara, who lives fifty miles downwind from the Ikata plant, discovered at Mr Hirose's lecture that the plant had already carried out, in secret, one 'potentially dangerous' power-reduction experiment and was planning another. She left the hall and immediately began collecting signatures to stop the next experiment. 'But despite the million-plus signatures delivered to the Shikoku Electric Company the test happened anyway,' she says. She seems genuinely surprised: 'Whatever happened to consensus, or consent?' She describes herself as an ordinary woman who brings up her children 'to be good Japanese,' who shops and does the laundry every day, and who gets up at five in the morning to cook her husband's breakfast. 'My husband is all right,' she says, 'but a lot of men are not. They don't want their wives being activists. They are threatening divorce over this.'

Divorce over such matters is no idle threat. In Rokkasho, a village in Aomori, on the tip of Northern Honshu, where the fight with the 'government in Tokyo' over the uranium reprocessing plant has been lengthy and acrimonious, several divorces have occurred with the wife's activism named as co-respondent. (Neglecting wifely duties for non-political reasons is grounds for divorce too, as in the highly publicized case of the husband who divorced his wife because her membership of the Jehovah's Witnesses took her out of the house too much.) The women in Aomori have also found themselves engaged in battle with the *uyoko*, which consider the housewives and their supporters to be 'left-wing agitators'.

The chief of the riot police is standing on top of one of the police buses, yelling through his bull-horn. The police want the area cleared of people immediately, he says, otherwise they will move in and clear it themselves. The riot police draw their body-length shields in front of them, looking both menacing and frightened at the same time, as if they expect to come to harm at the hands of these unarmed women, children and old farmers. The few young men in the crowd look like refugees from the West *circa* 1968, all beads and flowers, or are dressed in the uniform of the Japanese intellectual: hat (preferably a beret), corduroy jacket (preferably with patches), pipe (optional). The riot police seem overdressed for the occasion, as if they expected to be employed in riotous battle with seasoned left-wing demonstrators, decked out in facemasks, colour-coded hard hats and armed with lead pipes, of the type they use periodically at Narita airport.

Holding up their nightsticks and covering their bodies with their shields, the police jog into the crowd like a synchronized swimming team. They form a square pen around a group of demonstrators and run them out of the street. A second group of police try to do the same thing, but this group of protesters, having seen what has just happened to their colleagues, isn't so obliging. Some sit down while others try to push the police back; a strange, silent struggle ensues. Meanwhile, following a set of complicated hand signals like jobbers or footballers, another line of blue helmets snakes through the crowd, trapping Mr Shibata and the other singing farmers against the wall of the multi-storey car park. Their wives flip back from the parapet and disappear. I can see their legs, some wrapped in binding kimono, as they shuffle at amazingly high speed from one floor of the car park on to another.

The farmers are engaged in a silent shoving match with the riot police, their faces set in the sort of war-like expression you see at the kabuki. The action is balletic, hypnotic, completely surreal, a ritualized battle. The women push their way into the road, arguing with the police who are trying to stop them getting to their husbands. Mrs Shibata and half a dozen others attempt to pull off the riot police who are holding the farmers against the car park wall. Country women are not expected to wear the high-toned mask of deference as much as their city sisters and, like everything else, city or country, female deference is circumstantial. These are not the circumstances in which to be demure and the women silently wrestle with the police, their faces set in the same war-like masks worn by their husbands.

The riot police, having formed themselves into a pen capable of holding a dozen or so of the old men, including Mr Shibata, jog them away from the area of protest. Once they are out of this area many of the demonstrators simply walk off, as if their moment upon the stage has finished and it is time to go home. Mr Shibata and his colleagues remain, however, working their way back to the white mini-van where Ms Ohara is appealing through a bull-horn for the crowd to stay calm. One of the farmers yells something at her and she waves him forward. 'The police have severely hurt a demonstrator,' she yells in the direction of the riot cop who has been directing operations. 'The police should apologize!' The farmer is lifted on top of the van and stands beside her, theatrically rubbing his arm. The chief of the riot police clambers back up on to the police bus, bows deeply in the direction of the crowd and apologizes 'sincerely for this mishap'.

How marvellous a fellow is the sea god!

FROM AN ANONYMOUS *CHOKA* (LONG SONG)

In Kotohira Park, an hour from Takamatsu, is reputedly the oldest existing kabuki theatre in Japan. It was built in the 1800s and is still used once a year in April. The theatre, which was of course built to be operated without the benefits of electricity, still relies on manually produced and operated special effects, such as the eight harnessed men who rotate the stage. The light for the theatre's daytime performances is controlled by sliding *shoji* screens which regulate the amount and position of the sunlight filtering on to the stage. Since the late 1620s, when the shogun banned women from the stage (for the same reasons the English gave for doing likewise, namely the prevention of licentious behaviour), kabuki has been an all-male preserve in which the *onnagata*, the actors who play women's roles, are the big stars. However, kabuki was originally an all-female theatre.

The first kabuki was performed by a female troupe on a riverbed in Kyoto in 1603. The year, although accepted, is again perhaps rather too precise. Safer to say kabuki was originated by Okuni, a *miko* at the nearby Shinto shrine of Izumo, some time during the late 1590s or early 1600s. The original kabuki performances were dances not plays, based on the shrine dances enacted regularly by the *miko* and on other more ecstatic religious dances, such as those which derived from the tenth-century evangelistic movement of Pure Land Buddhism. The word 'kabuki' possibly comes from the word *katamukeru* (bent/inclined), a term then used to describe eccentric behaviour. The women soon began performing satirical skits and stories along with the dances, mostly about the relations between the sexes: assignations in the teahouses and bath-houses, encounters between men and prostitutes, and between husbands and wives. This new 'people's theatre', which was as raucous and accessible as noh was stylized and difficult, soon became an immensely popular form of entertainment and numerous all-female kabuki troupes set up business.

Three centuries earlier noh had also started from dance forms. The two most popular entertainments of the early middle ages were *sarugaku* (monkey music) and *dengaku* (field music). *Sarugaku* was so called because of the acrobatics and mime used by its performers; *dengaku* was based on the singing and dancing of peasants, literally in the fields, during the rice planting and harvest festival. The shogun Yoshimitsu loved *sarugaku*, especially the performance of two of its leading exponents, Kanami and his son Zeami. Yoshimitsu brought them and their art into high society where the two men, both playwrights, gradually transformed the happy-go-lucky *sarugaku* into the beginnings of the austere theatre known as noh (meaning 'talent/ability'), producing something that was more in keeping with the sombre aesthetics of the shogunate.

Noh plays are performed entirely by men, most often wearing masks. The style of the play is usually akin to a dramatic poem and is 'about' supernatural events. The plays are symbolic and the productions go out of their way to avoid the taint of realism. They are enacted by highly stylized ritualistic manners of speech and movement and there is little action or physical movement and less plot. The lead actor usually performs what is left of an original dance, something he achieves with the barest of movement.

After *onna kabuki* (women's kabuki) was forbidden in 1629, *wakashu kabuki* (young men's kabuki), which had developed in its shadow, came to the fore. As the eroticism of *onna kabuki* was found as much in the women playing *otokoyaku* (male roles) as in the often licentious scripts, so the eroticism of the *wakashu* was found in the personages of the *onnagata*. Homosexual prostitutes performing on the stage pleased the shogun as little as had the heterosexual variety, and *wakashu* were banned from the stage in 1652. Kabuki continued to be an all-male theatre, with adult men playing the role of *onnagata* as they do today. It was and is in essence a homosexual milieu, one in which the *onnagata* are the stars, adored and admired by the public at large.

The kabuki theatre reached its apogee in the shogunate capital of Edo, becoming part of the *ukiyo* (floating world) of courtesans, geisha and itinerant entertainers. The *ukiyo-e* artists, whose woodblock prints are perhaps the best known Japanese pictures outside of Japan, immortalized the great geisha and kabuki actors of their time. During the Tokugawa period, when art and theatre were heavily censored, the *ukiyo-e* artists also worked cleverly camouflaged political and social messages into their paintings. After censorship was relaxed somewhat in the Meiji era, kabuki plays tackled such subjects as 'living history', based on the thinking of the 'people's rights' movements. Nowadays, however, they have returned to performing the classic repertoire of historic and rather histrionic epics of love and war, leaving contemporary political and social issues to Japan's modern theatre.

Kotohira's kabuki theatre is located near the first flight of steps that will take you, eventually, to the Kotohira *jinja* (shrine). Kotohira is dedicated to Kompira, whose mythological identity has often been in dispute, but who is now widely accepted to be the god of the sea. Until the late 1800s Kotohira *jinja* was a Buddhist temple, and according to some records, it too was founded by Kobo Daishi. In 1872 Kotohira was given over to the Shintoists and until the end of the war was run by the Kunaicho. Perhaps because of its somewhat unusual background, Kotohira was one of the few imperial shrines that commoners were allowed to use before the end of the war. As a result, the god Kompira became popularized as the patron of all travellers, not just sailors.

Except for the small shrines located in many buildings, which are shrines in the common Western understanding of the word, *jinja* are usually a collection of wooden buildings which we would think of more as temples. Customarily there is a main shrine with its own building and a series of other shrines and related buildings, each with a particular function. Shinto shrines and Buddhist temples are frequently located on the tops of mountains. Kotohira, on top of Zozusan, is one of the largest and oldest shrines in Japan and is visited by some four million people every year.

I lug myself up the mountainside, clambering the first 365 steps to the main gate of the Kotohira *jinja*. On either side – as is true of most walkways leading to shrines – are tiny wooden shops selling amulets, prayer boards, eats and drinks, and others selling souvenirs of traditional wooden toys and knick-knacks. Inside the main gate the shops are replaced by stone lanterns showing the way to the other 420 steps leading to the main shrine. Should you find this somewhat arduous climb daunting, or physically beyond you, you may hire a palanquin and bearers to carry you, at a cost of about twenty pounds one way, thirty pounds round trip. Be warned, however – being bounced up a mountainside via a narrow stone stairway in the confines of a palanquin can be quite an alarming experience.

Kotohira *jinja* has a treasure house containing sculptures, scrolls and a collection of noh masks; it also has a small art gallery in a separate building which contains the works of the famous eighteenth-century 'back to nature' landscape painter, Maruyama Okyo. Now at the top of 785 steps, the main shrine is in front of you as you walk through the gate. It is of classic style, a Chinese whisper changed in the retelling, but resonate with its architectural beginnings. Its roof is layered like a two-tiered cake: on the top are triangles, with softly undulating sides that melt into each other. The bottom of the roof, which sticks out like a giant porch, is wavy. The shrine is open on all sides, its ornate shutters folded back and curtains woven of rice-straw hang a quarterway down at every opening. The inside is like a stage, flat and empty. The broad wooden boards shimmer in the diffuse light, glossy as a horse's back. Around one edge are white floor cushions. The *miko* come in and stand two deep at the back, in front of the rice-straw curtains.

The *miko* live in town with their parents. When they come to the shrine they bathe 'to wash off the impurities of the world'. Most of the *miko* will marry when they are older and, having officially lost their virginity, forgo their religious status. Although the majority of the *miko* you see around the shrines are young, there are old *miko*, many of whom, it is said, have become seers, predictors of the future. The role of the *miko* in Shinto is that of shamaness. She is the one who can bring forth the spirits. This is very apparent in some ceremonies, such as the *daijo sai*; but is also an integral part of the sacred dances, like those performed here.

The *miko* begin to dance, swaying their bodies, twisting their wrapped feet over the wooden floor; their faces are impassive, flat as a piece of paper; their waist-length hair is held in a loose, heavy pony tail. Their *tabi* (white one-toed slipper-socks) peek out from under their heavy, wide, dark trouser-skirts. Their feet whisper and gasp as they are dragged over the wood. Over the trouser-skirts are layers of kimono, the colours visible at the neck: white, red, white again. The over-layer is translucent, with an occasional bright green motif that looks like a painting of a bird woven in grass. The clothes make the *miko* look flat and wide like square tablecloths; their tiny oval heads appear too small for their bodies.

The *miko* are styled after ladies of the Heian court, as are the imperial ceremonial clothes for both men and women. At Heian-kyo women wore kimono, one over the other like this. Great care was taken to contrast the colours of each layer, which could be seen at the neck, within the sleeves and by the feet. This style of kimono was called *juni-hitoe* (twelve layers) although often more than twelve kimono were worn at one time – a woman might parade through the court in as many as twenty. The kimono were unlined, but still she needed to move slowly, carrying her 20-pound glory on her body like a snail's shell. Her sleeves swooped down below her knees; on each sleeve a little bell tinkled as she walked. Her toilette required twenty articles. There were fifteen ways she could style the front of her hair and twelve ways for the back. It took an expert six hours to dress her hair, which, like that of the *miko*, was left to grow as long as it could in the style called *kurokami*. At Heian-kyo eyebrows were shaved and crescent moons painted in their place. Sometimes women would paint two little black spots on their foreheads to match their artificially blackened teeth. (White teeth were considered revolting, an exposed part of the skeleton.) Men, who themselves were well rouged, also wore between two to twenty kimono, one on top of the other, colour-coded by rank. Many in the court developed a penchant for changing these clothes three times a day.

As the *miko* dance, the priests sit on the cushions playing ancient stringed instruments, plucking a discordant sad sound, a cry resonate with empty longing. The chief priest of this shrine was once a very important man: 'He commanded great patronage,' the old retainer tells me.

We walk through the grounds towards the chief priest's house. 'In the Tokugawa period he kept special rooms in the inner sanctum: one for entertaining the emperor; one for entertaining the shogun,' the old man says, shuffling beside me. He resembles an ancient English butler, as dry and dusty as the pages of the novel from which he could have emerged.

The chief priest's house is lovely, the sort of old inward-looking classical Japanese house that at once makes you feel a great sense of peace. It is concentric: on the outside is a verandah that wraps itself all the way round; immediately inside, and visible to the outside, is the ring of outer rooms; then, inward, a smaller ring of rooms, and then another, the innermost sanctum. The verandah and the house, like all traditional dwellings and shrines, are made of wood. The floors of the bare rooms are covered in *tatami*. We enter a small six-mat room. The size of a mat varies throughout Japan, but usually, as in this case, a six-mat room is approximately 12 feet by 9. Even if they are covered in carpet, rooms are still measured by the number of *tatami* mats it would take to cover them.

When he was Crown Prince, Hirohito slept in this innermost part of the house, the old man says. He points to the chrysanthemum carvings on either side of sliding doors, which, he states, are over three hundred years old. The chrysanthemum is the imperial insignia, the name by which the throne is known; Dietman (MPs) wear the insignia on their lapels, buttonholed into the past of *matsurigoto*, the old word for government, meaning Shinto (which is to say religious) ceremonial affairs. The old man opens a second set of sliding doors which leads back to the middle ring of rooms, and in turn another set which reveals the outer ring, the verandah and the garden beyond, beautifully framed in the wooden archway: the diminutive swollen bridge; the stream; the bent and twisted bonsai; the scaled-down hills; the landscape in miniature – a private world; a proxy, an echo of Takamatsu's Ritsurin Koen and of all the classical gardens of Japan.

Speak of this to no one
not even in dreams –
and in case the pillow
should be too wise,
we'll have no pillow
but our arms

LADY ISE (DIED 939)

From the street the house looks sleepy, just another old house that you cannot see into or out of. Nothing seeps out, not even sound. As I open the door, noise and smells rush at me. My wet raincoat is removed and spirited away. I slip off my shoes and follow a woman in a dusty pink kimono. She is as thin and droopy as the evening. The grip of the *obi*, the wide thick cloth that is wrapped round the waist when wearing kimono, makes her walk stiffly. The kimono is bound tightly around her body. Her feet are turned in; she pulls them one over the other, tottering on her toes and hurrying over the *tatami*, tripping along, past the little wood and paper boxes sunk down on either side, the private rooms full of deals and scams, smoke and laughter. She bows deeply and lifts her arm out like a statue of Progress, showing me inside one of these rooms.

The room is an oblong. The three windows are along one of the walls and are covered, as is usual, in *shoji*, shutting out the world. The long table, which takes up most of the room, is sunk down into a well. It is surrounded by floor cushions and backs, those curious half-chair contraptions that are made up of a chair back and arms. This seating arrangement, which is becoming more and more common even in very traditional places such as this geisha house, enables you to sit in a compromise East–West position: on the floor with your back supported but with your legs and feet dangling in the well under the table instead of tucked under you. The old people will tell you that this hybrid arrangement is necessary these days as the younger generation cannot 'sit' any more, which is to say sit in the cross-legged position for men or kneeling with bottom on heels for women.

The geishas flap around the room, six caged birds, holding their arms up and open in the shape of a half box; the palms of their hands push against the air. Tripping, half running, elegantly and quickly they manoeuvre us into our seats. These are provincial geisha, relatively unmade up and unornamental, not stylized dolls like their sisters in Tokyo and Kyoto. The face of the city geisha is a white, immovable, expressionless mask; the mouth is painted into a small pink bud; the eyes are kohl-encrusted.

Geisha are descendants of the *shirabyoshi* (the white gliders), female troubadours of the middle ages who, dressed in white, sang, recited epic poems, mimed accounts of clan wars and told stories based on historical events. Some of their repertory and ritual gestures also found their way into the noh theatre. By the seventeenth century, the geisha, memorialized in the *ukiyo-e*, were no longer itinerant but resided in special districts of the cities where other entertainers lived and performed. The most famous of these districts was the Yoshiwara, nightless city, the pleasure quarters of Tokyo. By then the geisha were part of a world known as *karyukai*, society of flowers and willows. The courtesans were the flowers, the geisha the willows.

Mr Watanabe is a local bigwig, sometime politician, businessman and fixer, a contemporary *daimyo*, and an honoured man in Takamatsu. He is already seated at the centre of the table, talking loudly and swinging his arms to and fro. Everything about him is round, from his bald, perfectly spherical head to his globular stomach. He is relentlessly jolly, displaying his squared-off teeth at each turn. Everything seems to amuse him inordinately. He reminds me of the members of Japan's cabinet, who are always shown before cabinet meetings convulsed with laughter like this. I suppose it is meant to be reassuring, to suggest confidence and control; but most people think it fatuous, even worrying. They wonder, not unreasonably, if the joke is on them.

This is Mr Watanabe's geisha house. He does not own it as such – it is owned by the senior geisha, whom Mr Watanabe, her patron, set up in business 'many years ago'. Mr Watanabe uses the house as a Westerner might use a club, to entertain clients, colleagues and visitors. He spends on average four nights a week here. Mr Watanabe is eighty-two, the same age as the senior geisha, whom he refers to as 'my outside wife' but calls '*okusama*' ('sama' being the polite form of 'san' which together with 'oku' means 'Mrs'. The connotation is of the more elegant 'madame' but it literally means something more akin to 'her indoors'. The *oku* – the depths within the house – is where the wife of an aristocrat dwelt, the wife of the peasant being outside tilling the fields). Sometimes he calls her *okasan* (mother), a common form of address by a husband to his wife. Being an *okasan* is what wives and all intimate women are to the men in their lives, mothering, coddling, chiding and anticipating his every need. If she worked in a hostess bar as the chief hostess or was the owner of such a bar, Okusama would be called by the Japlish (Japanese-English) appellation of '*mama-san*'.

Okusama has been Mr Watanabe's mistress for nearly sixty years, almost as long as he has been married. She kneels slightly behind us, close enough so that I can occasionally feel her breath on the back of my neck; as is the custom, she keeps refilling our tiny sake cups so that they are never empty; if you want to stop drinking in Japan you leave your glass or cup full. Okusama massages Mr Watanabe's shoulders. He tenderly pats her head. 'I tell him he must look after himself,' she says, 'but he doesn't.' Mr Watanabe laughs. Without him having to ask, she takes his cigarettes out of his jacket pocket and gives them to him. Our jackets lie folded on the *tatami* behind us. She massages my shoulders; her small, skinny, old fingers are hard and strong. Her face is very small and perfectly round; it is as smooth as butterscotch. It is only when she smiles that the lines appear.

Okusama entered a geisha house when she was five. 'Six under the lunar calendar [which was officially in use until 1873, but colloquially until well into the turn of the century]: in the sixth year on the six day of the six month,' that being considered an auspicious time for a girl child to begin her training in the arts. It was the atmosphere of the house that she was first supposed to soak up, learning the geisha life by osmosis. To begin with she just did housework and helped her 'sisters' and her 'aunt', her new family, to dress and to do their make-up; she learnt the singing and the dancing and the shamisen later in her apprenticeship. It isn't clear whether or not she was sold by her parents, but this is probable as they were very likely poor. Being sold to a geisha house was then an honoured route out of poverty for bright, pretty girls. It is illegal now to sell a child; and the youngest apprentice geisha, called *maiko* in Kyoto where they are most often to be seen wearing their distinguishing flamboyant make-up, are teenagers.

Okusama will be a geisha to the day she dies. As long as she can perform her dances and songs she will continue to be one. She is an endangered species, one of the now fewer than twenty thousand properly trained geisha in the country. As such she has the status and respect accorded to someone who is an artist: she is a 'repository of the culture'. She is happy, content. 'I have lived a long and interesting time,' she says, and she still has what is most important to her: her art and her business. She never wanted 'the eternal employment of marriage'. She never wanted to hear '*Meshi! Furo! Neru!*' (Food! Bath! Bed!), the late-night call of the half-pissed husband as he staggers through the door. She has had, she thinks, the best of Mr Watanabe – she sees more of him than his wife does and it is with her that he spends his evenings. She is part of his social life in the way that no wife can be. She smiles, a long knowing smile.

Mr Watanabe is giving his speech. He sits with his arms flat down on the table as if he is about to push himself up. He starts off by saying, 'In this era of internationalization . . .' I can hear the switch in my head click off: Script 21A, *kokusaika*, internationalization. It's like a form letter. 'We hope this opportunity to experience Japanese culture will bring about greater mutual understanding between our countries . . .' Mr Watanabe delivers this speech with concentrated sincerity; like a great actor he infuses freshness into every word. I wonder how many times he has delivered this same oration, using exactly the same words, with exactly the same emphasis in exactly the same places. In speech making, as in everything else, perfection is achieved by repetition.

Mr Watanabe tells me that he never met his wife before they were betrothed. She was taken by her family to the kabuki theatre, where she was parked outside the front and arranged decorously, the names of that year's famous stars painted on boards above her head. 'I walked back and forth several times,' Mr Watanabe says. 'I took a very good look. She was very pretty and from a very good family. From what I had heard I thought she would make a good wife and I agreed to take her.' He laughs his big, round, booming laugh which sounds as if it is coming from the inside of an empty cave. Being a traditional man he found love in the traditional place: outside of his marriage in the company of his mistress. He eats as if he were ravenous, hunched over his bowls and dishes, bolting down the sashimi and slurping the soup. His face is deep red where the sake has risen into it. 'Eat up, eat up, not so much playing,' Mr Watanabe bellows across the table to a man from the local TV station, who is deeply in conversation with one of the geisha. 'Playing' being the verb used to describe what you do inside a geisha house.

The foods looks lovely, a tray full of little bowls and dishes of all different colours and patterns, made of the finest lacquerware and pottery. There is blossom across the ice which holds the sashimi. Everything, as usual, has been arranged with great artistry: the bowls turned precisely to display the designs; the small portions of food arranged into pleasant shapes; a flower placed just so on most dishes. However, except for the sashimi, the soup and the rice, I don't really like *kaiseki* – the old court cuisine which is often served in geisha houses and top-drawer restaurants – it is too sour, too fundamentally unsatisfying. I like to look at it, but prefer to eat sushi or home-made noodles and the other common fare such as that brought in by the 'southern barbarians', the original Portuguese dishes of *yakitori* and *tempura*.

Okusama returns and sits behind us. She grins and pours us more sake. Mr Watanabe reaches to the centre of the table and takes an empty cup. He pours some sake into it and passes it to Okusama to drink. The men sitting closest to the other geisha do likewise. The geisha sip their sake, holding one hand beneath the cup to catch any spills. They are waiting for us to finish, to clear away the dishes so that the party can begin. Okusama finishes her sake and moves off on her knees three places down the table. She stops to chat and drink sake. The other women do the same, making a complete circuit of the table. The two youngest geisha, who are in their twenties, get up and clear, swaying gently as they balance the trays, moving unobtrusively in and out of the room.

One of the geisha plays the shamisen, the most melancholy of the stringed instruments. Okusama sings in a high-pitch warble, a poignant song full of the sounds of mourning, about a girl whose mother committed *shinju* with her boyfriend, a lovers' double suicide. *Shinju* literally means inside the heart, with the nuance of revealing the heart. Upon their death the girl realizes that she has lost everything. She had left her village as a bride and, being a neglectful daughter, had seldom returned to see her parents, not even bothering to attend her father's funeral. She now realizes that everything she had known as a child has been transformed out of all recognition. With the death of both her parents she no longer has a *furusato*. There are tears running down Mr Watanabe's face, two silent streams. He is half smiling, enraptured by the sound of Okusama's still strong and vibrant voice, playing against and with the shamisen, the discordant sound of a broken heart patched up with nostalgia: the sound of Japan.

At the far end of the room three of the geisha begin to dance, chafing their feet on the *tatami*, swaying back and forth and turning their hands in the air. It is not dissimilar to the sacred *miko* dances. There is scarcely any movement across the floor, more a bending of the legs and angling of feet and hands. The three dance with their sleeves, moving their arms inside them, making them flutter and ripple in slow motion so that they rustle and sigh like a willow's leaves shaken by a breeze. Two of the geisha begin to dance around the room, one holding on to the other's hips. They stick out their feet and waddle like penguins, sashaying their hips back and forth and calling to us to get up. Except for Mr Watanabe, everyone joins in, dancing around the table and kicking their legs in the air, clutching hold of each other in a drunken conga line. Okusama leads the line, delicately pointing her feet towards the table as we dance around and around; she is laughing, her face a deep red. She pulls me out of the line and takes me off to the far end of the room to show me another dance. I follow her, imitating the steps – three simple-looking moves that involve having your body, your feet and your hands moving at odds with each other. It is like patting your head and rubbing your stomach at the same time. I step back and watch her finish. She is known for her singing, but her dancing is exquisite as well. There is hardly any movement; she strikes poses, flowing one into the other, like a one-woman tableau.

At the door, Mr Watanabe and Okusama cuddle. He is crying and she is wiping away his tears. 'It's all right,' she says. I watch them out of the corner of my eye; the rest of us stand on the doorstep saying our elongated drunken goodnights. Okusama and Mr Watanabe have their foreheads pressed together; she kisses him lightly on the lips and holds his big, round, shiny, old face in her tiny gnarled hands. Now they are standing in front of the *shoji* screen, holding on to each other's hands. The light from the lantern by our feet makes them look like shadow puppets; for sixty years they have done this, watching each other ripen and then age, watching their bodies crinkle and bloat around them, watching his hair fall out, hers lose its colour and lustre. They are laughing now, uproariously, slapping their legs and bending over. She walks him to the door, her arms threaded through his. They look like the young lovers they once were; they seem so happy, as if nothing can touch them. She says goodnight to us. She turns to me and, pushing the hair back from my face, stretches up and lightly kisses both my cheeks. It is a startling thing to do, touching socially is something that is never done here. 'I am honoured that you could come,' she says formally, turning and stepping back over the threshold, my thank-yous trailing after her. The other geisha have filled up the doorway now, crunched together in a half-moon shape. Okusama stands in front of them. They all bow deeply, folding over in half.

Getting time off from the Buddha and doing the laundry

OZAKI HOSAI (1885–1926)

I am driven through Takamatsu encased in a waft of sweet plastic oranges. The smell is coming from the taxi's air freshener. Its vicious orange colour resembles the headache that gnaws at my forehead. Sake never gives you a hangover, you are told. This is a firmly held Japanese belief. It is, perhaps, true that sake will not give you a hangover – if you throw it up before going to bed. As we walked back to the hotel last night, the pavements were decorated, just as they are in Tokyo, with the little puddles of vomit that are always miraculously gone by morning.

The taxi driver tries out his English on me. He learnt it from the BBC, he tells me; it lacks prepositions: 'I have no one practice with,' he says. He is not a young man, perhaps sixty. It's impressive, all this time, effort and determination. From Japanese to English is a long journey, one he has taken alone with his radio. He has been studying for two years. He wants to go to England for a holiday one day. Perhaps when he retires, he thinks. He is saving up. I listen to him, perched on the edge of the back seat, my head shattering over every bump, straining my ears over his soft cadences.

'I bring you miniature forest,' he says with flourish, if still no prepositions. He indicates our destination – row upon row of bonsai trees stretch out before us. He is inadvertently right, it is a shrunken forest, and the trees look quite hideous like this, tiny, deformed and useless, as if the victims of some dreadful new miniaturizing experiment.

I walk up the narrow path, painstakingly placing one foot in front of the other so as not to kick over a precious specimen or knock off a branch. There are azaleas, pines, plums, apples, oaks and cypresses; none stand higher than a foot and a half: 'an imaginary, idealized landscape,' as bonsai lovers would have it. The cheapest of these bonsai will sell for around eighty-five pounds; a prime representative of the species for at least two hundred pounds and an exceptional tree for more than four hundred pounds. They need constant pruning and roping into position, even when they are 'fully grown'. Like the parrot, the bonsai is said to survive best with one owner. As each person has a distinct way of winding a clock, everyone, according to bonsai lore, has a distinct method of watering and tending plants. Like tea and much of the high culture, the bonsai, too, came originally from China. Bonsai cultivation has long since died out there, however.

It is unbearably hot and stuffy in the bonsai shop, dense with the smell of paraffin. Takayoshi, my minder, nods tersely when I enter, last night's happiness completely slept off. He is back to his tense official self: the bureaucratic mannequin, an official in the International Division at Takamatsu town hall, which is like the town halls in Norwich or Leeds sporting an international division (*kokusaika* is still the buzz word in the provinces). Sitting in the corner on a cushion by the paraffin stove is an embittered-looking *obaasan*; she hacks away at a bonsai, twisting the branches between her pincers. She is, apparently, the owner's mother. She looks like a bag lady in her open-fingered gloves, woolly hat and layers and layers of clothes. Like a Zen rock-and-sand garden, her face is lined with deep circular troughs. She barks something at her daughter-in-law and the younger woman nods frantically: '*Hai, hai, hai, wakarimashita, wakarimashita* [Yes, yes, yes, I understand, I understand]', she replies, barely audibly, as people do here when they are being chastised. Her thin voice is full of deference and fear; she keeps her head bowed, staring at the plum bonsai she is trimming. Her bent head bounces up and down like one of those nodding dogs.

The daughter-in-law is miserably thin, eaten away by misery; her skin and hair flake and crumble like old cement. Her husband, the owner of the bonsai shop, tells us that they have two children. I look at his wife, who is trying to pretend that she isn't here: she looks scarcely big enough to bear a mouse. This is a family business. The owner's family has been cultivating bonsai for four generations. Everyone works here – 'The children help out in their spare time,' the owner says – and everyone lives in the house at the back, a modern ferro-concrete building with a traditionally shaped curved roof of grey slate. 'My son will take over the business,' the owner says. 'My daughter will work here until she marries.' Perhaps what they want does not come into it; or perhaps they want to continue the tradition to such an extent that they do not think about anything else. I wonder, as is so often the case, whether his wife will get her own back on their son's wife in retribution for all the years of suffering at the hands of her husband's mother; whether this mousy, miserable woman will, too, sit in the corner chewing off bits of branches with her pincers and emanating hatred.

For most married women the choice of employment is usually stark. If there is a family business the choice is made for them; if not there is low-paid 'part-time' work in the factories, shops or offices. Most single women do not fare much better either, and are usually relegated to low-paid full-time work from which they are expected to 'retire' upon marriage or at the least on the birth of their first child (they can return to 'part-time' work after their children are in kindergarten). As far as I know no one has ever calculated the contribution to the economy of these part-time workers, always women or the elderly, who can legally work thirty-five hours per week, earn half the average full-time hourly rate, receive few or no benefits, and be laid off with little notice and no compensation.

Only about 25 per cent of all male workers reap the benefits of Japan's much vaunted lifetime employment system. These men (the number of women in the lifetime employment scheme is minuscule) are employed by the big companies or the bureaucracy. The big companies can afford such largess in part because of the cushion of underpaid part-time and full-time women workers, and in part because their myriad small sub-contractors bear the brunt of recessions and lay-offs. Lifetime employment is not always a panacea, however, as it can work against the employees' interests. Big companies who are part of this system will often not hire new workers during years of peak production because they will be stuck with them if production falls off, which means in the fat years their employees have to work longer hours to produce the goods faster.

Near the bonsai shop is Tadano. Like Komatsu, which is better known overseas, Tadano is a crane and heavy-equipment manufacturer. The Tadano brothers started their eponymous company after the war, 'from nothing,' Mr Tadano says. Mr Tadano, like Mr Watanabe, is also rotund and relentlessly jolly. He looks like Mr Pickwick, only smaller; a compact round man with a compact round disposition. The factory resembles an aircraft hangar. It is cold and damp inside and the workers wear gloves and hats. There are no windows. Much of what is going on is a typical production-line operation; it is labour-intensive and there is not a robot in sight. There are lots of women though, an entire line of them, constructing what looks as if it will be the cabin of a crane; it dangles precariously at head height.

Mr Tadano thinks women workers are 'better than men' – and 'much cheaper'. He redesigned the line so that it could be completely operated by women, installing hydraulic equipment to lift all the heavy machine parts. This way he can 'keep the line running twenty-four hours a day by using three shifts of women; it was expensive to install all this equipment but it will pay off.' He nods and smiles at me, admiring his own innovation.

Since Japan became an industrialized country at the beginning of the Meiji era, women have been employed in factories, especially, as in England, in the textile mills. Most were indentured servants. There was no industrial revolution as such here, more an industrial absorption. During the Meiji era, Japan lurched abruptly from the country to the city, importing its industrialization fully made, mostly from Britain and Germany. At the turn of the century 90 per cent of the weavers and silk spinners were women, as were 80 per cent of those employed in the cotton mills. In 1897, almost 50 per cent of the workers in these factories were girls less than twenty; nearly 15 per cent were younger than fourteen. However, they were not as cowed as they often are today and were prepared to fight their employers over wages and conditions. The first strike by women factory workers was in 1885 in a silk spinning factory in Kofu City in central Japan.

Mr Tadano's female labour force is employed 'part-time', for, as he says gravely, 'they are married women'. I watch them working on different parts of the line, solemnly inserting this bolt into that hole, fixing these parts together, drilling and hammering and riveting in silence. There is no talking, no music, only the thumping and caterwauling of machinery. They look miserable in their neat, clean overalls. They work on average thirty-five hours a week: 'As much as the law allows for part-time work,' Mr Tadano points out, but they usually put in some overtime. 'Sometimes they want to make more money,' he says beaming, confident that such transgressions would never be challenged by the women, or that if they were their complaints would never be upheld by the courts.

The fast-moving production lines look like scenes from Charlie Chaplin's *Modern Times*, with mechanical employees working at mesmerizing rates. This is true of many Japanese factories: on a routine day at the average Nissan factory, workers are given two and a half minutes to attach the petrol tank and ten other parts to each car. At peak times the line is further speeded up: the ten-second pause between tasks is eliminated and workers are required to carry parts on their person to save time. Full-time factory workers, who average a twelve-hour day and are employed under the lifetime employment scheme, are beginning to complain about such working conditions, something part-timers, with no job security, are less likely to do.

At the other extreme, in a country with an unemployment rate that has hovered around the 2 per cent level for many years, younger male workers are starting to vote with their feet, staying away from jobs considered to be in the three Ks category: *kiken* (dangerous), *kitsui* (difficult) and *kitanai* (dirty). Some of the more unpleasant unskilled work is now undertaken by the 200,000 to 300,000 illegal immigrants. Japan does not accept legal immigrants as a matter of policy and high-profile companies such as Nissan cannot employ illegal labour. So in the early nineties, worried about an increasingly fickle young workforce, the ever falling birthrate and the increasing demand for their product, Nissan opened a new prototype factory called Nissan Human Land. The show factory, located in Kyushu, was dubbed a 'dream factory' or 'friendly factory' by the company's managers, who seemed to be relying mostly on *imeji* (image) to entice the young. The employee cafeteria is called the Harbour View Restaurant and has a panoramic view of the loading docks, and the assembly plant is called a pavilion. But some of this nomenclature is translated into physical improvements: the assembly pavilion is brightly lit with sunlight filtered through skylights, and cooled by air conditioners to a constant 77 degrees Fahrenheit, unlike the assembly plants in other Nissan factories which are dark and noisy and where temperatures soar to 90 degrees during the summer months.

To keep silent and act wise – still not as good as drinking sake, getting drunk, and weeping

OTOMO NO TABITO (665–731)

'Fukazu Naoko was the 1965 World Table Tennis Champion,' the manager says proudly as we walk through the door of the tearoom which is located inside the Butterfly Restaurant, which she owns. Ms Fukazu is an adherent of one of the three schools of tea that were founded by the great-grandsons of Sen no Rikyu (1521–91), the grandmaster of *chanoyu*, the tea ceremony. The room is small and still like the inside of an empty cardboard box. To one side, sunk into the *tatami*-covered floor, is a hearth, above which hangs a kettle from a metal chain in the ceiling. There is a *tokonoma* (alcove) – a fixture in all traditional inns, tearooms and private rooms in elegant restaurants – with the usual hanging scroll and vase with a single flower.

We sit in silence in a semi-circle on the floor, watching the master wipe the tea bowls, the big round handleless cups. He wipes them this way and then that; every move is precise and deliberate, carried out in slow motion with elaborate care. The *chanoyu* flourished as part of the so-called Zen culture of the late middle ages; Sen no Rikyu and the other masters of this period were all Zen priests. Our master handles the pottery as a new parent handles a newborn, gingerly, as if fearful of dropping it. The kettle bubbles away. Listening to the sound of the kettle is part of the meditation, part of paying attention to the here and now, of being in the here and now, of being without thought, a fundamental principle of Zen Buddhism. A tenet of Zen is that all things, including of course Zen, cannot be explained or understood in words, but only grasped intuitively, known or perceived in a non-intellectual way. In Zen, *satori* (sudden enlightenment) comes from rigorous discipline and introspection which produces awareness and intensity of perception. Zen is the philosophical underpinning of tea as it is of *bujutsu*, noh and kabuki. A tea master is expected to possess the same state of *haragei* as any practitioner of aikido, kendo, karate or judo.

Before we came into the *chanoyu*, the tea master told me a story of a tea master who lived during Sen no Rikyu's time. This man was challenged to a duel by a *ronin* (masterless samurai). The master explained that he knew nothing of swordsmanship and asked to be excused but the *ronin*, whose real purpose was to extract money from the tea master, insisted. For the master to have paid him off would have brought disgrace to his *daimyo* and clan, so he accepted the challenge. Having resigned himself to dying, he resolved to do so with the honour of a samurai. He postponed the duel and went off to a nearby fencing school to learn to die honourably by the sword. The *sensei* (teacher/master) of the school asked him to perform the *chanoyu*. Watching the tea master perform the ceremony with total concentration and serenity, the *sensei* told him that he had no need to learn the art of dying as his state of mind was enough to cope with any swordsman and with his own death. He instructed the tea master to approach the duel as if he were about to perform the *chanoyu*. The *sensei* predicted that it would end in mutual death, an honourable outcome for the tea master. The tea master did as he was bid, and the *ronin* saw that his opponent's presence of mind was such that it was possible for the tea master to win. He asked the tea master to pardon his 'rude request' for a duel.

I think of this as I watch this modern tea master pour boiling water over the green powder, mixing it with a brush into a smooth, thick, frothy, vividly green liquid: concentration, aware-ness, a fusion of all one's mental and physical powers. We take the bowls in both hands and turn them, admiring their beauty. There is conversation now, low and restrained, on the quality of the earthenware in our hands and the attractiveness of the flower arrangement. The tea is good, strong and slightly bitter. 'If you drink too much green tea,' Takayoshi told me earlier, when I was swigging it back in the bonsai shop, 'you will hallucinate; so please be careful.' Drunk in sufficient quantities and at sufficient strength, O-cha evaporates a sake hangover. However, it takes a great deal more green tea to induce hallucinations.

O-cha was first introduced into Japan from China in the eighth century, but it was not until the early middle ages, when it was taken up and recommended as a medicinal drink by the Zen monks, that it became popular. In the fifteenth and sixteenth centuries, when local warlords and merchants met to discuss politics and business, it became customary to serve tea in a quiet room: in the world, but not of it. Politics and business have never been far from *chanoyu*. Sen no Rikyu, who is accredited with turning tea drinking into the art it is, also directed the fledgling Japanese pottery industry: the first Japanese bowls were made for the *chanoyu*. Pottery of this type had previously been made by Korean or Chinese artisans. Flowers had been put in vases for years, but the art of *ikebana* (flower arranging) was also developed for the *chanoyu*, as a way of heightening appreciation of the new Japanese vases.

Sen no Rikyu enjoyed the patronage of the shogun Hideyoshi, a poor boy who, quite literally, fought his way to the top. Hideyoshi spent much of his life at war, for the most part successfully battling local warlords at home or trying, unsuccessfully, to invade Korea. Hideyoshi liked to show off his wealth and power and built, at Osaka, what was then the most elaborate castle ever. He also loved to give huge parties, such as the Kitano Tea Party, to which everyone was invited, from the richest of his vassals to the poorest of his peasants. Kitano lasted for ten days and was attended by thousands of people who watched plays and sang and danced. At another of his famous parties, Hideyoshi handed round trays heavy with gold and silver from which his guests could line their pockets.

Despite Sen no Rikyu's plain rooms and less-is-more aesthetic, tea ceremonies as well as tea parties were often occasions of ostentation during Hideyoshi's time. In his castle at Osaka, Hideyoshi's own tea things were made of pure gold. The rich in general spent a fortune competing for rare and beautiful tea bowls, and collectors would do anything to keep their prized possessions out of the hands of rivals. In one celebrated case,

Danjo Matsunaga, a *daimyo* under siege in his castle, smashed his precious kettles and other priceless tea-ceremony paraphernalia rather than have them fall into the hands of a rival collector. This having being done, Danjo committed *seppuku* to avoid the ignominy of capture.

In the end, so the story goes, Hideyoshi turned against Sen no Rikyu partly because he thought he was plotting against him, and partly because Sen no Rikyu refused to grant Hideyoshi permission to marry his reputedly exquisite daughter. The grand-master of tea was accused of bribery and 'invited' by Hideyoshi to commit *seppuku*, which, of course, he dutifully did.

The esoteric world of tea is still, as it has always been, very much of the world: feuds, factionalism and petty jealousies consume the practitioners of this rarefied art. In the spring of 1991, four hundred years after Sen no Rikyu's death, his descendants, the masters of the now three separate schools of tea, gathered in Kyoto to honour him. It was the first time in fifty years they had performed the ceremony together. Things did not go well: the descendants could not agree upon who of their number would serve the tea in honour of their illustrious ancestor.

Tea is still big business, both for potters and teachers: as many as twenty million people worldwide take part in *chanoyu*, thanks largely to Sen Soushitsu, one of the gang of three, whose school, Ura Senke, has branches worldwide. Sen Soushitsu, 'the ambassador of tea', is almost single-handedly responsible for taking the show on the road – he has practised *chanoyu* for popes and foreign royalty – and, most importantly, he has kept the practice of tea alive in Japan. After World War Two, Sen Soushitsu made *chanoyu* an integral part of young women's bridal training. As a result, women, who were once banned from *chanoyu*, are now its main practitioners.

Let a stranger in and he will drive you out of your own home

PROVERB

'We are going to the best karaoke bar in town, Lisa-san,' Takayoshi says. 'The very best, I promise you.' He throws up his arms, jingling his hands at the plastic bunting flapping over our heads. All provincial and suburban shopping streets are festooned with these plastic triangular flags, like a cheap imitative Christo project, linking one island of consumerism to another throughout the length and breadth of this country. I look at Takayoshi and the men from the bank; they have their arms around each other; they rear up and down like waves far out to sea. I cannot see how they can be that drunk – we had a little beer at Maimai-Tei but not enough even to turn their faces red. The food at Maimai-Tei was delicious. Seto naikai cuisine: lots of fruit sauces and piquant flavours, without any of the nasty bitter surprises often found lurking in *kaiseki*. These regional sweet-and-sour dishes were originally concocted to give energy and sustenance to the pilgrims following in the footsteps of Kobo Daishi around the eighty-eight temple circuit.

We walk down a tiny crooked path, past a Buddhist temple that is run by Takayoshi's friend, a man in his early thirties who reluctantly inherited the temple from his late father. His friend, Takayoshi explains, was living the good life in Tokyo and was disinclined to return home to run his family temple. Temples and shrines are often passed on in this way here, kept in certain families which are responsible for their maintenance.

The o-shaped moon looks firm and close, thick and creamy in the coal-black sky. It makes shadows from the lanterns and the statues in the temple grounds; short, squat shadows, a whole field of them standing in the corner by the temple wall. The statues are raised up on an altar of earth. There are toy windmills stuck in the soil around them; the wind spits through their thick plastic petals, making a clattering, whining noise. The statues wear red hats and bibs. At their feet are open boxes with an assortment of things inside: a toy car and a rattle; jars with sweets and biscuits; tiny jumpers and sleep suits; an orange and apple; unopened packets of juice. These gifts have been laid here by women. The statues have an unpleasant expression on their faces, something between a smile and sneer, although I think they are supposed to look happy. They are child-guarding Buddhas, guardians of the souls of dead children, mostly these days guardians of the *mizugo* – 'water babies' or 'unseeing babies', the poetic phrases for an aborted fetus.

'To make a water baby' means to have an abortion. In practice, abortion is available on demand for unmarried women (and may indeed be demanded of her), and for married women who have at least one child. Surveys of women – as opposed to surveys of doctors and government health officials – show that Japanese women have more abortions than women in any other developed country: around eighty-four abortions for every thousand women aged between fifteen and forty-four, four times the official figure (doctors under-report abortions to escape taxation). Unwanted pregnancies are hardly surprising in a country in which 80 per cent of couples rely on condoms for contraception and the other 20 per cent use the rhythm method. There are no diaphragms available, no IUDs or any other kind of modern contraception. Thanks to the power of the extremely lucrative abortion industry, and a reluctance to let women inexpensively, and privately, control their own fertility, the pill is unavailable as a contraceptive. (The high-dose version is available on prescription to a few women for control of irregular or problematic periods.)

The government, which has consistently given reasons such as safety concerns, or the threat of promiscuity, or the declining birthrate, for not legalizing the pill, had agreed to do so by 1992. However in March of that year it said that due to the growing incidence of AIDS in Japan it could not make the pill legal 'from a viewpoint of public hygiene'. As of 1991, there had been 405 cases of AIDS reported in Japan, with just over 1800 people said to be infected with the HIV virus. AIDS has always been seen as a 'white man's disease', most easily fought by hanging 'no foreigners' signs on brothels.

A high-ranking official from the Ministry of Health and Welfare once told me that the spread of AIDS was so low in Japan because there were only about five hundred homosexuals in the whole country! Japan has gone from glorifying homosexuality during the samurai years to stuffing it so far back in the closet that most homosexuals now operate from within heterosexual marriages. Paul Schrader's wonderful film *Mishima: a Life in Four Chapters*, which, among many other themes, explores the novelist's homosexuality, is yet to be shown in Japan because of this 'revelation'. However, there is a homosexual world in Japan, especially within the traditional theatre such as the kabuki. And an active homosexual fantasy world, of which more later.

Some Japanese doctors think that the number is low because AIDS cases are under-reported or undiagnosed, but others contend that the widespread use of condoms has kept the disease under control (yet these same condoms fail to prevent pregnancy). There has been a reluctance to confront AIDS publicly – it wasn't until the government gave AIDS as its latest reason for not legalizing the pill that an advertising campaign began. Underground trains in Tokyo were suddenly covered in posters of Count Dracula saying, 'I'm afraid of AIDS.' He was soon joined by other personages from the crypt, such as Frankenstein, a mummy and a witch, all with the same message. AIDS, it appeared, was still something that happened only to foreigners and characters from horror films.

Although abortion is an accepted practice in Japan, both Buddhism and Shintoism are actually, if not especially vehemently, opposed to it. To be a mother is a woman's highest, often only, calling. Adoption is not much of an alternative: a 'not yet married mother' must list her out-of-wedlock children in her *koseki*, a document that any would-be spouse or employee is likely to want to see. Moreover, there is a reluctance to adopt 'illegitimate' babies. Three-quarters of the some 100,000 adoptions each year are of adults, usually men adopted by their in-laws for reasons of succession. Most of the rest are children adopted by new step-parents. The recorded percentage of babies born out of wedlock is lower than anywhere in the developed world, but this has as much to do with a reluctance to measure illegitimacy as the high abortion rate.

To take care of your water baby's soul you must buy one of these sinister little child-guarding Buddhas, for which some temples charge as much as seven hundred pounds. The mother's feelings of guilt or sadness are shamelessly played upon. There are signs in many temple grounds cataloguing the ill fortune that befalls women who fail to buy a statue or decline to pay the temple to perform memorial services for the souls of their water babies. High on the list is that subsequent children will be born handicapped. Like the *chanoyu*, Buddhism in Japan is never far from business. As well as the traditional money-spinners of wakes, funerals and the performance of regular services for the souls of the dead, Buddhist temples have branched out into running car parks, schools, restaurants, blocks of flats, and, in one celebrated case in Kyoto, a night-club run by an abbess.

The karaoke bar door is at the top of a flight of narrow steps. We go up them two by two, as if we were entering the Ark. The two local bankers, whose idea this was and who are the best known of our party here, go first, clinging on exaggeratedly to the handrails. Takayoshi and I follow. Takayoshi, having been sufficiently oiled to enjoy himself, is laughing so hard that he has to complete part of the climb on all fours. The bar is small, tinier than my living room. The interior and the furniture are white. There are wall mirrors everywhere. The furniture is overstuffed; white armchairs on stilts adorn the bar, large white banquettes surround the walls. The banquettes are covered with people: women sitting on men's laps, men sprawled out, some sleeping. The armchairs at the bar are empty.

The *mama-san*, a highly coiffured attractive woman in her forties, comes towards us. She smiles at the bankers and pushes open the door, forcing us all down a step. Her eyes flip up over us, settling on me and the two European diplomats who are with our party. Her face clouds over. She looks at the bankers. 'No foreigners,' she says to them, putting one hand on top of the other to make a T-shape, the sign that something is closed. Refusing to serve foreigners in bars and restaurants is not unusual, even in Tokyo. The bankers say nothing. I can hear them suck in air through their teeth.

'I am sorry,' she says to them, 'but we don't serve foreigners.'

One of the men speaks. 'Well,' he says slowly, considering his position, 'there are only three foreigners. They are very important . . .'

Takayoshi, who has been hovering silently at my side, his head hanging off his neck like a dog who has just messed on the carpet, jumps to attention. He pushes his way through the middle of the two bankers. The *mama-san* greets him by name and bows.

'This is very difficult,' he says. 'For the sake of my face . . .' He bows slightly. Even though this was not his idea, he is our minder; he will 'lose face' if we cannot get in.

She sighs, stands back from the door and opens up her arm like a flight attendant at the entrance of a plane. 'Please,' she says, 'please come in.'

There are two other hostesses inside, one in her thirties, the other in her twenties. All three are dressed in single colours: the *mama-san* in a white bodi-con ('body consciousness', which is to say tight suit); the older hostess in a red bodi-con suit and the younger in a short black skirt and tight black T-shirt. Their shoes match their outfits. On the bar are dishes of Twiglets and jelly-beans. It would seem that there are no foreign drinks allowed here either: the shelves are laden with Japanese gin, Japanese vodka, Japanese brandy and Japanese whisky. I order a dry beer. The *mama-san* puts my drink on the counter.

'I like your hat,' she says. 'Is it European?'

She is wreathed in smiles, as if nothing had happened, as if she couldn't be more pleased to see me. She seems neither surprised nor embarrassed that I can understand her, that I must have understood perfectly well what she said to the bankers. The other two women come up and admire my hat as if it is the most marvellous example of millinery they have ever seen.

'Where are you from?' the youngest says.

'Do you like Japan?' the thirtyish one says.

'How long will you stay?' the *mama-san* says.

The young hostess is sitting across the laps of two old men. She has her arms around the neck of one and her feet in the balls of the other. The old men look like lizards, still and crinkled, with eyelids that bat up and down slowly and seldom. They look like brothers, but they are probably not. Three OLs sit beside them, laughing into their hands. One of the young bankers is singing some mawkish *enka*, his mouth almost swallowing the microphone. Behind his head the laser disc on the karaoke machine shows a young woman wandering in a field of what looks like *bosozoku*, the motorcycle gangs whence the *yakuza* recruit their apprentices. The words of the song drift along the bottom of the screen, with a little dot bouncing on top of them in time to the music.

The corner where the karaoke machine is kept is covered in discs. There is a little fat booklet on the bar listing the selection. The machine does something wonderful to a voice as it passes through – all the men come out sounding like Julio Iglesius, the hostesses, the only women so far to have sung, like Barbra Streisand. The *mama-san* pulls a sleeping man up from a banquette and begins to dance with him, throwing him around the room, knocking him into tables. Like one of those rubber balls attached with elastic to a bat, he returns and bounces off her. He is asleep on his feet. She undoes his belt and dips into his trousers and, much to the amusement of the other patrons, pulls at his penis as if she were milking a goat.

The other hostesses and some of the men are rearranging the furniture, pushing the chairs and tables as far back as they will go, making a tiny space on the floor. The music changes to Madonna singing 'Material Girl'; the youngest hostess in the black mini-skirt races into the newly cleared space. She is wearing sunglasses. She begins to gyrate on the spot, working her arms and legs up and down as if she is at an aerobic class. She unzips her skirt and tries to wiggle out of it, but it is too tight and she has to wrench it off. She pulls off her shirt and chemise and then her bra, revealing tiny breasts, no bigger than those of a pubescent girl. Under her black tights are black see-through bikini pants. She pulls on a red garter, holds on to her breasts and runs up and down the room, finally landing spread-eagled on the lap of a grinning besuited fellow, who shoves his arm between her thighs, energetically rubbing her vulva with his wrist.

One of the bankers wants to sing something. 'You know,' he says to me and the *mama-san*, 'it goes da, da, da, da, da. It is the most famous song in Japan. It is what the passengers sang to keep their spirits up as the JAL plane was crashing. You must know it . . .' (In 1985, a JAL 747 crashed into a mountain outside Tokyo killing 520 people – the worst accident in the history of civil aviation.) I know of the event, but not the song. The *mama-san* knows both: she puts on the disc for us, and hands over the songbook and microphone for our duet.

Later, when we leave, the *mama-san* shows us out. She stands and bows as we descend the steps. 'Thank you very much for honouring me with your custom,' she says, without a trace of irony. 'Please come back soon.'

I look at my dirty hands –
it's just like coming face to face
with my mind these days

ISHIKAWA TAKUBOKU
(1886–1912)

The train had fled faster than panic, ripping into the darkness to get here, but now its movement is sluggish. It trickles past the cone-shaped volcanic mountains that edge the plain, pointed beads of black sweat wrapped around the severed neck. The mountains sometimes look dainty, squibs of icing decoratively bordering a cake; then they look insubstantial, as if they have been washed on to the stretched canvas of the grubby dawn sky.

Two men get on, middle-rank *sarariman* in blue single-breasted suits. '*Gaijin, ga!*' one says to the other, his voice choked with surprise. They plop down across the aisle from me, shifting around in their seats as if they are not comfortable. The one who has not spoken leans forward for a better look. 'She has a small nose for a foreigner!' he says with equal alarm. The other man grunts an assent and they dig into their briefcases for newspapers, holding them aloft in front of their faces, flapping them back and forth like sails. The one closest to me is reading a tabloid. Like most Japanese tabloids, this one has hard-core S&M serials inside. His friend is reading a broadsheet 'sports paper'. On the outside there are pictures of women, naked and spread-eagled, with (in keeping with the law) their pubic hair bleached out. (Battalions of housewives and students are employed by the government to ink or scratch out offending displays of pubic hair on imported copies of *Playboy* and *Penthouse*, and world-famous paintings featuring nudes with pubic hair have been turned back at Narita airport lest they shock the populace.) In the biggest photo, a woman who looks Filipina is performing fellatio; because the man's pubic hair is bleached out she appears to have completely swallowed his penis and be on the way to burrowing into his stomach like a mole. Perhaps this is a deliberate effect. The man in the photograph does not look very ecstatic – he is still wearing his glasses and his face is as composed as if he were walking down the street.

Pornography is very casual here, ubiquitous like advertisements. You can buy hard-core porno magazines and videos from vending machines on street corners, along with beer and sake, condoms and lonely hearts columns, rice, ice-cream, flowers and instant noodles. Vending machines are everywhere in Japan, even on the top of mountains, dispensing your every desire. Mainstream magazines carry photos of naked women too, usually trussed up like sides of beef and hung from the ceiling. In Japan most porn is of an S&M nature, with women overwhelmingly playing the M part of the equation, shown graphically as horribly tortured victims. This is as true of the porno *manga*, thick comic books, which are read in their millions each week by boys and men alike.

Manga come in many varieties and reading them is an extremely popular form of entertainment. Each of the half a dozen weekly *manga*, some thicker than an A–D London phone directory, sell between one and three million-plus copies. The monthlies, mostly aimed at girls, sell a couple of million each. As well as pornographic, *manga* can be instructional, chronicling the life of Buddha or explaining the capitalist system; can deal with social issues such as couples living together or divorce; or can be political and satirical. But mostly they are entertainment, using every possible genre, providing an easy and fast escape for the harried and weary.

As with clothes, many trendy magazines and *manga* have English names and mottoes. *Lady's Comic Loving* is a popular girls' *manga* as is *Lady's Comic Rouge*. The covers tend to feature young Western couples, with the female looking as if she is fourteen or fifteen years old. Like the corporately manufactured *tarento* (talent), the flat-chested, bow-legged teenage girl pop stars, these models are a testament of *rori-kon*, the Lolita complex prevalent among Japanese males. *Rori-kon* style and behaviour is the ideal; Western *rori-kon* is the apogee of this ideal. However, whereas your average fifteen-year-old Western girl likes to think that she is a woman, an average Japanese woman likes to act as if she is still a girl. There is a name for these ageing teenagers: *burikko*, 'pretending-to-be-children'. *Burikko* is the female response to men's *rori-kon*. Many women, especially those who are still single, continue to be *burikko* well into their forties, or for as long as they can get away with it.

Girls' *manga*, which are read by females of all ages, feature soft porn under such names as 'Passionate Roman'. These stories are usually set apart by an introductory full-colour page, like a *manga* within a *manga*. There are few words in *manga* stories. The heroes and heroines are often Western-looking; blonds predominate, but there is usually a black man with, of course, great *coitus* ability. The romantic action between the blonde women and the black men often takes place in large Western-style houses. Women in Passionate Roman, as in porn in general, are either innocent rape victims or lascivious insatiable male-hunters.

Stories depicting sex with a black man are common in *manga* aimed at young women. The fantasy is quite rampant – tales of *kokujin* (black person) groupies are common in women's magazines as well. These groupies are camp followers of authors, such as Yamada Eimi, whose bestseller *Beddotaimu Aizu* (*Bedtime Eyes*), about a Japanese woman who lives with a black American service man, sold over a million copies. Outside the diplomatic corps and the United States Army, there are few blacks in Japan's tiny foreign community, increasing their exotic/demonic appeal. When Mike Tyson fought one of his world championship bouts here he had a bigger battle outside of the ring, fighting off the fans who were hell-bent on sticking their fingers into his hair.

Fantasies about black men are eclipsed, however, by the most popular fantasy in girls' comics: romance with *bishonen*, beautiful androgynous young heroes. *Manga* tales under such headings as 'Sexy Boys', feature impossibly gorgeous, athletic, blond, bisexual, Western-looking boys. One half of the *bishonen* couple is always also the lover of a blonde woman with big breasts. The *bishonen* are invariably shown as great lovers of their female partners, bringing them to unrivalled heights of ecstasy, something that apparently is not happening to real women and men. Reports on single women and sex undertaken by the various women's magazines consistently show that more than 40 per cent of women are unsatisfied with the way their partners make love, because it hurts or is uncomfortable; and they are unsure whether they reach orgasm. Over half of single women report that they find masturbation more exciting than sex with their boyfriends. Married women don't fare any better: 70 per cent say they pretend to reach orgasm as a 'reward' for their husband's hard work.

The train lurches over the square plain, sawing through its middle, creaking and grumbling through the patchwork of pocket handkerchief fields which are dusted in silver and gold leaf, half lit by the tepid light. Men in wellington boots squelch and slurp through the fields, shadow puppets, black and flat as spilt ink. The plain stops before it gets going. At the base of the mountains lies a ghostly settlement, a town or even a small city. The air above it is grainy, like a badly developed picture. One of the tall wide chimneys on the outskirts of the town breathes brown clouds into the air. We cannot smell the smoke or the earth or the mountain air. The inside of the bullet train is hermetically sealed like an aeroplane; it even looks like a plane with cabin-style seats adorned with white headrests. The bullet train was designed and built in the sixties and the interior reflects this; but its exterior shape and line is a translated art deco poster – it belongs more to modernity than the newer trains.

The train has stopped at a station that appears to have no name. Three of the young women *obento* sellers have got off, their oversized trays now bare. The boxed lunches the Japan Railway caterers were hawking were wrapped in green paper with white circles criss-crossed with rails. They had lugged the *obento* from one end of the extraordinarily long train to the other, supported over their shoulders by thick straps. The ones who sold the drinks manoeuvred over-laden trolleys through narrow doorways. All bowed when entering and before exiting the carriage and thanked the riders sincerely for their patronage. They stand in a slanted line now, solemnly watching the train. As it drags itself away they bow towards it in unison. The station master is bowing goodbye to us as well, his hat precariously hanging from his head. This is usual everywhere, except for stations in the major cities where bowing a respectful goodbye to trains would be a full-time job.

Some of the fields are covered in what looks like miniature plastic igloos, each one connected to the other, left over I assume from a forced early crop, unseasonable melons perhaps. The occasional orchards are frail and sickly. Apples as large as grapefruit hang improbably from emaciated trees, each individual fruit lovingly wrapped in foil to preserve its perfect form and tended with devotion by teams of *obaasan*, small and squat, round as the fruit. The sun is unforgiving in August, cruel and close, it glares from the sky, a quivering white hole. The old of both sexes, the tillers of Japan's fields, respect its awesome power; they cover themselves in its presence.

The *obaasan* are adorned in the most fantastic overblown head-dresses: Victorian baby bonnets with shoulder-wide bibs in white and pastels and tied under their chins; or wide-brimmed straw hats under which they have stuffed white towels or head-scarfs of various hues. Some wear peaked caps with long wide tongues licking their shoulder blades. They all wear *mompei*, the baggy work trousers that were *de rigueur* during the war, and long-sleeved shirts or blouses covered by overalls that resemble artist smocks. Their trousers are tucked into their boots. As the train passes they look up and smile, often toothlessly, and wave like small children. Their faces are acorn brown, creased like discarded paper bags. We could be anywhere in Asia; anywhere but where we actually are: the heartland of modern Japan.

During the winter, my destination of Shiga Heights (in Central Honshu's Joshinetsu National Park) is a popular skiing region. There is a skiing *boomu* (boom/fashion/fad) among the *shinjinrui* (new human beings), a somewhat derogatory term used by their elders to describe fashionable and supposedly fickle young people. In common with all of the ski resorts in high season, the slopes in Shiga Heights are ferociously overcrowded: you cannot see the snow on the mountains for designer ski suits. One year's fashion may be for Descente one-piece suits, or Rossignol Virage skis with Marker M46 racing bindings and Rossignol Dynafit 3F boots. Every year's fashion involves a vast outlay, even for the amateurs.

Skiing, like all *shinjinrui boomu* sports, is as much about dressing up as about sport. Just as well: there are twelve million skiers trying to cram into six hundred resorts. Patrons, especially in areas close to Tokyo, must queue for two hours or so for a chair lift, and then dribble down the slopes *en masse*, their skis bumping those in front, an illustrated Malthusian nightmare: so many people, so much money, so little space.

Everyone in this carriage is fast asleep. The men are stretched out fully on the reclining seats, their heads lolling from side to side, their arms folded across their besuited chests. The women are more circumspect: they have tipped their seats back less, keeping themselves more upright, and they hold their hands together neatly on their laps. The woman sleeping next to me is called Yoko. She is an OL at a bank in Tokyo. She is going home for an *omiai* (an honourable meeting), a formal introduction to a marriageable man considered a good match by her parents and her aunt, who is the go-between (a common role for an aunt). Yoko has a pale moon face with barely discernible eyes; she is, in short, a classic Heian-kyo beauty. We have the same blood group Yoko and I, type A positive. It was the first thing she asked me. We went on to zodiacs later. According to Yoko, the concurrence of my blood group, star sign and Chinese year have given me altogether too much passion and strength which 'would be good for a boy' but which I should try to tame, something she assures me she has to be careful of as well.

Yoko talks, like so many Japanese women do, in the rat-a-tat-tat style of rapid machine-gun fire. Typically, again, she is intense, concentrated like a frozen can of orange juice that makes ten times its size; she holds her steady gaze on my eyes like a laser beam. You are frequently told by the Japanese, in a way that will brook no contradiction, that they never make eye contact and so you should not be insulted or suspicious at this. But I have never met a Japanese who didn't make eye contact, unless he or she was trying to sell me a bill of goods. If anything, eye-locking is more intense here. The only place where it does not go on is in formal situations, such as business relations between strangers where there are clearly defined social inferiors and superiors. The inferiors are too busy bobbing their heads up and down like buoys on the water to catch anyone's eye; the superiors too busy basking in their deference.

Yoko's sleep is restless. Beneath her eyelids her eyes are pawing over her dreams. Last night she was so excited she could not keep anything to herself. Her potential husband is a Todai (Tokyo University) law graduate, she told me breathlessly, *la crème de la crème*, one of the happy breed most likely to succeed. She mugs when she talks, widening her face into kabuki expressions of exaggerated surprise or shock, and this too is typical, funny and sweet. She has made up her mind to like this boy, as a lesser heroine in a Jane Austen novel might do. She is determined and resigned at the same time: 'I am sure I'll like him,' she says with considerable emphasis, seeing her future laid out before her, the cards upturned like a game of solitaire that came out quickly, deftly. 'I am very lucky that he is interested in me.'

The suitor's parents are of a higher social standing than hers. They are Tokyoites. His father was a Todai law school graduate too, and is now a bureaucrat in the Ministry of Finance; he is a descendant of some *daimyo* whose name, in her giggly fluster, she cannot remember. Yoko's parents live in Nagano. Her father is a small-time *sarariman*; her grandfather a fisherman. She is 'honoured' he would even consider her.

Yoko and the young man both live and work in Tokyo, as does her aunt, but it was considered 'better', she said, 'to meet the first time at my parents' home'. Dinner will be very formal. She will wear her best kimono. Now she is wearing a black bodi-con suit, a fashion that extends far beyond hostess bars. The suit is stretched over her body like a sweet wrapper: the skirt clings just above her turned in knees. This is Yoko's second *omiai*; the young man's first. Either party may refuse the other; but it will be difficult for her to do so as her parents also 'couldn't imagine a better prospect'.

Yoko wakes up talking. There is no transition between being asleep and awake. She opens her eyes and her mouth at the same time, sitting up, straightening her seat, brushing down her clothes and tossing her head. She swans off to the bathroom with her toilet bag. Almost all single people have at least one *omiai*, and just over a quarter of all marriages result from these arranged meetings. Among the political, bureaucratic and business élite, marriages are still very much arranged to seal alliances. In the Tokugawa period everyone, except for priests, had to marry. While not literally true today, much of this edict persists psychologically in Japan. Marriage is a social necessity for both sexes – without it people are not considered proper adults. Making a good marriage, in a social sense, helps the man up the greasy pole and gives the woman his status.

Divorce, although legal and simple if uncontested, is uncommon and frowned upon. The divorce rate has more than doubled in the last twenty years, but at 1.26 per thousand people it is still one of the lowest in the world. From popular literature one gathers that this is a function of social pressure rather than married bliss. In girls' *manga*, stories of OLs and their *sarariman* husbands invariably follow the same pattern. After the fashionable Christian-style white wedding, the cartoon-perfect couple take their week's honeymoon in Australia (as 80 per cent of Japanese couples do). Then back home to the reality of 'eternal employment'. The husband, naturally a young ambitious *sarariman*, does not come home until between ten and midnight every night. And when he does he is drunk. He eats all of his meals buried in a newspaper and disappears to the golf links at weekends. As the story unfolds the bride rants and raves at her husband to no avail.

Over 40 per cent of young housewives told the Hakuhodo Institute of Life and Living, the social research arm of Japan's second largest advertising agency, that they felt isolated from society and out of touch with their old friends; the same percentage of housewives between the ages of thirty-five and forty-four told the institute's researchers that they 'wonder what they are living for'. Hakuhodo entitled its survey 'Japanese Women in Turmoil'. Many women, as they will tell you, resolve this turmoil through their main pleasure in marriage: their children.

'I'm tired of children' — to anyone who says that, no flowers

BASHO

The school has sent a car to get me, a black car with white doilies on the seat arms and headrests. It is icy inside, like stepping into a fridge. The driver is wearing his jacket and tie. A small run of perspiration trickles down the nape of his neck. He had stood on the platform as the train drifted into the station, a solitary figure holding up a sign reading 'Yamada Juku' (Yamada Cram School). No one else got off the train and he bowed deeply as I walked towards him, keeping the sign in front of him just in case. He is pleasant looking, with a wide open country face, round as a smiley button, and his crew cut is like a nail brush. He is thirtyish, I should think, perhaps younger. In the mirror, I can see that his face is still damp from the heat. How long had he stood on the platform waiting, watching the snout of the mole-headed train burrowing through the fields? Perhaps he had been afraid that I should miss my stop, that I should be gazing formlessly out of the other window watching crossbred things, a mutation of a pear and an apple, or a grapefruit and an orange perhaps, grown in the greenhouse on the opposite side of the tracks.

The conductor had been worried too. He had flapped over at the previous stop to inform me to get off at the next one. He had stood fixedly by the door nodding and smiling, theatrically miming an exiting passenger as the train drew into the station. He needn't have worried, Yoko had everything organized. She fluttered around checking the overhead rack, ensuring that I alighted without forgetting anything. A foreigner is like a child to be coddled and chided through the vagaries of Japanese life, an incompetent in the face of food, bedding and being here. All this clucking and fussing is meant kindly; it springs as much from a horror of the very thought of being alone in an alien culture, as it does from a conviction of the uniqueness of this one.

Hanging off the side of one of the mountains, and clustered around a gigantic car park, is a complex of three large rectangular sixties-style hotels. The hotels, which in the winter house the skiers, will function as both dormitories and classrooms for the week-long summer *juku*. The lobby of my hotel is a secret grotto. A plethora of goblins grimace from every corner: water spirits, flower spirits, earth spirits, spirits of the lakes and the sky, and, of course, the unforgettable, ever popular *tengu*, the spirit with a huge phallic nose, said to dwell in the trees in mountainous regions. *Tengu* are small winged goblin-like creatures, reputed to be descendants of Susano-o. They are often represented, like this one, with red bodies draped in feather cloaks and wearing black hats. They are mischievous, not evil, fond of playing tricks on the gormless humans that wander in their way. Some of the other little wooden creatures have the roundness of Buddhist priests; others are pointed and knobbly, gnomic in all senses. It is dark inside and I wend my way carefully around decoratively carved laminated tree-stumps, stepping gingerly over those lamps with pink and blue globules of something unpleasant-looking swirling about in liquid.

The man whom I take to be the hotel owner takes my *meishi* (business card) and examines it carefully, in the standard respectful way. Almost everyone in Japan has a *meishi* to proffer. The less you have on it, the more important you are. Thus the prime minister's *meishi* simply bears his name. You cannot do business without a *meishi* and it is seen within Japan, as it is outside the country, as a quintessential piece of Japanese business paraphernalia. Yet *meishi* are a relatively recent foreign importation, an outgrowth of the calling card that was introduced to Japan by the European diplomatic missions in the late nineteenth century. Its use among Japanese started to take hold during the Meiji era, when modernization was synonymous with Westernization. Certain bureaucrats and businessmen who routinely deal with foreigners have their *meishi* in both English and Japanese, with their names in English transposed into Western style, first name followed by surname. This practice also goes back to the Meiji era when arranging one's name in a foreign order for foreigners was the equivalent of Western dress, part of the process of Bummei Kaika (Civilization and Enlightenment) as Japan called its imitation of Western ways. The hotel owner tells me his name is Ishikawa and that he will show me to my room.

Mr Ishikawa is angular and wiry as a coat hanger, a contrast to the smooth calmness of the *tatami* bedroom. We stand in the well by the door removing our shoes; he, with his back to the room, slips out of his, leaving them exactly aligned and pointing towards the door ready to be walked into when he leaves. Mine are askew, pointing in two directions: the manoeuvre of getting out of them, stepping backwards and pirouetting on to the *tatami* without touching the floor or disarranging one's shoes is quite beyond me. He bends down, quite unselfconsciously, to straighten them. He tells me that in the winter season the room is occupied by six, sometimes eight, people. He points at the linen cupboard which indeed has futons and bedding for eight. I see them lying head to toe over the *tatami* floor – eight futons would cover this room completely, leaving no space to spare. The room is dominated now by a large carved and laminated coffee table, a peculiarly unevenly shaped affair of the Japanese 'rustic' style. Around the table are big square green floor cushions with red plastic chair backs propped up behind them of the type seen in Mr Watanabe's geisha house. Behind the coffee table is a *tokonoma*. In some hotels, as in this one, the television is unbefittingly slumped in the corner of the *tokonoma*, there being no other place to put it.

At the other end of the room is an enclosed tiled verandah with two sets of tables and chairs. There are slippers on the verandah which we step into before walking out on to it. The mountains are heavy and mournful close up, jagged and black as a slag heap. Mr Ishikawa points at the view and bows slightly towards it, like an impresario introducing his favourite act. 'These are our mountains,' he says reverentially, 'the source of our good fortune.'

Our reverie is interrupted by a loud rapping at the door. Someone is talking loudly in a high-pitched voice. The door is thrown open and a large square *obaasan* blunders in carrying a thermos. She shuffles across the *tatami* mat, talking to Mr Ishikawa and waving her free arm about. 'Eh, eh, eh,' he says in reply, as if he cannot quite follow her drift. She plonks the thermos down on the coffee table, drops to her knees and begins to crawl about on the *tatami*, organizing the cushions and the backrests into even straighter configurations. She jabbers away, her voice rising and crackling like an intermittent signal on a short-wave radio. Mr Ishikawa is examining his slippers. This tirade has something to do with his wife; and this woman is apparently his mother. 'Eh, eh, eh,' he says. She hooks the sleeves of her kimono jacket into suspenders attached to her shoulders, then gets two of the small round handleless red teacups out of the side cupboard and slams them on to the table. They are plastic, but look like lacquer ware. She dips her hand into the tea tin and puts three big pinches of O-cha into the teapot. She stops talking at Mr Ishikawa for a moment and looks over at me.

'Can you drink O-cha?' she asks.

I tell her that I like it really strong. She thinks about this for a moment and then laughs uproariously, showing her gums and rocking back and forth on her knees, as if this is the most improbable thing she has ever heard.

Mr Ishikawa sighs and laughs nervously. He points at the table and seats me on the cushion most directly in front of the *tokonoma*. If there is more than one guest this is the position in which the most honoured will always be seated; if there isn't a *tokonoma*, that guest is seated furthest from the door and the others are arranged around him, or occasionally her, in order of importance, the least important being furthest from the *tokonoma* and/or the nearest to the door. There can be no mistaking how important or irrelevant you are to your hosts. Feelings are not spared. I have been at lunches and dinners where, following a noisy discussion by the hosts about their relative status, the already seated guests have been rearranged like cut flowers.

Mr Ishikawa's mother heads for the door, a great cruise liner sailing out of port, leaving a tidal wave of words in her wake. He laughs nervously again when she has gone. 'My wife and my mother do not get on,' he says woefully, shaking his head, as if this butt of a thousand jokes and the subject of anguished advice books actually still surprises him. His hound-dog expression displays the burden of his *mazakon* (mother complex) to its full effect. A *mazakon* is said to afflict the majority of the male population, who indeed do encourage their wives to be second mothers not partners.

It is customary to be served tea in your room when you arrive. In a *minshuku*, a relatively inexpensive bed and breakfast-style place, or an upmarket *ryokan* (traditional inn), the host or hostess will stay and take tea with you. Mr Ishikawa's establishment is a *hoteru* (hotel), which is to say a mixture of Western and Japanese rooms and styles. In Japan, in all but the most upscale Westernized establishments, the price is per person (which is why the maximum number of people are crammed into a room) and includes breakfast and dinner. Mr Ishikawa tells me about his *hoteru* facilities, which include an *ofuro* (communal hot bath) served, he claims, by a natural spring. All *hoteru*, *ryokan* and *minshuku* have a communal bath of some description, even if it's achieved by tap water; and a bath before bedtime is a nightly ritual, for children and adults, in almost all homes.

In front of the car park, a colony of Japanese monkeys is playing in the trees, its members screeching and fighting with each other. Presently, the monkeys disappear into the woods. It is silent now. There are no bird sounds. The sun crawls up the sky, expanding its white body to fill it. Inside the hotel pots are being washed and orders called out; a man laughs, a woman is singing something familiar, a tune that is always in the air. Mr Ishikawa rushes out and peers down the mountain. He has put on a navy blue jacket and a maroon tie. He taps his head with a white handkerchief that has been folded into a large square. He puts his head on one side, turns and rushes back into the lobby. There is a rumbling growl coming from the valley. It sounds like what, in retrospect, you often think you hear at the beginning of an earthquake. It is turning into a bellowing roar, thundering up the mountainside towards us, like an escaped animal, vociferous and insistent. Mr Ishikawa rushes back out of the hotel, buttoning up his jacket, a line of staff trailing after him as wispy as smoke. They arrange themselves in a line in the car park, standing to attention, their chins turned slightly upwards.

I can see it now, creeping up the twisted road below us, clunking, hissing, gasping and belching, a long white-headed creature crawling towards us on all fours, its blank square head peering around the bend. The first coach roars on to the forecourt, and flips up on to the car park, the next, almost touching the first, follows, then the next and so on. In a well-choreographed waltz, all sixty-one coaches find their place, without pausing or altering course. When the last coach is in its slot all the engines are turned off, letting out a collective sigh. The doors fling open and, in order of arrival, out they pour – three thousand children, their teachers and administrators: Yamada Juku's summer school is in session.

The hotel staff suddenly shoot out in all directions, waving and shouting at the silent children, rounding them up into ever engorging groups to march them off to their respective hotels. Inside the lobbies children stand quietly at the reception desks, whispering to each other and watching the staff tear around them, honking and flapping and crashing into each other, like geese being pursued for Christmas lunch. The children are frog-marched in battalions to their rooms and instructed to gather in the big hall in five minutes where the head teachers will address them. The children bounce their heads up and down: 'Hai, hai, hai, wakarimashita, wakarimashita,' they chant in unison.

'There are only one hundred and seventy-five days left until February the first,' the teacher says. His arms are crossed in front of him. He sways back and forth on the stage, solemnly eyeing the children, row upon row of them sitting on either side of the long lines of tables. He repeats this, isolating and leaning on every word. 'Think carefully about what you are doing here. If you don't pass the exam, all your efforts will have been in vain.'

The children sit motionless, rigidly upright, their hands resting in their laps. Their hajimaki bear the exhortation 'We Must Succeed!' They are too big for their heads, and have slipped or are askew, making the children look like demoralized accident victims left unattended too long in a hospital waiting room.

'It doesn't matter if you try hard and fail,' the teacher says, 'that is meaningless. It's a very tough world out there. If you say, "I tried my best, but I failed," people will say, "So what?" You must not fail.' He repeats this twice, prowling back and forth across the stage, watching the children, pausing to stare at one and then the other, looking at them sceptically, letting them know that he doubts they are up to it.

'Have you ever studied twelve hours a day?' he says. 'I don't think so. Here you will. You must all be quiet and concentrate and abide by the rules. You must be able to obey the rules. A lot of athletes have camps like this. It is important for people who have the same mission to live and study together, it produces the best results.' He stops pacing and stands centre stage again. 'We don't want to be too strict,' he says, softening his voice. 'We don't want to scold or hit you. But please remember, we are here as a group, moving, working, thinking together. If you behave as an individual you will cause trouble. Remember, work together as a group!' He pauses, looking slowly around the room and shaking his head dourly. 'I hope you will be able to smile on February the first!' he says.

The children applaud this, but they do not smile. Under the garish fluorescent lights the terror etched into their eleven- and twelve-year-old faces makes them look ghoulish, as if they are wearing Hallowe'en masks. The teachers, all men, are dressed in identical navy blue tracksuits with 'Yamada Juku' written in English on the back. They wear the same 'Fly High Eagle' T-shirts as the children.

'Every minute must be used in the most efficient manner,' the teacher continues. He speaks in a deep somnolent monotone now, which carries within it a timbre of unmistakable menace: 'Please remember that every minute is very important, so use your time well. Please remember that your parents paid more than one hundred thousand yen to send you here for this five-day camp. *Shiken jigoku* [examination hell] is just that. But it will give you a certain mental attitude, a strength, not only academic ability. You have to win against yourself.'

You have to win against yourself. This is a familiar litany, a first and often repeated message. The rounds of *shiken jigoku* for which these children are being prepared are for places in prestigious middle schools, many of them private. Children that fail to get into a good middle school will have little or no chance of entering the sort of high schools from where they may hope to apply to the top four universities: Tokyo, Kyoto, Keio and Waseda.

All of the children here spend on average three hours, four nights a week at Yamada Juku in Saitama, a well-heeled suburb of Tokyo, where most of them live. Yamada isn't the biggest of the thirty-six thousand odd *juku*, but it is one of the best known, and is well respected and representative: as with most *juku*, two-thirds of the children here are the sons and daughters of *sarariman* and two-thirds are boys. Many attend the *juku* every day for a full day during their holidays, and after a half day of regular school on Saturday. *Juku* is a way of life for 70 per cent of children of their age throughout the country. In the Tokyo metropolitan area 90 per cent of children attend *juku* during most of their school life, as do 40 per cent country-wide.

Many mothers try to get their pre-school children into one of the very few places at the so-called 'escalator schools', which operate a system somewhat akin to lifetime employment. Under this procedure, once a child has passed the kindergarten test he or she is on the escalator to the university to which the kindergarten is connected without having to undergo *shiken jigoku* – with the proviso, of course, that they can keep up with the work. Competition for top-class escalator schools is phenomenal; and the kindergarten entrance exams for these schools are very stringent. However, most mothers would rather the lesser evil of pushing their child beyond endurance at three than subjecting him or her to a childhood of *shiken jigoku* with no guarantees at the end.

There are only ten thousand places available each year at the four prestigious universities. The rest of the students who pass the university exams will be relegated to second- and third-tier universities, which will affect their job prospects: the big companies and the bureaucracy hire almost exclusively from the top four universities. (LDP politicians are overwhelmingly Tokyo alumni.) Of the million or so students who sit for university exams every year, around 400,000 fail to get a place anywhere. Most of these *ronin*, as they are called, will attend 'preparatory' schools full-time the following year and sit the exam again. Preparatory schools for *ronin* are like super-crammers where old exam papers are intensively reviewed.

Japan has a 99 per cent literacy rate, and in terms of overall results the standards of most, if not all, state schools are high. Japanese children go to school for 240 days a year, a school year much longer than that in the West. However, there is so much to remember in order to pass the exams, which resemble a vast game of Trivial Pursuit; so many countless facts, dates, and numbers to be regurgitated at high speed, that children cannot learn everything necessary in regular school hours. Hence the proliferation of *juku*. The best *juku* cost around 800,000 yen a year for each child; private schools the same again. Although basic education is free, an average family spends between 20 and 25 per cent of its income on *juku* and/or private schools.

All three hotels look like refugee camps. *Ad hoc* classrooms are strewn throughout the dining rooms, ski storage rooms, hallways, reception areas, corridors and bars, many separated from each other only by flimsy curtains so that the maths lessons can be heard in the Japanese classes and vice versa. Beneath this cacophony is a loud insistent droning noise, like an aeroplane being tested; it's the generator pumping power into the basements to fuel the makeshift cocoon-shaped workmen's lights illuminating the corridor and storage room classrooms.

The children are slumped over their books, furiously scribbling down what the teachers are saying. They are used to the overcrowding. A typical classroom in a regular school has over forty pupils and many have up to fifty. They are used to the tiredness too. In a recent survey of eleven- to thirteen-year-olds who were asked what they would like to be doing right now, a third answered 'sleeping'. Like everyone else, children sleep when and where they can: each morning on the underground in Tokyo there are rows of po-faced children between the ages of six and eighteen – the girls in their blue and white sailor suits, the boys in their high-neck brass-button serge jackets and peak caps – all clutching expensive oversized leather satchels, and all fast asleep. Sleep becomes an even rarer commodity during the period leading up to *shiken jigoku* when children follow the famous exhortation 'Pass With Four, Fail With Five,' meaning just that: if you are lazy enough to sleep five hours instead of four during this time you will surely fail the exam.

Apparently schoolchildren don't have much energy left over for what we might consider to be normal mischief. When you see them returning home from school in the evening their shoes are still shining, and their clothes look freshly laundered and pressed. There are no muddy knees, no ties askew, or hats hanging off, no shirts sticking out. There is no jostling, no shoving, no shouting, even among the big spotty youths who hang off the straps, clogging up the train doors. Their lives are carefully contained. The teenagers like to go to Makudonarudo or coffee shops between school and *juku* but often schools forbid this, not just between school and *juku*, but at any time. Many schools dictate precisely what children can and cannot do – down to the colour of their underwear – outside their gates as well as within.

Children occasionally release their pent-up aggression by physically attacking their teachers or throwing things, such as lunch boxes, at them. But more usually they single out a scapegoat for *ijime*, the systematic bullying of a child perceived to be different. The differences causing so much offence can be vague – perhaps his or her hair isn't quite the right shade of black, or his or her eyes not quite brown enough. If the child is too fat or too skinny, too short or too tall, too clever or too stupid for his or her own good, he or she is a tempting target. Children who have transferred from other schools or other parts of the country are at risk, but those most likely to be attacked verbally or physically are the *kikiku shijo* (the returnees), children who have, for part of their lives, lived and been educated abroad.

Ijime is different from the usual childish cruelties practised on outcasts in Western schools: it is systematic, relentless and carried out by the group as a whole. A child who is made a scapegoat for his or her differences will quickly be deserted by friends, will be cast out totally and persecuted for years. In a country in which belonging to a group is held in such importance, banishment is a terrible punishment. Teachers, if they see anything happening, are unlikely to do much about it. A child who is seen as wilfully different, such as a returnee, is likely to find him- or herself actively persecuted by the teachers as well as the children until he or she becomes a 'proper Japanese'.

The instances of *ijime* are estimated at several hundred

thousand a year, but no one knows the true extent of the problem. Schools are unlikely to report it and parents may either not know or encourage their offspring to fit in more rather than complain. A handful of children die every year at the hands of school bullies. Some victims kill their persecutor(s): in one infamous case, by smashing his skull with a hammer and gouging out his eyes. Grudges against former classmates sometimes last into adulthood. In the early nineties, a twenty-seven-year-old man was arrested for trying to murder his former junior high school classmates in revenge for the way they had bullied him fifteen years earlier. He spiked twenty-one bottles of beer with arsenic and made three bombs, which he took to the class reunion party. He had written down what he intended to do in his diary, which was read by his mother who alerted the police. He was remanded in a psychiatric hospital for tests which pronounced him sane and he was released back into police custody. The courts are reluctant to find against schools in cases of *ijime*, but in the early nineties the parents of one *ijime* victim, who hanged himself, were awarded eleven million yen in compensation by the court as, 'The school had made insufficient efforts to end the bullying,' giving some glimmer of hope that *ijime* will finally at least be condemned by teachers if not eradicated.

By 1 a.m. the children have been individually studying their weak subjects for four hours. Except for the sounds of pens squeaking over paper and the rustling of pages, the classrooms are still. As they have been told to do unless they are questioned, the children ignore my presence. There is no giggling or grimacing, no pointing or nudging. They look right through me like dolls in a toy shop. All have little pots of cream on their desks, which they rub on their wrists and smell. 'It is mosquito repellent,' a solemn little boy tells me, 'it helps us stay awake.' Between sniffs his eyes keep closing and his head falls back. One girl's lips are bleeding. 'I bite them to stay alert,' she says. 'The mosquito cream isn't enough.' Other children have bruises on their arms. I watch them pick up their flesh and twist it, gritting their teeth and closing their eyes until it has hurt enough to bring tears on to their cheeks.

Midori, a Yamada alumni and the class supervisor, claps her hands. 'Come on,' she says, 'you are here to work. You must work. You must overcome your tiredness if you want to pass your exams.' She sighs. 'It is only the first night. If they are ready to give up already, how are they going to make it through the week?' She walks over to a boy who has fallen asleep with his head and his mouth open. She grabs him by the scruff of the neck and shakes him violently. 'I am sorry, I am sorry,' he says. He bites his wrist, and looks at the impression of his teeth.

One little girl, sitting as still and stiff as a statue, holding her book up in the air in front of her, stares with unblinking eyes at the pages. Without any warning she collapses with a heavy sigh on to her desk. Her book clatters across the floor. None of the other children bend down to pick it up. None look at it, or at her. Midori walks across the room and prods her in the back with a wooden pole, as they do in a Zendo (a Zen meditation hall) if you slump or doze off. The girl sucks in her breath and pushes herself up. I pick up her book and give it to her. 'I am sorry to have been a trouble to you,' she says to me. 'Thank you very much for what you have done.' Her voice is cracked and scuffed like old lino. She is trying not to cry. She pushes on her eyebrows and her cheeks, literally holding her eyes open.

You have to win against yourself. She looks like the little girl I saw who fell off her bike as she sped round the corner near my flat in Tokyo. She lay dazed on the pavement, holding her eyes open and her tears in. She whispered that she was all right and lent on my shoulder to get up. 'I am sorry to have been so much trouble to you,' she murmured. Her left leg hung loosely, the bones of what had been her knee jutting out like kindling. She let go of me and reached for her bike. I grabbed her before she fell. 'I have to get home,' she said, as if she were forcing the words through a sieve. 'I'll be late for *juku*.' Her lips were bleeding from where she was holding on to herself with her teeth. The ambulance men stated the obvious: her leg was broken in several places.

The *ofuro* is inside, not outside as I prefer, but it is surrounded in glass so that the mountains and the trees are eerily visible through the steam. The sky is coal-black, potmarked by clusters of deep white shimmering stars. The moon is a perfect half, a cream cheese moon, seemingly suspended from the night sky, swinging in and out of view on an invisible rope. The water is inflamed, feverish; it turns you scarlet on contact, done like a lobster in seconds; it rips your breath out of you. Dense small clouds rise from it, drift off and dissipate. The clouds, like the water, smell of sulphur, suggesting that it really might be a natural spring.

At the edges of the room are the washing positions, each with a mirror, taps and hand-held showers, all at squatting height. Midori's colleagues, the other class supervisors, are washing, squatting down on the bathing seats, pouring buckets of water over themselves, consulting the mirror as they shampoo their hair. The buckets are small and plastic, blond-wood coloured, marked with black lines so they resemble the old-fashioned wooden buckets they have replaced. The matching seats, which are oblong, sucked in at the middle and narrower at the bottom, have about them something of the style of a forties couture hat. After at least half an hour of soaping and rinsing off, soaping and rinsing off, the women make their way through the fog to the kidney-shaped bath, holding their flannels over their pubic hair. Once they are in the water they put a soaked flannel over their faces or on top of their heads.

Most of them, like Midori, are employed by the *juku* to encourage the others; they are successful Yamada graduates who made it, first time around, to the university of their choice. Like Midori, most would say they had a *kyoiku mama* (education mother). Midori's mother pushed both her and her brother hard: 'She had to work harder for me because the majority of places at the best schools are reserved for boys – right from the beginning,' she says.

The better educated you are, the better a husband you are likely to bag. Midori's mother hopes she will be a bride-recruit for one of the big companies: 'Companies like their employees to marry each other, it cements bonds.' Although as many women as men go on to higher education, only a quarter attend four-year universities. Women make up nine out of ten students at junior colleges, which are often *ad hoc* finishing schools to turn young women into *ryosai kenbo* (good wives and wise mothers). Midori's mother didn't want that for her daughter so Midori went to university. 'Mama always wanted to go to university but she just went to bridal training classes, tea ceremony, flower arranging, cooking and sewing. She wanted a proper education for me.'

Midori talks quickly, in a matter-of-fact manner that is in complete contrast to the high-pitched, demure tones she employs while talking to the Yamada men, superiors on two counts: as men and as former teachers. When one of the teachers came into the classroom earlier, Midori's whole body language changed: her head dropped down, her hair fell over her face, her toes turned inward, she held her hands together in front of her. When she spoke to him, her voice flew up several octaves. (In women's speech, the higher the tone, the greater the level of politeness and deference being shown to the person addressed.) The teacher was telling her that he wanted her to take an extra class tomorrow. Afterwards, he sat down for a while to watch the children. She turned her back on him and, as if he wasn't there, resumed her former manner: stalking around the classroom with her head up, barking out instructions like a sergeant major.

The noise creeps into my dream, transfiguring itself into an air-raid siren above the sound of gunfire. I roll over for cover. I find myself crouched on the *tatami* floor staring at the clock: it's 6 a.m. Out of the tannoy above the *tokonoma* comes the most awful sound: a screeching, wailing bugle, playing some off-key version of reveille. Someone is rapping anxiously on the door. I jump up to see if there is a way I can turn the tannoy off. The door flings open. Mr Ishikawa's mother blusters in, mumbling and throwing her arms about. She stands in the middle of the floor, arms akimbo, staring at me, her mouth slightly open but momentarily at rest.

'It isn't possible to turn it off,' she says. 'It's for announcements. It will stop in a minute.'

Mr Ishikawa's mother lowers herself to her knees, complaining about the condition of her joints as she does so, and starts folding and rolling the bedding. 'Where do you come from? How long have you been in Japan? Is this the first time? How long will you stay? Do you like Japan? Can you eat Japanese food? Can you use chopsticks?' she asks, barely waiting for an answer before proceeding to the next question. I answer her in monosyllables, hoping she will go away, or at least stop talking. 'This is wrong, this is wrong,' she says, flapping the three thick pads I put over the futon, 'just one over the futon is correct.' I tell her I like the bedding to be soft. She shakes her head in dismay at my nasty foreign ways. 'Can you eat Japanese breakfast?' she asks. 'Or do you want toast?'

I want toast, Japanese style, which will come with a cold hard-boiled egg and some salad, two-inch slabs of thick white toast, made from 'English Bread', as it's called. Whoever brought the idea back from Britain must have spent a great deal of time in the old transport cafés. Even though I would bet ten thousand yen that the majority of the children will be eating toast, as they do at home most mornings, she looks at me triumphantly, as if I have confirmed something she always suspected: the inability of for-eigners to eat fish and rice in the morning. (What many foreigners, myself included, cannot eat in the morning – or at any other time – is the breakfast dish of *natto*, fermented soy beans, the taste of which is acquired, to put it politely. For those who did not grow up on the stuff, *natto* is often described as simply revolting in both texture, look and taste.)

I flounce off to the bathroom, careful to back up into the plastic shoes inside its doorway, the toilet slippers in which I must make the rest of the unsanitary journey. You never enter a toilet barefoot or in your house slippers in Japan. Toilets in private houses as well as *hoteru* are equipped with special plastic footwear like this. The toilet is of the traditional squat variety, flat on the ground, for balancing over not sitting upon. There are all sorts of toilets in Japan, from the Western style variety that have warm seats in winter and automatic flushes, others that are part bidet and wash you afterwards, to the prototypes that can analyse your urine for health problems. But mostly there are these squatters to contend with.

The children are already doing callisthenics in the forecourt, wan and bleary-eyed, but as coordinated as a professional chorus line, swinging their bodies from side to side, straight line upon meticulous straight line of them, swaying and dipping in time to sprightly marching music. The music, too jolly and enthusiastic for its own good, is blaring out of the tannoys hanging off the roofs of the three hotels. The tannoys are also strung all the way up the mountainside. Much of Japan is set to muzak: ski slopes, high streets, botanical gardens, zoos, beaches, parks; from one end of the archipelago to the other, incidental music opens and closes on your life, warding off the dangers of silence.

After ten minutes or so the music stops. The teachers blow whistles and the children are regrouped by the supervisors into smaller packs for a brisk walk in the mountains. As they march off, the tannoys on their route crackle into action, blaring out what could be martial music. Midori rounds up her group like a sheepdog, making it tighter and tighter. She is wearing a hat to keep the sun off her face, not so much out of fear of its debilitating heat, but to protect the lightness of her skin. Like that of most city dwellers in Japan, her skin is very light. As it was in Heian-kyo, a pale complexion is considered a thing of beauty and a mark of aristocratic birth: brown skin signifies someone who works in the fields or on a building site. Japanese people do not think they tan, but that they turn black, the colour of other Asians, a fate to be avoided.

Yamada Keisuke, the *juku*'s founder, lounges in the cafeteria finishing his breakfast of cigarettes and coffee. He is reading a newspaper, folding it in half and then quarters as if he were commuting on the underground. Mr Yamada started this *juku* a short time after he left university. There are branches, existing or planned, in London, New York, Paris and Brussels, where the concentration of Japanese families is large enough to make it worthwhile. Mr Yamada's business is not just *juku*. He owns a company which researches new educational techniques, and develops products such as the Mass Cubic Arithmetic System, with which you can teach your infant maths. His companies gross about four billion yen annually.

Mr Yamada is well known here as an outspoken and promi-nent critic of the education system, condemning its bias to rote learning and bemoaning its 'lack of creativity'. This leaves him in a curious position: an entrepreneur, nominally outside the main system, successfully feeding it what he says it should not not want.

It's as if Richard Branson opposed flying as a mode of mass transport, but determined to do it better.

Mr Yamada is heavy set, an intense man in his forties, clearly not given to smiling, vague remarks or chit-chat. Despite his feelings on the woeful nature of the education system, and its inability to foster creativity, his *juku* is based (as are all *juku*) on super rote learning and can scarcely be said to provide an alternative. He agrees and explains that, 'Parents don't want creativity in education. What they want is for their children to be successful and pass exams. They don't ask us to foster creativity. They expect us to supplement what's missing, to fill in the knowledge gap that will allow their children to pass the exams.' He lights another cigarette from the one he is about to stub out. The ashtray, just after breakfast, already has thirteen of his butts in it. (Sixty per cent of all men smoke, many heavily, but only around 15 per cent of all women.) He flops backwards, opening his body as if in a dead faint. He believes that even if he started an alternative school no one would send their children to it: 'They couldn't, because these children would then be failures. They could not possibly succeed in our system.' He shrugs his shoulders in a way that could either be fatalistic or cynical, or both. He is very recessed, hidden away under layers and layers of opaque material, mummified.

'Without rote learning children cannot pass their exams, which means no university, which means no good job,' he says. 'We are here because the schools cannot, or do not, teach children what they need to know in order to pass the exams. No mother would risk her child's failure. She would rather see him suffer if that is what is necessary.'

I know from my friends that he is right. No mother *would* risk her child's failure, but it begs the question Mr Yamada always raises: whether *shiken jigoku* should exist and whether these exams should be predicated only on the remembrance of facts.

'While it is true to say that the exam system is wrong,' he says, returning to his favourite theme, 'it is also true that the schools are incompetent.' Because of this he will not hire teachers who have taught in state schools: 'They have too many bad habits.' He thinks the schools, which is to say the teachers, should be able to equip the children to take these exams whether they are right or wrong. 'The schools spend too much time on peripheries. They should teach as we teach: concentrated bare facts, straight-to-the-point rote learning.' Never mind that he finds rote learning 'an abomination', it is 'the only way a child can possibly get through a Japanese exam'. As for using his status as a prominent educator to try to change rather than perpetuate the system, he thinks that this is impossible. 'There is nothing I can do, except talk about it. It's up to parents and Mombusho to decide to change it. *Shikatta ga nai* [What can you do]?'

Mr Yamada tells me he would change in a minute if the system was altered and 'creativity was valued'. He has a curriculum worked out. He can go either way. Japan is worried that its citizenry lacks the creativity that will be needed in the twenty-first century to provide a successive array of fancy consumer goods and so-called value-added products such as software. Mr Yamada's concerns are echoed in educational reports, even in some parliamentary ones, but are all ignored by Mombusho.

As for now, the most important thing the children will learn during this week-long *juku*, according to Mr Yamada, 'is how to concentrate. They will learn how to study no matter how they feel or what odds they face – through noise, distraction, tiredness, everything – and that is the most important lesson of all. Without that they cannot hope to succeed.'

Aiyako hopes to succeed. She is twelve years old. During term time, she attends *juku* four evenings a week for three hours each session. In the school holidays she goes every day for a full day. 'I like it,' she says, 'all my friends go too.' (Japanese children consistently report in surveys that they like school, both *juku* and regular. This may be true. They are expected to enjoy it. Going to school isn't seen as a chore or something you have to go through. Japanese teachers, along with parents, believe that all children want to do well in school and conduct their classrooms accordingly.) This is Aiyako's first time at summer school. She has come 'because I am particularly bad at maths'. There is nothing of the budding teenager about her, not even of the pubescent. This is true of most girls and boys her age in this country. She is unequivocally a child, a lively little girl, earnest, straightforward and wide eyed. There is no such concept, much less a word, for 'teenager' or 'adolescent' in Japan. Children – as they are still treated and referred to – between the ages of twelve and nineteen are not thought of as especially problematic. If they have problems at this age the source is looked for at home or at school, as it would be at any other time, not in their glands.

'My mother encourages me a lot in my schoolwork,' Aiyako says, 'but my father just says, "Good luck!" It is better to be encouraged.' She nods her head intently. 'Mama looks at all my work, she sits down with me when I do my homework and helps me. She keeps me awake when I am falling asleep. She encourages me to do better: "You can always do better," she says. It makes me try even harder. I want to make her happy. She has put so much into me. When I don't do well she becomes upset.' Aiyako's face darkens. I can imagine what she hears: 'Mama doesn't love you any more,' the high-pitched whine, plaintive and long suffering, beaten over the heads of children who step out of line or fail to come up to muster.

A child's failure is the mother's failure, she will be blamed by family and society alike; she cannot allow her son or daughter to fail. Another child might take advantage of the dynamic, play the game for all it was worth, as some children do with variations of, 'If you want me to pass my exams I'll need chocolate ice-cream' or a new bike or whatever. Not this one. She sits alert with her head cocked to one side, an anxious puppy panting to please. In her spare time she plays badminton or rides her bike and also reads for pleasure: 'I like magazines about movie stars,' she says. Despite all her schoolwork she reads a novel a week, 'On the train, to and from school and to and from *juku*. It's nice. It helps me forget my worries about the exams!' She is worried about the February exam: 'I hope this week I will learn to concentrate better. I cannot concentrate for more than forty-five minutes at a time – and that's no good. I will never pass the exam unless I can concentrate properly.' All children are taught such *hansei* (reflection/self-examination), and to be modest about their abilities, which of course can and must always be improved.

Aiyako doesn't know what she wants to do when she leaves school, she has no dreams of what or who she will be, or none that she will admit to. 'My mother says that I must pass this exam so that I can get into the school I want – it is for my future – I cannot even think about what I want to do when I leave school until I have passed this exam.' I press her on this. I want to know whether she has an idea of where she wants to get to, whether for her, like the boys, she sees this constant battle against examination hell as her one chance at upward mobility, whether she can imagine herself a *kyaria wuman* (career woman), bound to the best company for life, unable to move to another company lest she lose her place on the promotion escalator; or whether, in her mind, upward mobility will be obtained by the best marriage, a possibility enhanced by the best university. But she shakes her head and looks at her shoes, pursing her lips. It would be too immodest to speculate on her entrance to university, and what that could mean for her in the future; it might even bring bad luck.

The maths teacher walks into the classroom ahead of the children and throws his bag on his desk. He begins to write a problem and its answer on the blackboard, talking nineteen to the dozen as the children scramble for their desks, throwing their copy books on top of them and scribbling down what he is writing. Most of them are standing by the sides of their desks or kneeling on their chairs, gradually lowering themselves into a sitting position as they write. The teacher leaves the first problem on the blackboard and goes on to the next without pausing or turning around to look at the class. He holds a textbook in one hand, into which he burbles indistinctly, like a man trying to set the record for speed-reading the phone book. He appears to be completely oblivious to his surroundings.

The door creeps open and two girls sheepishly come in with their heads bowed. They are two minutes late. The teacher looks up quickly and turns on them: 'You worthless girls,' he bellows. 'How dare you come late to my lesson!' They are bent over at forty-five-degree angles like outstretched ironing boards. They whisper apologies. He storms across the classroom towards them: 'You have brought shame on your parents!' he screams. 'They have put their faith in you and how do you repay them? By behaving disgracefully! Come here! Kneel down!'

He points at the floor by his feet. The girls drop to their knees and collapse forward until their noses are almost touching the floor. The teacher picks up a *manga* lying on his desk. 'You are not worthy to have been born!' he howls. 'All the sacrifices your parents have made for you – and look at you – look at you!' He rolls up the *manga* in both hands, holding it like a rounders bat, and wallops the girls around their heads. They keep perfectly still. One of them digs her nails into the palm of her hand. The other children do not take their eyes from their books. The teacher throws the *manga* on his desk. 'You will stay there for the whole lesson,' he says to the girls. 'If you want to waste your parents' money, you will not waste my time.' He picks up his textbook and turns to face the blackboard. He cleans it and writes down the answer to the next problem, adding the question as an afterthought.

I walk to one of the English classes with Jun. He is eleven, but much smaller than an average child of his age. He is what we once might have called 'weedy'. Unlike the other children, he obviously finds talking to me excruciatingly embarrassing. We sit down in one of the lobbies; he squirms about in his chair, pushing his body to the far reaches of it. He, too, attends *juku* four evenings a week for three hours each session and every day in the holidays. Like most children, he likes to read *manga* in his spare time: 'It helps me to relax,' he says. I can see him on the train, weighed down by his heavy satchel, drowning like an unwanted kitten inside his black scratchy uniform, his mind awash in the *manga* world of heroes, villains and violent solutions.

'I have come to the summer school because I must get better grades in order to pass the exam,' Jun says stiffly. 'Regular *juku* isn't enough for me.' His parents, he tells me, say the same thing. His eyes dart about. All the colour has seeped out of his face. He is sweating. I get up and motion him outside. His relief is so tangible; I feel as if I have released an animal from a trap. We walk across the forecourt. It is a lovely day, full of yellow sunshine, thick with the smells of a mountain summer, like the days of an imaginary childhood. He walks like a crab, his eyes moving incoherently over the landscape: there is more than fear or anxiety in his face, it is sticky with dread. He agrees, somewhat reluctantly, that it is a lovely day, but denies that he would rather be outside playing. 'Play today, cry tomorrow,' he says, repeating it like a mantra, 'play today, cry tomorrow.' This, too, he would have learnt from his *manga* heroes, this and to keep his head down, to struggle against impossible odds, to win, to fulfil the fantasy of the poor boy who succeeds by his merits, who becomes the best in the land in his chosen sphere. It's a universal fairy tale; but in Japan it is as if the midwife whispers it in the newborn's ear.

It is cold and damp in the basement where the English class is being held. It is lit by ghostly green-tinged lights that might have been designed to give you an instant headache. As the area is normally used for ski storage, there are no windows. The English teacher glances up and immediately looks away. He doesn't seem pleased to see me. After a minute of sitting in his class I realize why: he cannot speak English. Moreover he cannot pronounce it, making the clichéd error of substituting Ls and Rs. As if caricaturing himself, he says, 'When in Lome do as the Lomans do.' In Japanese there are no L or R sounds as such but a cross between the two, usually slightly closer to our L sound.

But I suppose it doesn't matter, there is no conversation going on here, nor is it expected. The children are writing down in Japanese the English phrases he is reading from their textbooks, practising the written translations that the exam requires. By the time they reach university Japanese children have studied English for ten years. Like British school-taught French or German, few pupils actually learn to speak the language they study. However the teaching methods and exam requirements here result in students unable to say even simple words or phrases. Apart from those who deal with foreigners professionally, few people can speak a second language. More can read. Of those who can speak English reasonably fluently most have taken private conversation lessons, studied abroad for a while, or tuned into the BBC World Service or the Voice of America.

Two girls and a boy at the back of the class are sound asleep, the pens have fallen out of their hands. One of the girls lies across her desk, the other girl and the boy hold their heads in their hands. The teacher, who is staring at the textbook he is reading, doesn't seem to have noticed. He reads a story about a Japanese man in New York who was surprised when people said, 'Excuse me,' if they wanted to get past him in the lift, instead of silently barging him as they would in Japan. 'He was also surprised when he bought a doll which had "Made in Japan" written on it,' the teacher says. 'Translate into Japanese the word "surprise".' The children lean forward and copy out the translation from their specially prepared textbooks.

Things are more cheerful in the Japanese class, which is being held on the ground floor in what would usually be a games room. I sit in the middle of the room behind a boy wearing a black silk bomber jacket bearing the Japlish legend: 'Capital Success. Living a Free and Easy Life.' The girl next to him wears a similar jacket with 'Artistic temperament. Workmanship and Quality Guaranteed' sewn on. Another girl's sweatshirt bears the statement 'Atelier Meiku: The United Kingdom of Great Britain and Northern Ireland 1974.' The girl next to me has a knapsack which proclaims on the flap, 'Sun House: We'll feel the light warm our hearts.' Nonsensical Japlish phrases permeate everything and are particularly used to sell products: 'I feel Coke,' scream the mob of ecstatic teenagers; 'Speak Lark,' says James Coburn, puffing on a macho American cigarette; 'For beautiful human life,' says the robotic voice at the end of the Kanebo cosmetics commercial. Japlish is commonly used to make clothing trendy, like these children's clothes and my bum bag, which tells me: 'They were getting off to a bad start but they tried hard to make a fresh start. Their courage will carry them through.' Or today's T-shirt, which everyone is wearing, with 'Keep Your Spirits' emblazoned across the chest.

Japanese advertising is a great employer of foreign stars, models and settings, sometimes with peculiar Japlish scripts to accompany them, such as that energetically conveyed by Paul Newman in an ad for the JCB credit card. Sylvester Stallone sells a sausage; Brooke Shields smiles from Sansui music systems; and Sting sings for something incomprehensible. Black stars get a look in as well. The opera singer Kathleen Battle sings the praises of Nikka Whisky, and in his pre-prison heyday Mike 'Iron' Tyson punched for a beer. However, almost all of the ordinary foreign models are white, bone-thin and very young, part of the aforementioned *rori-kon* that Japanese men have developed as a counterpoint to their *mazakon*.

Japanese television shows are punctuated by ads of American homesteads full of young Americans on the porch in rocking chairs, or prairies full of doleful blonds, or preppy male glee clubs. The fantasy of American culture infiltrates much of youth culture. Twenty per cent of the country's teenagers wish they had been born an American, slightly more wish that they had not been born Japanese. But still, 51 per cent of these teenagers believe that the Japanese are superior to other races.

The Japanese teacher is pleasant. He looks kindly at the children and smiles as he talks. 'I will read you the story and then I want you to write about the feelings of the characters and the meaning of the text, taking not more than twenty minutes, and using no more than forty *kanji*,' he says, opening the textbook and holding it in the palms of both hands, although it is neither particularly big nor heavy.

'In the first story I want you to think of what the expression "This is really life" means in the context of this story,' he says.

The children have opened their textbooks to the relevant page, their copy books at the ready beside it.

'No matter how far she went, she couldn't find the post office,' the teacher reads. It is the first line of the story. He pauses. 'How would you feel?' he asks. 'Insecure, uncertain – these are the best answers.'

The children write the words 'insecure' and 'uncertain' down.

'She tried to cross the bridge, but the wind was so strong,' the teacher reads. 'In this case the feeling is fear.' He pauses while they write this down: 'fear'.

'Then the wind stopped and the girl ran across the bridge,' he reads. 'Halfway there the wind started to howl so violently again that she couldn't go backwards nor forwards.' He looks up from the text at the children staring down at the books on their desks.

'How would you feel now?' he asks. He waits for a moment. '"Desperate" is the best answer,' he says, nodding his head.

He runs his finger down the text: 'Now we come to the end of the story. She is almost over the bridge and sees the post office right in front of her. Now at this moment how would you feel?'

The children stare at their textbooks. The teacher looks at them smiling. Seemingly all at once they realize that this is a question they are supposed to answer: every hand in the room goes up. The teacher signals to a boy at the back by a window. He stands up quickly, scraping his chair over the wooden floorboards.

'*Ando*,' (relief that difficulties have been triumphed over) the boy says, 'she would have felt *ando* because she would know her parents had been worried about how she was doing, and if she had had to turn back before reaching the post office she would have failed them.'

The teacher nods and smiles. 'That's exactly right,' he says. '*Ando*, as your parents will feel when you pass your exam in February. So in this story the phrase "this is life" means that the determination to win is the most important thing of all. You may feel desperate, but you must go on and achieve your goal. Now, as quickly as you can, please write about this story, using no more than forty *kanji*.'

The children write down the above summation, copying it out neatly from the notes they took as he spoke.

'Now for the next story,' the teacher says. 'This is about the different feelings people get from the same experiences. I want you to remember that as I read.'

The story is about two boys who do everything together when they are young, but as they grow up they slowly begin to realize that they see and understand things in different ways.

'The conclusion of this story,' the teacher says, 'is that we are all isolated because we cannot share our experiences.'

THE

CITY

AT

THE

EDGE

Tokyo on first, or even second, sight often disappoints. In part because of the images we bring to it. Despite the catchphrases associated with modern Japan – 'economic miracle', 'Phoenix risen from the ashes', 'second largest economy', 'technological wizardry' – it is often still thought of as a *ukiyo-e* filled with delicate geisha and elegantly formed wooden structures, an image stuck in the nineteenth century. Tokyo's *omote* disconcerts: the city is a cacophony of neon signs, crowds and chaos.

The city's buildings are, for the most part, concrete and glass, grey and sand-coloured, stocky like one-time boxers, jammed together randomly, filling nearly every inch of space. The signs and billboards in *kanji*, *hiragana*, *katakana* or *romanji* (the Roman alphabet) reflect the eclectic style of the city and its dissonance. The streets and the buildings are stitched together with string upon string of thick black utility cables (only 20 per cent of Tokyo's cables are underground whereas all are in London). The neon signs hang down the sides of the buildings from top to bottom, like the old-fashioned cloth banners they replaced. They advertise the shops, cafés, restaurants, cinemas, beer halls, sushi bars, *yakitori* joints, night-clubs, sex shows, galleries, in short anything that is available within the building.

A bar, club or restaurant often reconstructs another world, giving the city the feel of a giant multi-faceted theme-park. In Tokyo's contemporary public interiors you are always somewhere else, down to the last, if sometimes wrong, detail: the American fifties; France through a film noir lens; the year 2000; an Italian holiday; a British railway station; an aeroplane; a château's wine cellar; Liverpool in the sixties; a German country inn; a Japanese seventeenth-century farmhouse. Fantasy is aggressively sought out, not so much for whither but whence it takes you.

Tokyo is an enervating city, heavy with crowds like Trafalgar Square on New Year's Eve. It merges into Kawasaki which merges into Yokohama and so on halfway to Osaka, hundreds of square miles of urban conglomeration without an empty bit of land in sight. Thirty-three per cent of Japan's population lives within one hundred miles of the Emperor's palace. Of these forty-odd million, thirty million live within a twenty-mile radius of the palace. Scarcity and politics have driven land prices wild. Mortgages are now taken out over three generations. For the 40 per cent of families who are not landowners, the idea of buying a house has also been relegated to the realms of fantasy.

You move through the city as if underwater. Above and around, zig-zagging over your head, are the elevated Shuto expressways, numbers one through nine, licking office and apartment windows. The roads look like murky rivers. Yellow cabs and white cars predominate, a custardy mess choked with dying yellow and white fishes. Inside the cabs the taxi drivers, like the politicians on the campaign trail, wear freshly laundered white gloves, and there are spotlessly clean white headrests in faux lace on which to sleep off an interminable journey. Even in the capital most of the roads are tiny *ura dori* (backstreets), barely wide enough for one car. Often on the *ura dori* there are no pavements, just painted lines. In Japan more people are killed *by* cars than in them.

At the centre of the city is the palace, where the shogun's castle once stood. It is still castle-like, wrapped up like a present, encircled first by the Uchibori dori (Avenue outside of the Moat), then the moat itself, widest on the western edge, where it is called Sakuradabori, the Moat of Cherry Blossoms, after the trees that grace its banks. At the front of the palace grounds, facing Marunouchi, the business district, is a wide spread of pale grey gravel, a vast gathering place which is often covered by busloads of elderly people from the countryside, and identically dressed schoolchildren, gawky in their ugly blue and serge uniforms. The old and the young wait their turn to stand, kneel and squat for group photographs in front of the Nijubashi, the Double Bridge, the most photographed spot in Japan. It is

picture-perfect: behind the Nijubashi is a white turret, a classical piece of Japanese castle architecture, with its grey sloping
and pointed roofs, its slanted walls drifting into the moat. The
bridge itself is made up of a balustrade with two half-gaping
mouths. Centred in front of each mouth, on the commoners' side
of the moat, are two shivering willow trees. The Nijubashi is an
exemplary corner of the past, in a place where there are few
physical manifestations of history. This is a city which has been
rebuilt twice from scratch this century, once after the Great
Kanto Earthquake of 1923, and again after the firebombings of
1945.

Here in the centre of the city the office blocks rarely rise much
over twenty floors. Only Shinjuku in western Tokyo is considered
topographically safe enough for real skyscrapers. That is where
Van Gogh's 'Irises' is, at the top of a life insurance company, so
far from its birthplace. Despite the sophisticated earthquake-proof
technology built into the city's structures, people fear that Tokyo
will have to be rebuilt again after The Big One, as the inevitable
next big earthquake is reverentially called. There are earthquakes
all the time of various degrees of magnitude – things fall off the
shelves and walls, buildings quiver and slop from side to side.
Being in a lift is the worst. The lift stops and shudders in the shaft.
Will it break? Will this be it? This is what we dream of here, a
country set adrift from the world, broken in two, sinking. This
nightmare is the stuff of *manga*, restless nights or a best-selling
novel. It is how the country sees itself. The very earth beneath our
feet shifts and realigns. This is what reality is like here, shifting:
the Japanese have an earthquake psychology. In political or trade
negotiations this is called, by the hapless foreigners, 'moving the
goal posts': the point of agreement once in sight slips away like a
mirage, reforming as something else momentarily unobtainable,
to be negotiated for again. Internally, this is in part how the status
quo is maintained for it is difficult to fight a constantly changing
reality.

As well as the palace district, the city has several other major
centres. Among them the Ginza, the most famous, is a short walk
from the palace; the working-class districts of Ueno and Asakusa,
which make up the Shitamachi (the low city) is to the northeast;

and brassy Shinjuku and trendy Shibuya are both to the west on the Yamanote (high city) side. Just below the palace is Hibiya Park, the first park in the country to be laid out on Western lines. Overlooking the park and the palace is the Imperial Hotel, not, unfortunately, the Frank Lloyd Wright version, which was destroyed in the sixties in favour of something commodious and more modern. The new Imperial is indistinguishable from the offices of the life insurance company, telephone company and bank which also stare at the park with blank glass faces.

By the side of the Imperial is the Takarazuka Theatre, the Tokyo home of the eponymous all-female troupe, purveyors of romantic musicals and titillation. On nights when the troupe performs, it is almost impossible to pass – the area surrounding the theatre is clogged with giggling, shivering, trembling female fans, calling out the names of their idol; oooing and ahhing, squealing at the sight of her; pushing flowers and presents of clothes and handmade dolls into her arms; reaching out gently to touch her, their hands vibrating in the air like tuning forks. Others bring love letters, which they will pin on the stage door.

Almost all of this adulation is directed to the stars of the Takarazuka, the *otokoyaku*. The *otokoyaku* wear their hair cut short and slicked back like James Dean, sometimes shaved at the sides to give the appearance of sideburns. A thick forelock usually dangles over their right eyebrow, which is pencilled in to appear bushy, wide and straight. Their eyes are covered in blue, pink and mauve make-up, under the lid and over, to give the impression of long wide orbs. Their jackets, shirts, trousers, suits and tuxedos are all cut on male lines. An *otokoyaku* strides out like a man; she does not mince, take dainty steps or knock her knees together like a woman of her culture. The *otokoyaku* smile and wave in wide broad generous strokes. Everything about them is expansive, impressionistic, drawn on an ample canvas, larger than (a woman's) life. They walk the earth fearlessly, like men. But the fans want the tension in tact, want the woman visible beneath the boy. When Haruna Yuri, one of the older and most famous *otokoyaku*, wore her stage moustache out in the street, the fans complained. She had worn it to play Rhett Butler in Takarazuka's musical version of *Gone With The Wind*, which over one and a half million people, most of them women, flocked to see. The *otokoyaku* wears her 'male' costume off stage to 'preserve the dream' that she is a boy. She too is a *bishonen*, like those in the *manga*, a hybrid of sex and race: neither male nor female, neither Oriental or Occidental, but a big-eyed, stylized betwixt-and-between.

Androgyny as a sexual ideal is an old idea in Japan even outside of the kabuki and noh. In tenth-century Heian-kyo, a female beauty had a plump white face with a tiny mouth and the narrowest eyes. This was also true of a male beauty – the only difference being his wispy beard. Men in Murasaki Shikibu's famous novel from the period, *The Tale of Genji*, are termed 'beautiful as women' – a great compliment. Men in this time were expected to display emotions – tears were a sign of sensitivity in both sexes, not weakness. The sophisticated court at Heian-kyo was, to an extent, of a kind unseen in Western history – one culturally dominated by women. *The Tale of Genji*, probably the first novel in the world, was penned by a woman. In Japan the tenth century is considered the Golden Age of Literature, and the writers were overwhelmingly female. Once the warrior culture of armoured masculinity took hold, men found this unsettling. Throughout subsequent centuries men sought to discredit these writers, especially Murasaki, claiming that her father wrote the outline of the book and that some unknown male the best of the rest. Such desperate 'scholarship' has since been abandoned, and Murasaki's authorship is now unquestioned.

The Takarazuka almost always perform musicals, mostly ones especially written for them from such epic tomes as *War and Peace*. The troupe's taste is eclectic, and without fear. It will perform almost anything it thinks can be rendered romantically: *Antony and Cleopatra*, the life story of James Dean, Harlequin romances, *Me and My Girl*, and *The Rose of Versailles*, which the troupe adapted from a *manga*-telling of Marie Antoinette's life story. The troupe has also danced for Japan – in the thirties in military garb, and in the sixties it undertook a world tour to convince sceptical foreigners to buy what were then considered 'inferior' Japanese products.

The Takarazuka Theatre was the invention of a railway magnate, Kobayashi Ichizo. In 1914 he was the not-so-proud owner of an underused railway line between Osaka and the then Takarazuka spa. Mr Kobayashi dreamed up the idea for the theatre and the all-female troupe to provide entertainment for the masses, whom he hoped would then ride his Hankyu railway to see the show. The Hankyu Corporation still owns the railway and the troupe, as well as being a property developer and owners of department stores and the Hankyu Braves baseball team. Nowadays the Hankyu line from Osaka to Takarazuka is permanently packed with women – the Female Express as it is sometimes jokingly called – groups of housewives, young singles, old women and teenagers. There are only ever a handful of men, mostly elderly, smiling indulgently, accompanying their wives who have spent a lifetime as Takarazuka groupies.

The Takarazuka village itself is as pink as a little girl's bedroom. It has a permanent fairground and lots of little shops selling food and Takarazienne (as the actresses are called) paraphernalia: posters, mugs, buttons, and dolls in the idols' likenesses. There are a multitude of fanzines, in which the Takarazienne are written about exhaustively. The mostly manufactured gossip about the favourite stars, especially the comings and goings of the *otokoyaku*, is written in syrupy gushing tones, in the language of old Hollywood fan magazines.

The actresses, many of whom live in the company dormitories, walk around the village as they do in Tokyo, careful to keep in role. Those who play the women's parts are excessively dainty and demure, caricatures of modern Japanese womanhood. They, too, wear the eye-rounding make-up but generally they are smaller than the *otokoyaku*, as delicate and clean as tiny dolls wrapped in cellophane. Like overdressed little girls their long hair is kept back from their faces with bows, slides, ribbons and Alice bands. Some have fringes, some ponytails or plaits, others topknots, pigtails or braids. They wear big earrings and necklaces as they do on stage. They smile prettily with small half-closed mouths, so in contrast to the *otokoyaku*'s wide grin. When their faces are in repose, the female players look pleasant, half smiling, like Japanese air hostesses; the *otokoyaku* look serious, with their pouting expression, almost sullen: sexually aware Peter Pans.

The following of the Takarazuka is a phenomenon in Japan, a rite of passage for many teenage girls, some of whom continue the practice into old age. I have been to the theatres, both in Tokyo and Takarazuka, with friends who had been fans as teenagers. All were immediately swept up in past reveries. Every seat in the almost three-thousand-seat theatre was filled with women and girls enraptured by the corpulent sets and overblown plots. The actresses are always dressed in violently vibrant gowns, the *otokoyaku* in Liberace-style tuxedos of various hues or, if the script calls for it, brightly coloured army uniforms which resemble commissionaires' outfits. The acting however, like most Japanese acting, is very good, especially considering the nonsense they are expected to spout, but the music is forgettable and the dancing basic. In *War and Peace* the refrain sung over and over throughout the show, at the oddest moments, is: 'Everyone must love their life, life is everything for us.' In a Takarazuka musical when the lovers (many) kiss (many times) they do so passionately but with their backs to the captivated audience. At the end of the show there is always a finale which usually takes place on a derivative set borrowed straight from a Las Vegas show. Up and down a two-sided staircase of extraordinary size, glittering Takarazienne, in Busby Berkeley costumes, sing and dance. Every show uses up to four hundred costumes and at least three hundred pairs of shoes.

There are four separate Takarazuka troupes: Moon, Flower, Sun and Star, with eighty-five actresses in each. The girls usually join the theatre between the ages of fifteen and eighteen, training at the Takarazuka school for two years before they appear on stage. About seventy-five current Takarazienne are the daughters of former Takarazienne, and about half of those are third-generation players. Takarazienne are forced to retire when they marry because, as Araki Yoshio, one of the managers (all of the managers, directors, producers, composers and choreographers of the Takarazuka are men) explained, 'This theatre provides a dream for the audience, a romance. Most fans come to see the *otokoyaku*. If an *otokoyaku* is married it shatters the illusion [of her being a boy].' As for the actresses playing the female roles, 'Marriage adversely affects their glamorous image,' says Mr Araki. He thinks that the theatre is so popular because it provides a welcome escape from what women have been taught to desire since childhood: marriage. 'Most women come here to escape from their marriages,' Mr Araki says. 'They come to see the *otokoyaku*, an ideal man created by a woman. He is a romantic illusion. This is what the fans want. The kind of men these girls play – dependable, strong, kind and gentle – does not exist in the real world. This is why we do not perform modern plays, and when we perform a Japanese historical play we shift the setting to Europe. Mostly we perform European plays because Europe is more romantic.'

For the *otokoyaku*, playing the part of the *bishonen*, in a society in which male and female roles are strictly differentiated and tightly prescribed, can be a liberating experience. Asaka Jun, an *otokoyaku* probably in her late twenties (Takarazienne do not disclose their ages), is a rising star; tall and elegant, gorgeous rather than beautiful, she looks as if she stepped out of a glossy black and white thirties Hollywood publicity shot. Offstage she wears a beautifully cut expensive-looking man's jacket with, needless to say, trousers. Under a tailored shirt she sports a cravat. Her presence so close at hand is disconcerting. No woman on the streets of Japan looks like this. Gone is the campness of the stage *otokoyaku*, what is left is what titillates her fans: erotic ambiguity. Here is a girl plastered in make-up like an adolescent boy trying to look like a woman playing the role of a man.

Her fellow actress, Mito Hibiki, who plays female roles, sits daintily beside her. She too is in costume, wearing a little girl's dress, with a fussy collar and a female persona. A *burikko*, she is a caricature of many of the younger and would-be younger fans. As Jun sits with her body open, relaxed back in her chair, one leg flipped over the other, so Hibiki keeps her body closed and held tightly against the seat. Like most of the girls, when Hibiki joined the company she wanted to be an *otokoyaku*, but was found to be 'too petite'. I try to imagine what she would look like if her hair was cut like Jun's, if she moved and spoke in the same way.

These days the majority of *otokoyaku* are chosen primarily because they are tall. This wasn't always so: most of the older *otokoyaku*, from a generation in which most people were short, are the same height as their partners.

Echoing Mr Araki, Jun thinks the Takarazuka is so popular 'because it provides such a nice fantasy. It's a chance for women to escape from daily life.'

'The women come for the romance,' Hibiki says, 'to fantasize about their favourite *otokoyaku*; that this perfect boy is their lover. This is why the *otokoyaku* are the centre of the performance. We, the actresses, are the housewives, or the young girls' stand-in on the stage. Together we make the lovely dream.'

Jun's fans buy her flowers 'and sometimes on my birthday they buy me men's clothes, jackets and shirts. It's not like other areas of show business. In the Takarazuka, fans and stars are close. There is no wall between us. They are not kept outside. Fans come into the dressing room and talk. They give us advice on hairstyles or acting techniques. We have a close relationship with them.'

The fans are sometimes ardent in their declarations of love. 'They get so caught up in the illusion,' Jun says, 'they say to me, "You are such a beautiful young boy, I am in love with you." And then I have to tell them, "Look, I am a woman, I am not a boy. This is just the theatre." It isn't only the young girls that get so caught up, which one might expect, but even married women!' She laughs and looks at me with a stylized expression of wide-eyed surprise. These fans, Jun says, 'want to believe' she is boy, 'want to believe in the dream'.

Like the kabuki actors, the actresses sometimes fall in love with each other as well. 'We are playing roles,' Jun says, 'and our roles extend off the stage. It's not as if we can walk off and leave them behind.' Playing roles has changed them. Especially Jun who has the bigger role to play. 'Before I joined the Takarazuka,' she says, 'I was just an ordinary Japanese girl. But now many things have changed inside of me. My ideas have changed. I don't feel like an ordinary Japanese girl any more. I feel protective of women. I don't know if I can explain.'

For both of them acting is 'freeing'. They have been with the company for ten years now and if they are going to marry they will have to do so quite soon. (After twenty-six a woman is considered to be on the shelf or, as it is often put, like '*kurisumasu keki* [Christmas cake] the day after *kurisumasu*'.) Both Jun and Hibiki want to get married and have children, but as Jun says, 'To be a Takarazienne is everything for me.' It is difficult for them to choose an ordinary life over an extraordinary one, to choose to be in the audience rather than on the stage. Both say they can no longer 'imagine being anything other than a Takarazienne'.

The area around the Takarazuka Theatre in Tokyo has become as hip and fashionable as the young women who crowd in front of it. There's a small ritzy *depato* (department store), all chrome and glass and foreign fashions. The area is dotted with ethnic restaurants of every hue. There is an ultra modern cineplex nearby as well as the Nissei Theatre, a venue that tends to put on the Japanese version of foreign musical blockbusters. Underneath the arches of the railway line that slices the Hibiya and Yurakucho districts from the Ginza is another world, dark and cavernous, crammed with bars and eateries, full of small-time *sarariman*, ties askew, washing noodles and *yakitori* down with copious amounts of beer and sake.

Above the *sarariman* the trains of the Yamanote Line, the Tokaido Line and the Keihin Tohoku Line, haul millions of commuters back and forth from central Tokyo to the suburbs. The Yamanote Line encircles central Tokyo. To live within it is to be wealthy. Most people commute from the suburbs, an average of an hour and a half each way. The commuter trains, frequent, efficient and cheap, are never sufficient. At the most crowded terminals *oshiya* (honourable pushers-in) are employed to do just that: shove the passengers into the train, packing with their white gloved hands as many people as they can into every carriage. You cannot move. Often your feet do not touch the floor. You have to keep your arms close to your sides so that they don't get broken.

It is for such times that the Walkman was invented: tune in, tune out. Most people close their eyes between stops. Those sitting sleep. Well over half the population describe their favourite recreation as sleeping. A man once stood next to me learning English, eyes closed, repeating the phrases after the tape – 'Haalow,

I yam a Japanese mahn . . .' – as if he was alone, in the 'privacy of his own home'. The *puribashi* of his home is, however, likely to be limited both by size and inhabitants: wife, children, perhaps parents. A third of all households are still three generational and the houses so small that it is common for parents and children to sleep in the same room, and when they are little on the same futon.

Most people who visit 'Love Hotels' – those extravagant palaces designed to look like mediaeval castles, the QE2, European cathedrals, New York City, a space shuttle, ten-tiered wedding cakes iced in pink, etc. – are married, but to each other. Around sixty million couples frequent Tokyo's Love Hotels every year, renting by the hour the *puribashi* in which to make love. Inside the rooms are pure kitsch: jungles complete with full sound effects and gorilla costumes; Elizabethan banqueting rooms with clanking suits of armour; boats sailing on artificial seas for the nautically inclined; baths as copious as small swimming pools complete with water chutes; beds that are stage coaches, Coronation coaches, luxury cars, or space rockets; beds that move and hoot at the first moans; beds that rock, roll, and rotate; cameras to record it all. As the adverts promise: it will put some umph back into your marriage, or at least, it is to be hoped, some laughter. But perhaps not giggly laughter. Like the Takarazuka, the Love Hotel is not seen as camp or kitsch – there are really no such concepts here. It is a fantasy world in which you have the *puribashi* to be someone other than your socially assigned self.

A man gets on the bus carrying a doll as big as a two-year-old child. He plops down in the seat across the aisle to the side of me and sits the doll carefully on his lap, rearranging her legs. 'Comfortable?' he asks. The doll has masses of thick blond hair spilling over her white round face. Her eyes are China blue plates, her mouth is a tight rosebud. He holds her hand and whispers in her ear. Most children's dolls have Western faces like this, some are black, few of this type are Oriental. A modern play doll is an outsider, separate from the traditional wooden play and display dolls which have Japanese faces. The black dolls are called Little Sambo. They are what you might expect from such a name: thick lips, wide eyes, wide nose, a racial stereotype like the white dolls. Despite the ruckus Little Sambo caused when news of it reached the US, prompting Japanese promises to withdraw it, the dolls are still available. No one has complained about the white dolls; perhaps the Americans think they are flattering. All the little girls have them. Little tots who can barely walk stagger up to you and point: '*Gaijin ga!*' they exclaim breathlessly, faces full of awe at the sight of a doll come to life.

Sitting next to the old man is an *obasan*. 'What a cute girl!' she says to the doll. She touches its cheeks. Like her older counterparts, the *obasan* is wrapped in kimono, around which is bundled a three-quarter-length kimono jacket in muffled pink. The costume and style and muted colours are the *obasan/obaasan* uniform. Although over 80 per cent of Japanese regard themselves as middle class, *obasan* in uniform like this tend to be either working or upper class, unselfconsciously traditional, neither aspiring to, nor flaunting, wealth like middle-class contemporaries. *Obasan* is a respectful term, but there is a whole genre of *obasan* comedy, akin to mother-in-law jokes. *Obasan* are derided for their nosiness, bossiness and carping. Through this comedy they are presented as scolds, mother-in-laws without portfolio.

The *obasan* and the man are talking about the doll as if she is his granddaughter. They talk as though they really believe this. The *obasan* doesn't seem to be humouring him, but rather accepting his reality. She reminds me of the spectators I saw standing around a painting party in Shinjuku Gyoen. The party comprised men and women from the silver (older) generation, as the euphemism has it, decked out in matching yellow floppy hats like kindergarten children, sitting easel to easel on the grass staring at sky then canvas, observed by inquisitive onlookers. I glanced at one canvas and then another as I passed, staring in astonishment at the realistic and almost identical renderings of Fuji-san executed as if you could still see it, as once you could, from almost everywhere in Tokyo. The spectators had joined in, offering advice. They could see it too. The cloud that covered its tip should be denser, whiter, the plain on which it stood flatter. These paintings were of an actual mountain on an actual plain, not even reconstructed half-remembered Edo prints. The painters were somewhere beyond imagination, wallowing in the muddy realms of belief, making a picture of an inner Tokyo – a concept, the paintings suggested, that everyone shared and saw in an almost identical way.

From a distance Fuji-san, with its perfect cone shape, is majestic, a truly magical mountain. In Shinto all mountains are sacred and Fuji the most sacred of all. When the bullet train passes Fuji-san it slows and the guards bow towards it; when a plane soars close an announcement is made; when a ship drifts in sight the sailors stand on the deck, awestruck like love-sick boys. I climbed it once, overnight so I could be at the top for sunrise, which in the land of the rising sun is the most glorious and romantic time of day. Once women were not allowed to climb Fuji as it was said that the mountain goddess would become jealous if she was trodden upon by a woman. Up close Fuji-san is a tired and bedraggled goddess; she looks battered and scraggy; she has been tamed. A road has been laid part of the way up; at 7600 feet, almost 5000 feet from the summit, is a car park (there are plans to turn this into a four-storey garage with room for five hundred cars); and steps have been carved into her flinty body to make the remainder of the climb easier. She is a terrible disappointment.

A terrible disappointment to a foreigner, that is. If you are Japanese you learn to close your eyes and create your own worlds. Men play imaginary golf at the traffic lights, or on crowded platforms, practising their swing, watching the imaginary ball soar over the fairway, smelling the grass, which, with million-dollar golf club membership fees, few will have seen. Golf takes place on a practice range for most players. Many *sarariman* have told me that they rather enjoy the *tsukin jigoku* (commuter hell – there are lots of hells) because it gives them a chance to be alone with themselves, unobserved, without expectations put upon them. These men, even if they are quite senior, work in the Big Room, the vast open-plan offices without a partition in sight where everyone watches everyone else. They work in their shirt sleeves to denote industry. Once, as a visitor to one of these offices, I was sitting clearly in view as I was announced by an OL to a man who appeared to be oblivious to my presence. He responded to what she said, but although looking in my direction appeared not to see me. Unacknowledged I sat and watched him get up, put on his jacket, comb his hair, pick up his cigarettes and walk through some invisible door about a foot from his desk. Then he saw me – at this clearly delineated point he had entered the waiting room. Virtual Reality will find a vast market in Japan.

I stand up and try to say something, but no sooner have I got to my feet than the words slip away

MURAKAMI HARUKI (1949 –), *TV PEOPLE*

It is Sunday morning and Akira is asleep on the floor in front of the television set. He had been watching a recording of one of the Jeremy Brett *Sherlock Holmes* serials which are popular here. Like the British, the Japanese love mystery stories, their own and other people's. Akira, a member of the Japan Sherlock Holmes Society, likes Brett's neurotic portrayal of the detective better than anyone else's. He has videos of all the screen adaptations of the stories, even some that are not dubbed into Japanese or are without subtitles. He knows Conan Doyle's stories off by heart; he has no need of subtitles. He watches these videos over and over, like a child listening to a favourite bedtime story. He is becoming more and more disinclined to do much else in his free time. Often, like today, he will fall into an exhausted sleep in the middle of one of Brett's dubbed soliloquies. Most Japanese television is Japanese-made but the few foreign programmes there are are always dubbed not subtitled. It is odd to watch Brett's body language so at odds with this deep dramatic Japanese voice. I swear it is the same man who dubs every male part into generic Japanese TV masculinity.

'He has changed since the baby,' Junko says of Akira. It is true. He has gradually reverted to cliché: the Japanese husband. Perhaps it is only temporary I tell her. And perhaps it is. Clearly he loves his son, Tomo, dotes on him, plays with him when he is home, but he has withdrawn from her, shut her out, she is no longer his friend, his lover, his comrade. She is *okasan*, mother. That is what he calls her now.

Junko and I had met in the midwife's house where our sons were born, clanking into the world one after the other like dolls on a conveyor belt. I heard her cry out in the labour room, make that gargling noise in her throat, the life rattle which becomes unstoppable as you shove the baby out.

My son was fast asleep on a futon beside me, wrapped up like a samurai doll in layers of white spreading gowns. When, at last, I had forced him out I had felt as if someone else had come into the room. His reality was shocking. I had forgotten what I was doing – that I was giving birth no longer occurred to me. 'You were very brave,' it was said afterwards. But it wasn't that. What was the point of making a fuss? I had thought I was dying. I was ready to die. I would have done anything to stop the pain. At one point I must have been moaning. 'Stop making that noise with your mouth,' the midwife had said. Four women were in labour in that tiny house that night; except for the gurgling at the end of their labours it was as hushed as a library. You are not allowed to make any noise. The pain must be endured in silence. '*Gambatte*,' the midwives say, 'think of the baby!' It would have been worse in a hospital, where, as in the midwives' houses, there are no pain-killers, no gas and air, no epidurals. In the hospitals they cut and shave you and move you from room to room at various stages of labour, changing your slippers and socks at the doorways. Here there was only one move, from the *tatami* room to the labour room at the point of giving birth, only one change of footwear, from socks to white leggings. I watched the younger midwife bathe my son in the sink. His eyes were startled and all over the place, trailing after the lights. She bathed him in his vest, her hand propping up his head. His body floated like styrofoam.

The next day Junko and I sat beside each other on big floor cushions, forcing down a lunch of pancakes and salad. The house was small. Upstairs was, by Japanese standards, a largish *tatami* room in which four women and four babies were housed; it doubled as the dining area. In the middle of the upper floor was the examination-come-labour room, which, when filled with patient, husband and two midwives, felt very full. On the other side of the labour room was a six-mat room where the midwife had put me, perhaps mindful that Westerners like a certain amount of privacy, or that many Japanese would feel extremely uncomfortable in such close and intimate proximity to a foreigner.

As she talked, Junko kept pushing her glasses back on her nose. It was painful to sit and everyone around the table kept shifting about. Our husbands had gone back into the world. Akira was why Junko had used a midwife. In most Japanese hospitals husbands are not allowed at the birth though some, such as the Hamada Hospital in Osaka, have gone to the other extreme, inaugurating the 'Angel Room concept' with twin beds like a hotel where the husband and wife can stay during the lying-in period, typically five days. An Angel Room costs 450,000 yen, including delivery, 150,000 yen more than normal. 'Akira wanted to be with me,' Junko told me. 'We try to do things differently, not me in one world, him in another. But it is difficult. He was severely criticized by his boss for taking this time off.' 'Severely criticized', a common Japanese phrase accurately describing an all too common Japanese experience. We ate in silence for a while and then she said, 'It was terrible, wasn't it?' Her labour went on for thirty-six hours. I nodded, surprised that she would admit so much. I told her that in Britain, the political correctness of natural childbirth acts as a gag on the truth of the experience; pain has become something else that is the woman's fault – either she didn't breathe properly, or she was tense, or afraid, or wasn't prepared, or is a wimp. Junko smiled. Here it is more straight-forward: 'Women are made to bear this pain,' you are told over and over again. It's the way it is. There is nothing to be done. '*Gambatte!*'

We had given birth to Dragon Seeds, as boys who are born in the most auspicious Year of the Dragon are called. According to Chinese astrology, Dragon Seeds are blessed, they lead charmed lives, they are leaders of men. The number of births increases during Dragon years in China, Japan and other countries where the Chinese cultural influence is felt. Girls born in the Year of the Dragon are not so blessed, however. Dragon Seeds are too dominant personalities to be females.

Akira and Junko are one of those couples that look like brother and sister: both wear glasses, both have what are thought of as aristocratic faces, long with high cheekbones and elongated ears. Both are intense and wiry. Akira is a *sarariman* who works in the international division of one of Japan's major corporations, where, as he says, 'My English is welcome but my foreignness isn't.' Akira is a returnee, and as a result is regarded as *hena-Jap* (strange Japanese), tainted by foreign ways, someone who is not proper Japanese. As children, returnees are part of an official problem, the subject of editorials and wrung hands. They laugh in the wrong places, speak when they should shut up, question their elders and argue rather than agree. Their cultural ambiguity gnaws at the social fabric, threatening its flimsy cohesion. Like former prisoners of war, when they return from their sojourn abroad they are subject to constant debriefing. As Akira said, 'We Japanese are too fond of the proverb "Hammer down the nail that sticks out". Not to stick out is to be Japanese.'

Akira's story is typical. He was thirteen when he came back from the Philippines, where his father had been posted. He had been away 'in a different world' for four years. Later on he found out from a boy in his school that the teacher had forewarned the class: 'Here comes this boy who isn't Japanese any more. He is *hena-Jap*.' The teacher had set him up for *ijime*. He was beaten up and robbed repeatedly at school. When his mother complained, she was told, 'Well, you've got to make this boy into a proper Japanese and then the bullying will stop.' But it didn't. 'Once you step outside of the group you're always different,' Akira told me. 'Something foreign to be rejected, like a virus to be fought off. In the Tokugawa period if you left Japan and came back you were murdered. Now it is just your soul that is destroyed.'

The Japanese still have souls. Souls pepper the conversation like money in England and problems in America. Japan is losing its soul, it is often said. Through crass materialism and Westernization its traditions, its cultural soul, is being destroyed. It's all of a piece – *kokoro*: mind/heart/soul. Japan could as easily be losing its mind, or losing heart. The older people especially talk of the 'double life' they are forced to lead, by which they mean a Western *omote* smothering a Japanese *ura*. In classical Japanese, *ura* means *kokoro* too. This double life is described in terms of frivolous things: watching Hollywood films, sleeping on beds and eating European food. It is a theme in Japanese history, this obsession with what it means to be Japanese, its apparent fragility. Japan has always had a staggering ambivalence towards foreigners and foreign things, a repulsion in many senses of the word. The country is always flipping the superiority/inferiority cultural coin, always finding itself wanting only to find its former mentors even more so.

When Buddhism was brought to Japan from China that country was then the richest, most powerful on earth, one in which the arts, architecture and printed literature were flourishing. Japan was a primitive society without so much as a written language. The highly sophisticated T'ang culture, which followed Buddhism to Japan, was overwhelming. The Japanese decided to emulate their culturally superior visitors – as the Chinese had an emperor, the Japanese now invented theirs, giving the title to the chieftain of the predominant Yamato clan, and endowing him with a splendid mythical Japanese lineage, as a direct descendant of the Sun Goddess Amaterasu. Chinese political and bureaucratic institutions were imported wholesale as were writing, literature and the visual arts. The new imperial court was moved from Nara to Heian at the end of the eighth century, a Xerox of its Chinese model.

But by the tenth century Heian-kyo was a place of egregious aesthetic refinement beside which the Chinese court paled. Now, having spent several centuries indiscriminately and feverishly borrowing from the Chinese, Japan turned its back on China and the world. No ambassadors were sent abroad, none were received. Unlike other great cultural capitals, Heian-kyo in the tenth century was bereft of foreigners and foreign influences; the coin had been flipped.

Akira is awake now, playing with Tomo. It isn't just his attitude to his marriage that changed with the birth of his son, but his attitude to his country. He has become what is termed a 'soft nationalist'. His form of nationalism isn't particularly bellicose, and he has little time for the mystic atavistic mumblings of the visceral Japanist right. He would describe himself as a pacifist.

He, like the majority of his compatriots, was violently opposed to the Gulf War. Equally, and as typically, he opposes the deployment of Japanese troops overseas, in any capacity, including as part of a UN peace-keeping force. (In the summer of 1992, after a lengthy and acrimonious debate, Japan decided it could, for the first time since the Second World War, dispatch a limited number of troops overseas, but only in a peace-keeping capacity.) Akira thinks, however – and this is an increasingly common view – that 'a war with America in my lifetime is inevitable'. It is a war in which he would feel obliged to fight for it would be in 'defence of Japan' as Americans 'will inevitably try to destroy us economically'. What he feels towards the once mighty and greatly admired United States is unabashed *kenbei*, a dedicated word meaning dislike of America, mixed with *bubei*, contempt for America. *Kenbei* came into vogue in Japan shortly after Hirohito's death, when this talk of a coming war with the US gained currency. *Kenbei* soon turned into *bubei*. Both words have replaced *hanbei*, the traditional post-war anti-Americanism that was based on feelings of inferiority, of having had the culture taken over by the foreign barbarian. Again, the coin has been flipped. The Japanese who once felt inferior to their oversized occupiers now feel smugly superior, though still threatened by this behemoth of a country which may turn out to be a very sore loser.

The boy had often seen this kind of expression on the faces of people who had lost something or missed a train

MISHIMA YUKIO (1925–70), THE BOY WHO WROTE POETRY

Junko is an editor on one of the trendiest 'style manuals' in Japan: 'A glossary of frenetic boredom,' as she puts it, a phrase that conjures most accurately the mentality of young Japan. 'Single aristocrats,' the young and wealthy are called by the marketing people. They shop often in Shibuya, a district which resembles a giant mall for the twenty-to-thirty set, at the most fashionable *depato*: Seibu, Marui, and Parco; at the new-wave shops of Loft which is six floors of hi-tech gadgetry; at Seed, with its nine floors of top designers; and at Wave, a building without windows, the world's most fully automated 'audio visual paradise'.

Style manuals like Junko's are instruction kits that tell the gilded youth what to buy and how to behave. Read a book while waiting for your date, they are advising men this year, it will make you look more intelligent. Here is a list of what to read. The Latin Americans are the 'must read's of the moment: Puig, Allende and Marquez are especially recommended, and it is their works you see boys reading in the cafés. 'Must' lists are prevalent in all magazines with pretensions in most countries, but nowhere is the advice taken so literally, so precisely as in Japan. As Junko says, 'To be a Japanese is to live always in dread of what others think of you.'

Junko looks as she feels: enervated. It's a permanent state, something she hadn't realized until she and Akira went on holiday in Australia. After a couple of days it was like a great weight had been lifted, something that had never happened to her on holiday in Japan. This effort of constantly keeping yourself in check grinds you down, Junko told me, it is what enervates people, it is why they sleep so much on trains, on buses, in meetings, at funerals and concerts, in gardens and parked cars. It isn't just a dearth of sleep: the exhaustion starts from the moment you are born and are wrapped up in a papoose on your mother's back. You cannot move your arms and legs; the more you fight, the more exhausted you become. It is the way she feels now. She bucked the system, insisting that this so trendy magazine take her back after Tomo's birth. (The law is more actively on her side now – the government has panicked because of the falling birthrate and is 'encouraging' companies not to force women to retire on marriage or even at the birth of their first child.) But she has to block out the whispers and snide comments about what a terrible mother and wife she is; she has to cope with her own parents' disapproval, ditto that of her parents-in-law. She doesn't openly fight back, she doesn't try to change their minds, she fights a guerrilla war, behind a cloak of conformity, something she learned to do at a young age.

As a middle-class girl Junko underwent the typical middle-class experience: when she was three she attended one of the best kindergartens in Tokyo. To get in she had to pass the usual battery of behavioural tests. She had been prepared for this by what in effect is a toddlers' cram school. She was taught not to cry when she was left alone in an unfamiliar place. She was taught to fold the wrapper of the proffered sweet in a very precise manner before discarding it – 'Fold it in half from left to right, fold it in half again from top to bottom and once more from bottom to top.' She was taught the right answers to the questions that would probably be asked. As might be reasonably expected, she was terrified when her mother and the head teacher left her at the top of a dark corridor and hid in one of the classrooms. Which one? She didn't know. All she knew was that she was supposed to walk down this corridor slowly and look for them calmly, without crying, without running, without showing how scared she was. The corridor was long. There wasn't a sound anywhere. She felt as if she had a bucket of water slopping about in her head. She thought she would fall over. She thought she would wet herself. She had never been apart from her mother before. Even though the cram teacher had told her otherwise, she believed her mother had left her in this dark place, that she would open door after door and never find her. She was afraid she would fail her mother. She was afraid she would fail to get into the kindergarten that was so important for her future.

By the time Junko was eleven she was attending cram school five days a week from 6 to 9 p.m. Every night she also did three hours of homework from regular school. She was permanently tired, falling asleep on the underground, wishing, like many children, that she had more spare time in which to sleep. Nevertheless, and although she doesn't really want him to, she has decided that Tomo will go through the system in the same way. Already she has put his name down for a kindergarten that he will need to be taught to get into. '*Shikatta ga nai?*' What can you do? 'You cannot be Japanese and be an outsider in Japan. You must learn to wear the right masks.'

Masks have always terrified me. Kabuki masks, noh masks, hand puppets, string puppets, the truth that you can never know anyone, not even yourself. I think of what Junko says: 'Behind my mask I can hide myself.' It was a statement of fact. It didn't bother her. I had seen her do it on so many occasions. She is as proficient as a Body Snatcher, a liquid-quick change artist, sliding from persona to persona. We would be sitting in a restaurant talking, or walking down the street laughing, and she would meet someone – the wife of her husband's colleague, or an old school friend, or someone from her office. Quite literally, she would turn around and become a 'typical Japanese woman', deferential, reserved, speaking only when she was spoken to. Like a great actress her body would change into the part. I barely recognized my lively opinionated friend with the theatrical gestures. Her body would instinctively implode, her arms fold in, her knees knock together, her head drop, her voice simper. It always discomforted me. I never knew where I was; it made her seem like the country itself, without an immovable core, as if she had no constant being. The self in Japan shifts with its role, like the traditional house which has no centre and no fixed walls, just rooms that change shape with internal *shoji* screens. All Japanese slip in and out of their roles in this way; but I know her so much better than anyone else and the gap between who I think she is and her social personas seem therefore so much more extreme and irreconcilable. But as she explained to me, her public face does not impinge on her private self hidden behind it. She sees no necessity to reconcile the two. Just the opposite in fact, for such separation is socially sanctioned, even expected. It is how she, and many Japanese people, protect their souls.

This is what is 'wrong' with the returnees, of course. They never learn to hide properly. They can never get the masks screwed down tight enough. It takes a lifetime of training, a lifetime of reinforcement, to learn how to be Japanese. Some returnees, like Kimiko, an acquaintance of mine, cannot even walk properly – she does not knock her knees and send her heels flying out, she does not dawdle or mince as if she is in kimono. Girls are trained by their mothers to walk as if they are always dressed in kimono, it's the feminine thing to do. There is nothing of trained Japanese femininity about Kimiko – she does not keep her head down, she walks in strides one foot flung out ahead of the other as if she is in a hurry, she walks without deference. People look at her as if she is in drag. Kimiko speaks English with an English accent, clipped and cockneyfied. Her mannerisms are as English as her body language. Her mind is bifocal. What she thinks and how she thinks is spliced through a prism; the thoughts are refracted by two cultures. Kimiko was twelve when her father, an importer, sent her off to boarding school in England. 'I have always had problems with foreigners,' he told her, 'and I don't want it to be that way for you.' She arrived on the doorstep of the school's Victorian manor in the Kent countryside unable to speak a word of English.

I always picture her alone, waiting for the school to come to collect her, sitting in the station on her trunk, holding on to her boater, surrounded by words she could neither read nor comprehend, trying to make sense of the gestures, the smiles, the hand movements, the facial expressions. Looking at blue and green eyes for the first time, at red and yellow hair, looking at people so different from herself, people coloured so differently from each other: blacks, browns, whites – even the whites were many-hued. To stand in a street in Japan is to float in an abundance of black hair, to be looked at by a million brown eyes, to notice only the slightest variation in skin tone: there are no other colours. This is what she had known.

Kimiko had some images of 'England' – a backdrop for a romantic *manga* story or perhaps the setting of an even more romantic Takarazuka musical. England could have as easily been France or Germany. All European countries are blended into a generalized Occidentalism, an unknown *muko* (over there/the other side/abroad), a flirtation which includes food, fashion and romance, a field of otherness through which someone might stretch their legs.

'It wasn't so bad,' Kimiko always says. For three months the only lesson she had was English, all day, every day. One or another of the girls would come and get her for meals and mime what she was supposed to do, or take her by the hand to where she was supposed to go. The girls were kind, she told me. The kindness of strangers. I could see what would happen to her. She would always be a visitor now, raiding other people's lives, sticking her fist into their density, travelling alongside them like a shadow.

Kimiko returned to Japan when she was nineteen to attend university. Having spent eight of her most formative years learning to be English as well as to speak it, she found she was no longer Japanese. The better universities rejected her. Keio wouldn't consider her at all because she had been educated abroad. Tskuba University wanted to know why she was sent to England. 'As if it meant that I had done something wrong.' They gave her a Japanese language test. She failed. Her Japanese wasn't up to their standards; they said that she spoke and wrote it like a foreigner. So she ended up at Sofia with the other returnees and foreigners. She claims that she still cannot really speak Keigo, ultra polite Japanese which, as she says, 'even young people speak to each other when they are in a *sempai–kohai* relationship'. Kimiko's *sempai* (seniors) were then the students in the years above her, to whom she was a *kohai* (junior). *Sempai–kohai* relationships exist in all institutions. In companies, those who have seniority over you, by dint of joining the company earlier, are your *sempai*. *Sempai* are social superiors, deferred to and addressed as such, but are also benefactors and protectors.

Kimiko worked in a publishing office part-time, translating Japanese into English. She didn't understand the rules. When the manager asked the ritual question, 'Any suggestions?' she gave hers. Her boss told her off: 'Why don't you grow up? No one expects you, a female and a junior, to speak.' When she was given press releases in English to look over, she corrected them, changing phrases such as 'We go most honourable before you', to something resembling a living language. 'Look,' her boss told her, 'I know you can speak English, but please do not correct mine.'

After years of independence, of emotionally fending for herself, she lived at home with her parents. Her mother was afraid she would get lost in Tokyo and treated her like most Japanese mothers treat their grown-up children – as if she were five years old. She wanted her to say exactly where she was going, with whom, why, for how long, and when she would be back. Some young Japanese rebel against this, often violently (it is not unknown for boys to beat up their mothers or for girls to attack them verbally). But not Kimiko. Her mother was a stranger whom she was trying to get to know, to whom she was trying to be kind.

Kimiko hated Tokyo, 'the crowds, everything'. She remembered England wistfully, not so much for what it was, but for what it wasn't: Japan. 'I don't know how to behave here. If you look Japanese but act differently the Japanese can't take it. All they can think of is "Oh, she's so different; oh, she's so weird." You cannot be Japanese and be an outsider in Japan.' At first she wanted to stay in Japan, although she really missed England. 'But basically I am Japanese and I don't want to be any more strange than I already am. I want to be accepted in Japan – perhaps I don't try hard enough – especially at work, everything I say just gets on their nerves. I think I must stay and just try harder to be a good Japanese.'

Japaneseness is not a given, it is something to be worked at, achieved. To be 'a good Japanese' is an especially onerous task; it is like the archipelago itself, thin with narrow boundaries. When he was prime minister, Nakasone Yasuhiro, oddly thought of in the West as an internationalist, set up an institute in Kyoto dedicated to uncovering Japanese identity. In a famous speech to the party faithful entitled 'Establishment of a Japanese Identity', Nakasone stated that 'to become more international we must become more Japanese'. Japaneseness, in a country 99.9 per cent Japanese, is apparently so opaque and ephemeral that it is in constant need of defining, reinforcing and repair.

In the end, Kimiko gave up. She decided she didn't want to be Japanese after all and went back to England to work, luxuriating in her foreignness, rather than having to smother it, enjoying the ocean of space it forms around her within which she can quietly swim.

At school we learned the same kanji. *Being Japanese, we were taught there is no greater blessing than to be Japanese*

KANEKO MITSUHARU,
THE SONG OF LONELINESS

Around the corner from our flat stands the Boei-cho, the Defence Agency. For all the time I lived there I believed it was on this Boei-cho balcony that Mishima Yukio, Japan's most famous novelist, stood addressing the Jieitai, the troops of the so-called Self Defence Forces, trying to incite them to rise up and restore Emperor Hirohito to his pre-war glory. I could never pass the square, bull-headed building without thinking of that November day over twenty years ago when Mishima committed *seppuku*, after failing to convince the Jieitai to follow him into the past. There were pictures taken and printed in the magazines, photos of Mishima's head propped up by the side of his body, his bloody severed neck, his stomach covered by a cloth blackened with dried blood. The explanation was there. He had taken a sword and slit his belly, spilling his guts on to the carpet. His friend had chopped off his head with another sword and then also spilled his own guts on to the carpet. He sat beside Mishima with his head on the floor, which apparently someone else had obligingly chopped off. I wondered what happened when you were the last in line to spill your guts on to the floor, what it felt like to die slowly like that with your head still intact. I thought about dying like this. *Shinda tsumori* (imagined death), 'Imagine you are dead,' the Japanese say to each other when in despair. How bad can your earthly suffering be? In part *shinda tsumori* is so that you don't actually have to do it, just imagine dying and then start again afresh.

There was another picture of Mishima, always with an eye for drama, standing precisely at noon that sunny cool day. He was wearing the sickly yellow brown uniform of the Tatenokai (Shield Society), his own private army, the army Nakasone, the then head of the Boei-cho, had allowed him to form and instructed the Jieitai to train. Mishima liked to march about with his troops on Fuji-san, and this too was allowed. From below the balcony, the Jieitai could see only Mishima's long dolorous head, tied up with a Rising Sun *hajimaki*, of the type worn by the kamikaze pilots. Mishima's student soldiers of the Tatenokai had thrown his last manifesto out of the window. The papers frittered to the ground. The text was based on the attempted *coup d'état* by young soldiers of the Jieitai in the thirties, the so-called Two Twenty Six incident, named for the date when the uprising occurred, 26 February 1936. 'We have waited in vain for the Jieitai to rebel,' Mishima had written. 'If no action is taken the Western powers will control Japan for the next century!'

Mishima wanted a Showa restoration to re-elevate Hirohito to his wartime greatness, to go back to a real, pure Japan, the country's spiritual core. Despite this the writer lived in a house that was the epitome of British Victorian style, not so much straddling two cultures but at war with both. This is not an uncommon phenomenon. Often the more 'Westernized' a person appears, the more Japanist he or she will be: the Western dragon, the enemy within, must be slayed. And the more Western the country seems, the more Japanist it will be. Before the Second World War there were cartoons depicting young women scratching their heads, their imported ideas falling off like dandruff. The text read: 'Purge the United States and Britain from your head.' Even before a war with the West was a real concept, propaganda films condemned the wearing of Western clothes, the viewing of Western movies, the reading of Western books and the playing of Western sports, such as golf. Purge the West from your head.

The soldiers were not impressed. Those who read the manifesto seemed not to understand. Mishima spoke, competing with the noise of the helicopters circling warily overhead. 'I thought,' he said, 'that the Jieitai was the last hope of Japan, the last stronghold of the Japanese soul . . . Japanese people today think of money, just money. Where is our national spirit today?' Those who could hear above the din screamed at him that he was an arse-hole, an idiot, that he should get down. 'Are you *bushi*?' Mishima asked. They were not. You might have seen it coming then – the *shinju* of the soldier-lovers Mishima and Morita (the student leader and Mishima's disciple). Samurai lore is full of such things. Mishima was nothing if not *bushi*.

The crowd seemed to find him comic in his Gilbert and Sullivan uniform with its tight waist and big brass buttons. He had gone to the Boei-cho with every intention of committing *seppuku*. He had taken the two necessary swords – the short sword for the belly, the long one for the neck. If they had upped and followed him and let him lead them into a *coup d'état* I wonder what he would have done. But they called him an idiot, a madman, and so his path to self-destruction was cleared, he was free. He would slit his belly and his lover-disciple would lop off his head before slitting his own belly: *bushido*, the way of the warrior. *Shinju*. It is all of a piece *kokoro*, mind/heart/soul.

Later I discovered that Mishima had not killed himself in the Boei-cho site in Roppongi, as I had unquestionably believed, but the one in Ichigaya, on the other side of the palace. There was nothing casual about Mishima's life and the date of his suicide was thick with meaning. He had committed *seppuku* on 25 November, often the date of the Niinamesai, when the emperors offer the newly harvested rice to the Sun Goddess. I still sometimes forget that Mishima's fastidiously timed exit took place in Ichigaya. It worked better this way, near my flat, and near the house and shrine of General Nogi Maresuke, Hirohito's mentor and father figure, into whose care the future emperor had been entrusted as a child.

General Nogi was a war hero too, of the Russo-Japanese war. He was a virulent Japanist who taught Hirohito to be likewise. When Emperor Meiji, Hirohito's grandfather, died Nogi committed *junshi*, following him as any proper subject must into the next world. It too was a *shinju* of sorts, his wife went with him. Hirohito was eleven when Nogi killed himself; as a future emperor he was not allowed to show any emotion. By all accounts Nogi was a powerful personality who influenced Hirohito in the way you can be influenced only when you are a child: indelibly. Nogi left a suicide testament decrying the moral weakness of Japan and appealing for a restoration of the Japanese spirit, a cry echoed by Mishima after him and many of their compatriots today. The Nogi Mansion, now a museum of the General's life, is a gloomy Meiji style Western structure. The General is enshrined in the garden, deified as a god of war. Outside General Nogi's house and tomb is a bus stop. From here you can ride through Aoyama to the top of Omotesando dori, the great thoroughfare that leads to Emperor Meiji's shrine, with whom the first stage of Japan's modern history begins.

The Emperor Mutsuhito, as Meiji was in life, was not quite fifteen years old when he was dusted off and hauled out to oversee the beginnings of the Meiji era, Japan's equivalent of the Victorian Age: steam trains and imperialist power. *'Sonno joi!'*, the anti-shogunate slogan and rallying cry, echoed the meaning of the title 'shogun', a derivative of 'Seiitaishogun', 'Commander in Chief against the Barbarians'. Thus the country's abrupt lurch into modernity came about by returning to the mythic past. The past was, of course, sequestered, utterly Japanese, eminently suitable for quelling the nationalistic fears aroused by Perry. Mutsuhito was removed by Japan's new leaders from the Imperial Palace in Kyoto, the 'spiritual home' of the emperors, to the former shogun's castle in Edo, now re-labelled Tokyo. Japan looked West for technology and government structures, importing foreign experts and sending off expeditions of high officials to Britain, Europe and the United States to study Western institutions. The first constitution was written at this time. Known as the Meiji constitution it was, like the uniforms still worn by Japanese schoolchildren, based upon the Prussian model. It was enacted to give Japan prestige and standing in the world; to give it the appearance of being of the world from which it had been so long apart.

As the court paintings show, even the clothes and the furniture changed: one year Mutsuhito, his family and retainers, were cross-legged on *tatami* in kimono, the next they were sitting stiffly, bolt upright like corpses, on French baroque chairs wearing the latest Paris fashions. Mutsuhito was made over like a political leader. The young Emperor – who had favoured Chinese-style costumes of long dolorous kimono over wide trailing silk trousers, and whose eyebrows were shaved off and repainted high on his forehead, whose cheeks were rouged and gilded, whose teeth were blackened – was refitted with a Prussian military tunic, a white horse and teeth to match. Like now, it was all dressing up: a Western *omote* over a Japanese *ura*. The cracks soon poked through: '*sonno joi*' became a war cry against *kokusaika* and the ever dangerous outside world.

Whenever he could spare a few moments, he headed for the store. He stayed there as long as he could

KOBAYASHI KYOJI (1957—), *MAZELIFE*

You can buy anything you want on the Ginza: sushi sprinkled with real gold flakes; an oxygen shot; favours, sex and politicians over a hundred-pound glass of Scotch; Louis Vuitton handbags, Yves St Laurent dresses, Hermes scarves, Paul Stuart suits; bamboo boxes of fireflies; a Gauguin; a ten-pound cup of coffee served with a choice of cup selected from the world's array of exorbitant china; a thousand-pound mink toilet seat cover; a loaf of real French bread flown in from Paris that very morning costing twenty pounds. Anything. In survey after survey shopping is perpetually listed as a top leisure activity, and the more expensive items are the more desirable. (The Japanese are the most researched and surveyed people in the world: '1 per cent of the population makes live recordings of birds, trains, etc.; 8 per cent of women stand in the bath when washing; 100 per cent of women in their sixties are home at midnight.' Not a day passes without a survey in the paper, most of them undertaken by subsidiaries of the advertising companies; much of the rest by the government.)

The Ginza oozes money, old money, pre-war money, middle-aged money, aspiring money, bad money, good money. It is on the Ginza's edge that the Recruit company sits, the overflowing font of one of the biggest post-war political corruption scandals, the eponymous shares-for-favours affair. Every major politician, including the current prime minister Miyazawa, the then prime minister, Takeshita, and Nakasone his predecessor, had been sold, through aides and relatives, pre-floated company stock by the Recruit company founder Ezoe Hiromase, stock which was then sold for a vast profit. There seemed to be no one of importance Ezoe had not bribed. If the whispering campaign is true he needed to buy all the help he could get. It is said, *sotto voce*, that Ezoe is a *burakumin*.

Money never speaks *sotto voce* on the Ginza; it shrieks good taste. Women and men, more expensively and uniformly dressed than on Bond Street or Madison Avenue, cruise the backstreets with heavy wallets. The hunger for luxurious foreign labels is insatiable. Louis Vuitton sells more of its bags in Japan than anywhere else. Japanese sales for Chanel represent over 40 per cent of all its worldwide sales. Most of the women still have LV bags slung over their shoulders, although the over-forty set has moved on to Gucci and some of the younger women favour Chanel. Hermes scarves are a must for those who have been to Europe this year, as are lots of real gold chains worn with real Chanel suits. The men leave their Burberry raincoats open, exposing the unmistakable lining. The younger men from certain ministries are easy to spot in their Italian three-piece suits in charcoal-grey, a marked contrast to the blue *sarariman* suits of ordinary or older ministerial or corporate warriors. The semaphore of clothes is very precise. Chukuka ha, and the other extreme left cells, riot in their own colour-coded hard hats and facemasks, and the *yakuza* are blanketed in tattoos, over which they wear Jimmy Cagney-style wide-striped suits with jackets that look as if they have forgotten to remove the hanger.

The crowds swill up and down Chuo dori, the Ginza's main drag, pouring in and out of the big *depato*, the exclusive Waco and Mitsukoshi on Ginza Corner. To enter these shops is to be excessively attended to. At the doors young women in uniform suit, hat and gloves, bow at a forty-five-degree angle and welcome you in shrill, surreal voices. Other young women stand at the foot of the escalator bowing and pointing upward with their arms in a ballerina pose. In the lift you may get caught alone with the lift operator, who is bent over in a forty-five-degree bow, her eyes examining the floorboards, explaining in an excruciatingly simpering tone, exactly what is on every floor. She holds her hands together tightly in front of her knees as you stand behind her in the ascending lift. You are the object of her servile pose and patter, and are either filled with an urge to laugh very loudly or die with embarrassment. Every morning the women in the *depato* gather together for the meeting and to practise their servile bows and patter. If you come upon them unexpectedly you will find them talking quite naturally to each other. The change is instantaneous when they turn to address you; the voice becomes shrill and the body implodes. You cannot see the join.

A little further up Chuo dori is Tiffany's, on the spot where the first Makudonarudo once stood. The same young people that once ate at this branch of the Golden Arches now shop at Tiffany's with comparable nonchalance. The jewellers made the 'must' list in the style manuals last *kurisumasu*: 'Be sure to buy Christmas presents at Tiffany's or Cartier this year,' the magazines gushed. 'On Christmas Eve have an Italian dinner for two, and spend the night at a hotel in the Tokyo Bay area.' *Kurisumasu* used to be simpler – just the year before presents were ties or scarves and dinner for singles was French and taken with a group of friends, while married couples with children ate roast beef and *kurisumasu keki* at home.

Over 50 per cent of the population actively celebrates *kurisumasu* with a meal and presents for the children, lovers or spouses, but the *kurisumasu* revellers worship Santa-san not Christ. From Hokkaido to Okinawa, the country throngs with the 'Jingle Bells' variations. Banners bearing messages such as 'The More Love and Santa Claus, the Better it is: Merry Xmas from All Over the World!' hang inside the *depato*. This widespread commercial celebration of *kurisumasu* has been going on for only about twenty years. It has caught on with such fervour partly because, unlike the traditional gift-giving seasons of *chugen* at mid-year and *seibo* at the end of the year, you give presents to loved ones not to those you have *giri* to and/or want something from, such as your boss or your MP. Bringing in a completely new, alien, and essentially meaningless system from the outside in order to do something utterly untraditional is the traditional way in Japan.

An extrinsic festival of personal gift-giving does not interfere with the intrinsic *giri* system. Nothing is changed, threatened or modified, it is added to, not superseded by.

Most Japanese say they are a mixture of Buddhist and Shinto. Shinto ceremonies are favoured for marriage and inducting the child into the family house, a sort of Christening rite. Buddhism is for funerals. But for cool *shinjinrui* a white wedding, complete with some sort of Christian ceremony, is a must and now precedes the Shinto wedding ceremony. It is for the gown and the unfamiliar. That's how it's sold on the posters in the underground and the ads inside magazines: 'White Wedding' with pictures of the bride draped over an exotic foreign setting wearing one of the most lavish and frou-frou gowns imaginable. In a circumstantial, contextual society, death is best served by one set of practices, marriage another, fashion something else again. Some critics consider this frivolous, which it may well be, but it is more accurately capricious, a habit of mind in which consistency and reconciliation are neither valued nor practised. Things are lined up side by side – there is no necessity to connect.

I bump into someone, a man in a hurry. After three years my directional signals are sometimes still wrong; my radar worse. The crowd is relentless, blind and single-minded – full of some hidden purpose, it comes at you, unyielding, or, to be precise, the male half of the crowd does. With women the usual adjustments are made without thinking to avoid collision with each other, as they are in most Western countries. But with men and women it is the women who must make all the adjustments, moving like agitated crabs to the side of any oncoming male. It isn't particularly a question of male rudeness, but of male certainties. As boys men are taught that, as social superiors, they go first: in and out of the lift, in and out of the door, up and down the street. Men are served food and drink before women in restaurants as they are at home. In short, they are taught that girls always give way to boys; boys always have the green light, there is no need to look to see if anything or anyone is coming.

The grey helmet of the smoggy sky is browning at the edges like singed paper, casting a dingy pallor over the city. On the *ura dori* people are disappearing into the bars and coffee shops. It is beginning to rain, a slow nagging drizzle. In the old *ukiyo-e* of Edo the rain fell like this too, in sheets of tadpoles, a mesh screen in front of the tottering women and men clattering through the streets on *geta*. The inhabitants of pictorial Edo clutched crinkly paper umbrellas and never looked wet. Edo, a mercantile centre with a rough bawdy culture, is rendered by its artists as a mellifluous fusion of colour in the rain, sweetly sticky.

A bicycle nicks at my heels, ringing its bell incessantly. I step to one side and it passes, meandering down the pavement like a drunk; it seems to have a life of its own. Its load, a housewife overladen with shopping, grips an orange plastic see-through umbrella in one hand. Her bags droop off the handlebars. Because of the density of the crowds she travels slowly, one foot scarcely off the ground. She swerves to avoid another bike heading towards her. Its passenger is a delivery boy; in one arm he clutches half a dozen big round red bowls full of sushi, the handle of his black umbrella intertwined between his fingers, resting precariously on top of his load. Bikes are not allowed in the road with the traffic, it is *abunai* (dangerous/look out!) as the police constantly chide. The police stand in the *koban*, the prevalent mini police stations that resemble oversized gazebos, yapping through the loudspeaker system, whining and pleading: 'Stand back on the pavement. Be careful you don't fall in the road. Watch where you're going. Take care of your belongings . . .' This sort of thing goes on in the trains and in the shops too. We are, it seems, always in mortal danger. The constant exhortations make me edgy. It's the sort of nagging that can drive you mad. Though you never see this. No one goes mad and throws a chair through the window or smashes a loudspeaker. No one screams or breaks down weeping. I have never seen a mad person here, not the sort that stands in the middle of the road and rants and raves about God and justice. Madness in Japan manifests itself in high levels of neurosis and acute introversion: acting in, not acting out.

Because the traffic light is against us, everyone waits at the intersection, even though there is nothing coming. I walk out into the road feeling weightless in the temporary void around me, as if I am going to detach, float off into space. The multitude follows, as if it has just noticed the absence of traffic. The crowd closes around me once again, rubbing shoulders and umbrellas – cheap, small clear-coloured plastic for many of the women, sombre black cloth for the men. The spikes grind against each other like teeth. I never carry an umbrella here, it is too confining. The cars slouch somnolently towards their destination. The road has been turned into a car park. The drivers, waiting to move, read, doze or stare out the window. The cars are pristine and freshly minted. Every six months a car more than three years old has to take a stringent and expensive road-worthiness test. There are lots of foreign cars: BMWs, Mercedes, Rolls-Royces, big cars that swell out all over the road. Like Britain, Japan drives on the left, but most of the foreign cars are left-hand drive to differentiate them at a distance as the status symbol they are.

I see only him at first, a small thin man wearing a black T-shirt, soggy with sweat and rain. He rounds the corner with his arms stuck out behind him. His face is saturated with a lifetime's worth of worry. The *jinrikusha* clatters after him, one of its huge wooden wheels mounts the pavement, precariously tipping the carriage. He steadies it, rights it, pulls it firmly into the road without stopping. He is running against the traffic, hoisting up his broom-handle legs so high that he looks like a cartoon mouse running from a cat. The cars edge away, squeezing tight against the far pavement, rubbing their squealing wheels against it. This is nothing akin to the tourist rickshaws you see in other countries. It is like a miniature stage coach or a palanquin. It is deathly black and enclosed.

Inside the *jinrikusha* the upholstery is white, silk probably – I cannot see much of it, as the passenger takes up most of the seat. She is staring out of the window. She looks through us, her plump moon-shaped face is white and immobile, an indifferent death mask. On her white lips she has painted a perfect tiny red Cupid's bow, her bitter-chocolate eyes are outlined in black. She is wearing a heavy off-white kimono of raw silk. Around her neck is a *han eri*, a white half collar, threaded through with silver star-like shapes; beneath the collar, a red and white under kimono is visible at the top of her neck. Her *obi* is exceptionally wide, stretching from her de-emphasized bust to her thighs. It is blue and gold brocade. On the lap of her kimono is painted a carp swimming towards some wavering plant. Her hair, which at least in part is probably a wig, is abundant, swept up in two corpulent knolls on either side, with a cottage loaf at the back. It is heavy with silver and red ornaments that shake as the *jinrikusha* does. Everyone turns to watch her trundling past. People smile at each other. To see an elaborately attired high-class geisha on her way to work in a *jinrikusha* is hardly a common sight in Tokyo. I expect to see a trail of cameras thundering after her, perhaps shooting an ad for sake, lipstick, or for 'Japan'.

Although Japan has its share of loud, repetitive hard-sell ads, it is more famous for its so-called mood commercials, in which the product's name is gently mentioned as an aside, if at all. More than any other country I have been in, much daily life in Japan looks as it does in these ads. In the hundreds of branches of Makudonarudo, smiling counter assistants call out a cheerful welcome, and neatly dressed smiling staff point out vacant seats, just as they do in the ads. As billed, the floors and the tables are immaculate. The bins are never allowed to be full. The customers, most of them between fifteen and twenty-five, look like the actors in these commercials; fashionably dressed, they sit quietly animated, discussing the latest fashions and pop stars. Nobody sprawls, talks too loudly or puts their feet on the seats. No one has a hair out of place. The young women eat their hamburgers with great delicacy, holding them in one hand, carefully encased in a napkin or the paper they were wrapped in, the other hand underneath lest any crumb should fall away. After taking a bite, they hold their free hand over their mouths and nod their heads in jerky agreement with whatever is being said. Young men are not subject to quite such decorum – they slouch forward, pull up the sleeves of their new jackets and eat the Big Mac with gusto.

Table manners were once as important as religion, and women are expected to be the custodians of the culture, maintaining continuity in Makudonarudo as in the *jinrikusha*. There were rituals to be observed when consuming food. The quantity of each nibble was strictly prescribed, as was the way of sitting and the body's posture at each stage of the meal. Women were forbidden to make a sound while eating or drinking, men were permitted to belch. Now everyone is expected to slurp noodles or soup noisily, but men are expected to be louder than women. This is offensive at first, but you get used to it, becoming deaf to it and then gleefully joining in; it is so much easier to eat dishevelled food in this manner. Certain habits remain forever alien, however, such as everyone sniffing on the underground, in the bus, the shops, restaurants and on the streets. To blow your nose in public is considered rude.

Business in general – and our enterprise in particular – is a holy mission

MATSUSHITA KONOSUKE, FOUNDER OF MATSUSHITA ELECTRIC

Up from the Ginza and back towards the front of the palace are the business districts of Marunouchi and Otemachi. The trading house of Mitsubishi, the biggest of the seven giant trading houses, controllers of vast swathes of the world's trade and resources, owns much of the former. At the turn of the century Josiah Conder, a British architect, built Mitsubishi Londontown here. From the photographs, the streets of Londontown were a pastiche of their namesake: lines of Victorian red-brick structures with white brick around the windows, like the flats on the Chelsea Embankment. Because of its proximity to the palace – which the Americans (fearing that if they killed the Emperor it would only strengthen the Japanese resolve to fight) declined to bomb until towards the end of the war – and because it was made of brick, Londontown survived the firebombing of Tokyo. After the war, Mitsubishi did what the B29s had failed to do: destroyed the district, but with the wreckers ball. The business district is unremarkable now, a series of unmemorable glass and concrete buildings enlivened only by the maze of colourful, noisy eating places and bars in their basements or upper floors.

This is where Akira works, in the heart of Tokyo's *sarariman* land, home to the blue-suited 'corporate warriors', as they are called, who take much of their '*sarariman* culture' from the samurai culture that defined it. In the language of *sarariman* culture business is war, *sarariman* are soldiers, and death due to overwork or work-related suicide is death in combat. Like that of the samurai, the *sarariman* dress and lifestyle are precise. His glasses are square with metal frames; his short hair is worn in the seven-three style — seven-tenths of it on one side of the parting, three-tenths on the other. His single-breasted two-piece suit, which he wears with one button done up, is usually a shade this side of midnight-blue or tin-grey. (As has been noted, certain younger upper echelon *sarariman* in the bureaucracies favour charcoal-grey Italian-made three-piece suits.) Under his blue or grey suit he wears a white or light blue shirt with a pocket for his Mild Seven cigarettes. Around his neck is a red tie with diagonal stripes. His slip-on shoes are black leather. In his inside jacket pocket he keeps a small Filofax-type contraption. He carries an attaché case and a rolled up newspaper. On his belt is a *poketto beru* (pocket beeper); on his wrist an equally aggravating beeping alarum watch, which nags him from one appointment to the next. He carries a change purse and a separate wallet stuffed with cash, which is still the main form of payment in hi-tech Tokyo, although he will possess a bank card and the increasingly customary credit card or two (more if he is younger, for the Japanese are discovering the joys of debt). His phone calls are made with phone cards, many given to him by other firms, who have them designed with the company logo and message as a way of cheap advertising. All sorts of businesses do this, including prostitutes and, naturally, telephone cards have become collector's items.

Akira and Junko live an hour's train ride from Otemachi station, half an hour closer to the city than the average commuter. Before Tomo was born they would both get up at six-thirty and scramble for breakfast. Now Junko gets up at six, feeds and dresses Tomo and makes their breakfast, usually toast and salad with perhaps a hard-boiled or fried egg. (Recently Akira has developed a taste for a more traditional breakfast of rice, miso soup, broiled fish and a raw egg.) Akira gets up at six-thirty, washes, eats breakfast and leaves the house at ten past seven to walk to the station. Sometimes he manages to get a seat on the train.

Junko is usually out of the house by seven. With Tomo strapped to her back, she cycles twenty minutes to her mother's house where she leaves him for the day. By the time she gets to the station and parks her bike (all suburban stations have vast cycle parks), it is nearly a quarter to eight. Junko never gets a seat. Too often she has to cope with *chikan* (foolish men), gropers who prowl the underground and the streets in search of hapless females to molest. The *chikan* on the underground are almost always ultra respectable-looking *sarariman*. Groping or rubbing up against women in this way is socially indulged behaviour, excused as a necessary outlet to dissipate stress. 'It is not their fault, they work so hard,' one woman victim told me to explain why she never made a fuss. Most Japanese women do endure such humiliation in silence, waiting until they can escape from the train at the next stop, not necessarily a safe move as in many residential areas in Tokyo there are printed signs hanging off the lamp posts warning women to beware of local *chikan* who prowl the streets for stress relief. Junko quietly steps on the offender's toe if she can, or kicks him in the shin. She too never says anything. It would be too embarrassing to call attention to herself in that way.

Akira and Junko begin their work day with morning meetings. For both they are fairly low-key affairs, having more to do with the business of the day than listening to inspirational words from the *bucho* (department manager) as is common in some firms and certain departments within their companies. (The morning meetings for the salesmen in both their firms resemble the start of a military campaign, with loud chants of victory, calls for death to the opposition and raised fist salutes.) All big companies in Japan have slogans, a song, and often a written corporate philosophy or a mission statement, which serve to portray the company as a quasi-religious entity whose only purpose in life is to serve humanity.

'Our primary concern is to eliminate poverty and increase wealth,' Mr Matsushita wrote in his company mission statement. 'How? By producing goods in abundant supply . . . I would like you all to keep in mind that the true mission of Matsushita Electric is to produce an inexhaustible supply of goods, thus creating peace and prosperity throughout the land.' This mission, which *of course* has nothing to do with making a profit, is later described as a 'sacred calling', 'sublime and far reaching', comparable in fact to the life of 'Buddha, whom it is said, remained in the womb for three years and three months, and his achievements were tremendous. We ought to take courage from the fact that Matsushita Electric has been in the womb much longer, and strive for even greater and more ambitious achievements.' This is not an unusual stance, nor is the language or meaning regarded as grandiose. As the samurai had his elaborate codes of conduct to glorify his certain death, so the sarariman has his company mission to glorify his certain sacrifice.

Akira is already seated when I arrive, shoving my way through the jam of sarariman who have congealed around the door of the sushi shop, waiting for tables to clear. Lunch is normally early in Tokyo, from noon to one, but some sarariman manage to get out of their offices by a quarter to twelve to miss the midday crush, thereby creating an earlier crush. Business lunches start at noon and are usually over by two. Unlike evening entertaining there is no, or very little, drinking during lunch. Akira has his head stuck in the Yomiuri Shimbun, Japan's biggest-selling newspaper with a circulation of fourteen million. (The other two big-selling broadsheets are the Asahi, which sells almost thirteen million copies daily and the Mainichi with just over six million. The Japanese read voraciously from manga, newspapers, magazines and novels to heavyweight tomes on politics and economics. Women, generally speaking, do not read newspapers in public, however, as it makes them look too serious, too pretentious, as if they are poking their noses into men's business.)

On the shelves behind the sushi counter are the whisky bottles with name tags around their necks that regular customers keep for evening socializing. The counter, the place where sushi aficionados prefer to sit and banter with the chef, is quite literally elbow to elbow. There is no way to eat without rubbing shoulders with both of your neighbours. The waitress welcomes and greets me. 'Isn't it cold?' she says, lifting the end of the sentence above her head, as if she is affronted by this dry frigidity. The Japanese, like the English, use weather talk as a greeting and to punctuate silence. Akira looks morose as he always does in repose. Hearing the conversation he looks above his paper and nods.

We both order one of the large sushi specials. It is part of the '*onaji desu*' ('the same') phenomena. The guest orders first and everyone else says, '*Onaji desu*' to whatever they have asked for. If you are a guest you are plagued by the responsibility of ordering things which (you hope) everyone will like. Tokyo restaurants, like those in Paris, are so much cheaper to eat in at lunchtime than in the evening. This special, which comes with a cup of ubiquitous miso soup, costs two thousand yen, about a fifth of what it would cost here at night.

Akira looks what he is: hung over. It is a permanent state for the average *sarariman*, who during the day often seems not quite mentally in the present tense. The average *sarariman* is said to limp along through life, a soldier in the army of the walking wounded, with a permanent headache and a weak liver from the booze, aching lungs from chain smoking, haemorrhoids, stiff shoulders and neck pain from being chained to his desk for hours at a time, a touch of VD from too much fooling around, and the obligatory ulcer which is so prevalent it is looked upon like the common cold. Those who do have colds stagger to work wearing surgical masks, both unhealthy and uncomfortable for them, to stop the spread of illness into the workforce.

Shortly after Tomo was born Akira became a *kacho* (section manager), a high middle-management position that, as he is in his thirties, signifies he is an 'élite *sarariman*', someone who is headed for the executive suite. He was told that he was lucky to have been promoted as he had blotted his copy book by taking time off to attend the baby's birth. He got the message. The role of *kacho* is said to be the hardest act in the life of a *sarariman*. It is the period when he needs to work the hardest and when the pressures on him from the top and the bottom can be close to unbearable.

Those who have been chosen for the 'élite course' are continually put through endurance tests. These are often run by management companies and involve tests that are diametrically opposite to those 'outward bound' type of team spirit exercises offered by their Western counterparts. Whereas the emphasis in the West is to learn to work as a team, the emphasis in Japan is often to learn to be alone. Akira, who so far has been on three such courses, has been sent alone into the Japan Alps in inclement weather to test his ability to deal with adversity; has stood naked, except for a *hajimaki*, under a freezing waterfall for several hours; and 'sat' for a twenty-four-hour period in a darkened hall where he was required to chant a mantra continually without falling asleep. When he did fall asleep (often) he was whacked none too gently on the back with a thick stick. Although he underwent the latter two trials with other élite *sarariman*, they were not operating as a group but as individuals undergoing *seishin* (spirit/mind/soul training). Ironically, because of his brief sojourn in the Philippines as a child, which has forever shut him out to a certain extent in Japan, Akira finds the individual state easier to bear than some of his 'proper Japanese' élite *sarariman* colleagues who have spent their lives huddled inside various groups.

Another variation of *sarariman* training takes place at the foot of Fuji-san in one of the most famous business schools in Japan, known colloquially as Hell Camp. The recruits to Hell Camp are sent there by their companies for thirteen days. Between the ages of thirty and fifty these *sarariman* fall into two categories: those who probably will be promoted and those who probably will not but are being given a last chance before being consigned to the role of *madogiwazoko* (window watcher), a *sarariman* who has been put out to pasture and has nothing to do all day but stare out of the window.

At the beginning of the course, the *sarariman* are given fourteen 'badges of shame', ribbons that are shed as each test is passed. To graduate you need a bare chest. Once in the camp, which holds about 250 *sarariman* at a time, the men are dressed in karate-type outfits. The training at the school is modelled on the kamikaze schools that existed towards the end of the war. Everyone has to shout when talking, especially when reading off their inadequacies. There are vast tracts of information to be memorized and regurgitated loudly at high speed, including the school's anthem, the Sales Crow song, which graduates claim never to forget. Parties of *sarariman*, dressed up in their blue suits, are bussed to the local station each day where they are required to sing the Sales Crow song word perfectly at the top of their voices over and over until the instructor decides they have passed that particular test. Every morning they are raised from their futon at four-fifteen for sunrise callisthenics, which are done facing the rising sun, while rubbing towels over their bodies, samurai style, to tighten the skin. During the thirteen days there is at least one 'endurance hike' in which squads of *sarariman* are marched off into the wilds with deliberately confusing maps and little food. The idea is for each squad to compete against the others, with the first one back, typically in seven or eight hours, the winner.

When tests are failed they are retaken again and again with individual training given by instructors, into whose arms, on passing, a sobbing *sarariman* will gratefully fall. There is a lot of weeping in Hell Camp. Emotions are raw. Careers, which is to say lives, hang on the outcome. After thirteen days only about twelve to twenty of the original 250 students will have shed their fourteen badges of shame and be entitled to graduate. The rest will be given an additional three days to do so. Half will fail. Now all chances of promotion have gone. After sincerely thanking their instructors and apologizing for their miserable existence, most of these failures will collapse sobbing on the floor and will have to be physically removed.

Although there is more movement of staff than the cliché of lifetime employment suggests (the average *sarariman* stays fifteen years with one employer, out of an average working life of thirty-seven years), job changing mostly takes place between small companies, and even among these companies a confirmed failure is hardly likely to find another employer. Hell Camp is used mostly by the larger companies, who are part of the 25 per cent of employers that operate under the lifetime employment scheme. These firms have agreements not to hire each other's staff, and again no one would hire a failure anyway; for those who do not graduate there is nowhere to go but to the limbo world of the *madogiwazoko*, a daily humiliation that can make firing in contrast seem humane.

In the early nineties, Japan, which was undergoing an economic slump (for Japan that is), went through one of its periodic fits of angst over the supposed irresponsibility of the young, and especially of youngish *sarariman* who in attitude surveys were called 'new breed *sarariman*'. A study undertaken in 1992 by the research group Hakuhodo entitled 'Japanese Sarariman at the

Crossroads' found that having grown up in post-war abundance *sarariman* in their thirties were much less interested in sacrificing their lives to the company. This is a constant refrain. When I first came to Japan young *sarariman* were said to be doomed by *mai homu-ism* (my home-ism), a condition manifesting itself in the *sarariman*'s claim that their home life was as, if not more, important than their working life.

What is true in someone's heart is not necessarily true of their behaviour. *Sarariman* of Akira's generation do wish they had a job that 'makes full use of their abilities,' although most are unsure what those abilities may be. Those who can will opt for jobs with less overtime and weekend work; and most draw a 'clear line between the company and their private life'. But these rather modest slippages in the servitude ethic are attitudes not actions. Japan's thirty-something generation may wish it was otherwise but it isn't.

Every time the country goes through an economic tremor it finds its younger workers wanting of the necessary diligence to meet the challenge. Every time this 'new mentality' is written about it is as if it is occurring for the first time. But like Akira, once *sarariman* stop being *hira* (rank and file workers) their dedication to the company takes precedence. It cannot work any other way. Whatever Akira feels in his heart, his behaviour has to change if he is to stay successfully within the system. He knows this, and so does Junko. But, working where she works, and being a woman, she is slightly to the side of this system, though certainly not outside of it. It isn't quite right to say that you 'cannot be an outsider and a Japanese in Japan,' but the gulf from inside to outside is so wide that it can only be traversed once. When you become an outsider, like the political extremists, you have to become incredibly extreme. There is no middle ground and there is no way back.

Akira has finished his sushi. He pats his shirt pocket. He gave up smoking last year; it is a reflex, something he always does after a meal. He used to 'speak Lark', choosing the American brand as an act of benign defiance within a sea of domestic Mild Seven, the *sarariman*'s obligatory cigarettes. He watches as the waitress empties an ashtray and winces as if the sight revolts him. He said nothing to his colleagues about quitting smoking, but they noticed immediately, ribbing him as if such an act was a sign of moral turpitude, a lack of masculine resolve. He gets up. It is nearly time for his first afternoon meeting. He sighs when we get outside; he hates office meetings. Like most *sarariman* he has two, usually three, sometimes four, formal inter-office meetings a day, 'to decide what has already been decided upon'. This has become worse since he became a *kacho*, as have the expectations of weekend socializing. Akira, as he always has, usually works at least half a day every Saturday. But now he is as likely to spend the other half of the day (or a Sunday) playing golf with superiors and prospective clients. There are frequent company outings or sports events over the weekend which he must also attend – some with Junko and Tomo – and of course co-workers' weddings. The idea of Sunday as a day of 'family service', that is, one which is spent with his family, becomes even more remote at this stage of his life. These days, Sundays that are free are more often than not spent sleeping, dozing in front of the Sherlock Holmes tapes.

Evening socializing is a given, right from the beginning of a *sarariman*'s career. Now he has clout in choosing where to eat and drink, Akira, like the bureaucrats from the Gaimusho, favours the steak houses. Such Tokyo restaurants are emphatically not Berni Inns, but the ultimate in 'power' dining. You eat in private rooms and are cooked for by your own chef. The rooms are designed along the lines of sushi bars in as much as you sit around a wide counter. The exorbitantly expensive Kobe beef (culled from beer-fed cows which had their bellies stroked daily to tenderize their meat) and the vegetables are cooked on a big flat griddle between you and the chef. It is performance cooking. Like the sushi chef, the beef chef behind the counter is there to entertain you with his skill in chopping the steak and vegetables into perfect squares and oblongs.

You do not beg off nightly entertaining. It is an extension of work and for most *sarariman* and bureaucrats is done either with customers, contacts, bosses or colleagues every night of the week. These evenings are oiled by copious quantities of booze. Japanese people get drunk quickly. After about two drinks most faces have reddened like slow-burning coke. Drinking and drunkenness are

more than acceptable for Japanese men, they are a social require-
ment – and a psychological necessity: it is the only way of publicly
being yourself, the safety valve which keeps this highly structured
society from exploding at the seams.

Anything can be said when you are drunk. The next day
everyone must pretend to forget what was said (while taking it on
board of course). *Said*, not *done* however. I spent much of my life
in Japan slumped on a bar stool, poking at a dinner, drifting
around yet another cocktail party, one of the few, if not the only,
female present. Spouses, which almost always means wives, are
not invited to what, after all, are really business meetings. Only
once did anything untoward ever happen and that took place not
in a dark bar stuffed with politicians or in a geisha house, but at
a formal banquet. An ancient scion of one of Japan's most famous
breweries, having swigged back slightly more Scotch than even he
was used to, planted both of his knobbly little hands on my
breasts under the full glare of the tinkling chandeliers and the
swiftly averted gaze of many a startled guest. With this, four of
the minders who float like driftwood around all such occasions,
appeared at his chair, pulled it back from the table with him still
on it, and when he showed little inclination to leave it, removed
him bodily from it. They carried him from the room still in a
seated position, his little legs quivering as if he thought he was
walking, his head turned back towards his meal which he seemed
to regret not having eaten.

The following day a member of the brewery's board was on
the phone, apologizing profusely for what had happened and
insisting that he come to seem me in person. I got more than I
bargained for. Almost the entire board of directors appeared
bearing a selection of the company's finest products, proffering
meishi and deep, deep bows with their apologies. I was informed
that the ancient groper had resigned, 'to take responsibility' for
his actions. I had lived here long enough to suspect it was
a Japanese resignation and that he would reappear somewhere, probably back on the board as an 'adviser', after enough
time had elapsed, but I was impressed and not a little puzzled.
Seku hara (sexual harassment) is an everyday occurrence in
Japanese women's lives, from the *chikan* to the rapist. As one OL

sardonically explained to me, 'We are expected to serve tea, look decorative and giggle at racy remarks. We are not expected to complain when we are touched "playfully", but to understand the stress men are under. This is our role in the economic miracle.'

Women who work with the public, such as exhibition guides, are routinely taught to fend off *chikan* by saying, 'I am so sorry!' when encountering any stray uninvited hand, as if they had accidentally bumped into it, reinforcing the idea that women have to put up with such behaviour, or worse, that they are responsible for both provoking and controlling it. This mentality extends to rape. The Rape Relief Centre in Tokyo reckons that the two to four rapes per one hundred thousand people reported on average each year under-records the actual number of rapes by as much as ten to twenty times. The reasons for not reporting rape are myriad. As the then director general of the cultural affairs bureau in the Ministry of Education wrote, 'Rape, while not gentlemanly conduct, is not so bad if practised on a modern woman whose moral standards have slipped anyway.' Even if a conviction is secured, the rapist will probably not go to prison. Moreover, the victim's potential compensation of between two thousand and twenty thousand pounds is determined by her age, occupation and, yes, whether or not she is a virgin.

Akira subsequently explained to me that just as in the way the Japanese were 'honorary whites' in South Africa, by virtue of my job I was an 'honorary man' in Japan, illuminating the *gaijin* joke: 'There are three sexes in Japan, men, women and foreigners.' And because of my status as such, I ranked this elaborate apology for *seku hara*. 'It would have been the same had he punched a man on the nose,' Akira said. It made perfect sense to him.

He bows slightly now when we part and sticks out his hand, giving the lacklustre handshake prevalent in this country, where the idea of touching a stranger like this is slightly unpleasant. A bow and a shake, the fashionable cross-cultural greeting and parting.

An evil rumour is forgotten after seventy-five days

PROVERB

Diagonally opposite the business district, across Hibiya Park, is Kasumigaseki and Nagatacho, Japan's Whitehall or Washington, home to the ministries, parliament, the prime minister's official residence (where he doesn't live) and the headquarters of the LDP and the socialists. The Diet Building, as Japan's parliament is known outside of Japan, was built in 1936. A pinkish brown Western style edifice, with a 200-foot clock tower in the centre, it looks as Germanic as its external name. On the right- and the left-hand side of the clock tower are both houses of parliament, respectively the upper House of Councillors and the lower House of Representatives.

In form the country is governed by this bicameral parliamentary system in which both chambers are elected. There is a prime minister and a cabinet. However, neither the cabinet nor the prime minister have anything like the executive powers they have in Britain. Power is diffuse, with the ministries and the various government agencies operating in an autonomous and sometimes contradictory manner. Political power rests on the ability to dispense favours, not to set or define policy. As one academic said, pointing out a truth self-evident to the Japanese, policy and actions concerning the Gulf war, 'should have been left to the Gaimusho as the matter was far too important to be left to the cabinet'.

The Recruit affair, coming to the fore as it did at the time of Hirohito's death and the start of the new imperial era, had momentarily threatened to effect change on Japan's moribund political system. Or so we thought at the time. But evil rumours and facts are soon forgotten in Japanese politics. Nakasone, who had resigned from the LDP over his role in the scandal, had not been indicted, despite all rumours emanating from the prosecutor's office to the contrary. He had run for parliament again as an Independent, sending out his sobbing son to speak for him (Japan is a very lachrymose country), and had easily held on to his seat. Takeshita, who had been forced to resign the premiership, continued to operate the party from the back room and then emerged before the 1992 Earth Summit in Rio as Japan's eco-*éminence grise*, protection of the environment having been 'identified' by the country's bureaucrats as an area in which Japan could play a leading world role. Miyazawa, who was forced out from his post as Finance Minister over Recruit, was now the prime minister.

The 'government in Tokyo' is a mirror image in modern dress of the Tokugawa government in Edo: an unmovable shogunate. It is even hereditary: a third of lower house MPs are the sons, sons-in-law or legally adopted 'successor sons' of LDP MPs. Almost every post-war prime minister has a son or son-in-law in parliament. At any one time, at least half of the twenty-member cabinet is made up of 'hereditary' MPs. All but one LDP MP under the age of forty is related by birth or marriage to a sitting or retired member. Moreover, the families of all but five of the country's twenty post-war prime ministers are tied to the Imperial Family by marriage.

The electorate's choice at the voting booth is within the LDP. In almost every constituency the LDP sponsors several candidates representing the different factions within the party, who run against each other for the same seat. The factions are not ideological, but personal power bases: the Takeshita faction, the Miyazawa faction, etc. The leader of the biggest faction is the man with the most power within the party and the biggest war chest for faction leaders must fund their members to run in the elections. The socialists do not sponsor enough candidates to cover every constituency, and even if they won every seat they contested they could not form a government alone; neither could any of the other opposition parties. After the Recruit scandal, the opposition parties, except for the communists who were not invited and would not have joined in, moved towards forming a coalition party, the only possible way of beating the LDP. News of this brave new world, and deep anger over institutionalized political corruption, immediately gave the collective opposition a majority in the following upper house election. But the coalition came to naught. The fractious politicos, who are, as the Japanese say, 'opposition for opposition sake,' could not agree on anything. And by the time of the last elections (in which the socialists lost over half of the seats they had previously gained) the only thing that had changed was the socialists' name in its English rendering: from the Japan Socialist Party (JSP) to the Democratic Socialist Party (DSP) of Japan. In Japanese it is still Nihon Shakaito, the Japan Socialist Party – the ultimate in useless window dressing.

It has long been rumoured that the opposition parties, again except the communists, are to some extent in the pay of the LDP. This had been something that was in everyone's interest to keep quiet, except when the proposed opposition merger looked viable. At that time, the then Minister for Construction, Okonogi Hiko-saburo, announced in parliament that he had bought ninety thousand pounds' worth of tickets to a socialist's fundraiser. The secretary-general of the JSP, Yamaguchi Tsuruo, not surprisingly denied this, saying that Okonogi's comments were designed to discredit the opposition parties. But Oide Shun, chairman of the JSP parliamentary policy committee, without commenting on the specific fundraiser, said that such payments were routine and made in both directions: 'Sometimes we buy fundraising tickets for LDP law-makers,' he said. 'These purchases are one of the things you just have to do when you are in charge of parliamentary management.'

Many people – if they think about it at all – have come to the conclusion that this modern shogunate will prevail, becoming more entrenched and more corrupt by the year until it either implodes or is violently routed. For, under the current political arrangement, there is in practice no possibility of a peaceful transference of power from one elected party to another.

*Not that I have found
loneliness only in Japan's ancient
heritage. I see it just the
same in men wearing business
suits, smoking cigarettes,
mouthing Western ideas*

**KANEKO MITSUHARU,
*THE SONG OF LONELINESS***

From Kasumigaseki through the winding and dilatory *ura dori* it is about a twenty-five-minute walk to our flat. Tokyo and the other major cities are organized as if they were theatres. The main avenues, generically the *omote dori*, are the stages on which the current play is unfolding; the *ura dori* are where the actors live. The *omote dori* are the flashy city; the *ura dori* a series of villages. The *ura dori* were originally laid out to confuse the enemy; they meander back on to themselves, curling and twisting, suddenly disappearing, to reappear elsewhere. Even when they seem to be parallel often they are not, leading you unknowingly astray. Most *ura dori* have no name. An address is made up of the *ku* (district), the *chome* (areas of several streets within the district) and the number of the block of flats, house, or office. None are numbered sequentially but in the order they were erected: number four may be next to number thirty-four, and so on. When you are invited anywhere you are usually faxed an area map with detailed instructions on how to find your destination. The map invariably comes with a walking route from the nearest train station or bus stop pencilled on it by a series of arrows, resembling the winning solution to a particularly difficult maze puzzle. This situation exists in every city, town and hamlet in the land, but is exaggerated by the sheer density of the capital. The vague addresses, coupled with the complicated street layout, can give verbal directions a whimsical quality. You will be asked whether you know where Ginza station is, only to be directed to somewhere that is nowhere near Ginza station (Ginza being the one firm rock from which to build coherent directions). Or people will direct you on the most roundabout route because it is the one way they feel you will not get lost. Generally speaking the Japanese are very nice about helping you if you ask and sometimes will take you all or part of the way. Fearing an embarrassment of non communication, however, few will volunteer to rescue a lost foreigner.

To reach our flat via the simpler *omote dori* route is to walk in the shadow of the Shuto expressway, past Ark Hills, a complex of buildings that includes the ANA Hotel, the news studios of TV Asahi, the Suntory concert hall, restaurants, flats and 'intelligent' office blocks, which is to say, computerized and centrally controlled. The ANA's vast lobby is an atrium filled with greenery, a waterfall and a stream; it suggests a rainforest and always reminds me of one of those natural habitat cages in a modern zoo. The hotel is so angled that every bedroom has a view either of Fujisan or the Tokyo Tower or the palace. The thousand-feet Tokyo Tower was built in 1958 as an answer to, and echo of, the Eiffel Tower. It is surrounded by motorways, perched to the side of Shiba Koen, a former burial ground of the Tokugawa clan. The gardens are truncated and noisy now, chock-full of entertainments such as a golf-driving range. In the middle of Shiba Koen is the lovely Zojoji temple, also a former possession of the Tokugawa shoguns, and a favourite spot at New Year when, along with the other Buddhist temples, it rings out 108 chimes.

What the Ark Hills complex replaced, and from where it takes its acronym, was a small residential district of houses, bars and local shops on the hills between the districts of Akasaka, Roppongi and Kasumigaseki. The complex was completed in the mid-eighties after twenty years of brouhaha as, finally, the people who had refused to sell their homes and businesses either relented or died. The complex is the flagship of the ubiquitous real estate magnate Mori Taikichiro, the octogenarian builder of modern Tokyo, and Japan's third biggest landowner after Mitsubishi and Mitsui. The Tokyo skyline is littered with buildings labelled Mori Biru (building) followed by a number – Mori Biru 49, etc. In this complex only an 'intelligent' office block, the Ark Mori Building, bears his name.

The existence of Mori's Ark Hills saddens those who knew the area before and who seemingly without exception, regard its character to have been assassinated. For those of us, myself included, who have known only Ark Hills, the complex, this windswept mountain of white daydreams, exemplifies new Tokyo, what it is becoming and what it might be, for better and for worse. Ark Hills is self-consciously hi-tech – you can stand on one of the open forecourts and watch the TV Asahi news studio at work. It is also self-consciously expensive. Top tickets at the Suntory concert hall are over five hundred pounds each. This is a lot of money even in Japan, where the average salary is eight million yen, about twenty-four thousand pounds – although for *sarariman* twice-yearly bonuses, averaging two to four times the basic monthly wage, combined with an assortment of housing, commuting, marriage, family and educational allowances, increase this figure by sometimes as much as double. Everything is expensive in Japan, and especially in Tokyo, from basic foodstuffs to the ten-pound cinema tickets, the forty-pound melon and the infamous three-generation hundred-year mortgages, with which you literally mortgage your children's future.

The *omote dori* upon which Ark Hills sits leads to Roppongi Crossing, the centre of a hip night-club area. The *ura dori* that weave between Roppongi and the older entertainment area of Akasaka are sedate and residential, graceful streets of houses, most made of concrete now, but designed along traditional lines with roofs like curled-up toes. The houses, hidden behind high walls, are slowly being surpassed by low-rise blocks of flats, each with a parking forecourt. You cannot own a car in Tokyo unless you have offstreet parking, a difficulty that doesn't seem to deter drivers as the ever increasing number of cars clog up the city's streets. This area is very pleasant and convenient for the centre of town, but you might want to live elsewhere, somewhere in the old

Shitamachi perhaps, the other side of the palace, the wrong end of town where the Yoshiwara once was; an area still more resolutely bawdy Edo than sophisticated Tokyo. If you are Westerners, you would probably be politely, but firmly, steered to the Yamanote side of the city where most other Westerners live. This is a continuation of an old idea: the foreign settlement.

In the Meiji era, when the country was first reopened to foreigners, Tsukiji, now the home of the famous fish market, was the designated foreign settlement in Tokyo, separated from the rest of the city by canals, gates and an expanse of meadow. Today our real estate agent is one of the few who will take foreign clients. Estate agents routinely post 'no foreigners' notices in the middle of their windows and most landlords will not rent to foreigners. In a study undertaken in the early nineties, 86 per cent of landlords said they refused to rent accommodation to foreigners. As in the countryside, blatant exclusion extends to restaurants and bars too, with some posting 'no foreigners' notices on the door and the others telling you simply that the restaurant is for 'Japanese only'.

This can be an embittering experience, or at the least a wearing one. It is difficult to feel well disposed to a country which excludes you as a matter of course. Foreigners who, as we say, 'have lived here too long,' tend to see discrimination and slights everywhere, from the taxi driver who does not understand what they say, to someone bumping into them in the street. For Koreans who have lived here over three or four generations, housing and entertainment are the least of their problems.

Koreans are seen as unfit both to guard the culture and to transmit it: they cannot become civil servants, teachers or police officers; they cannot vote and major corporations will not hire them. Until 1992, like us real foreigners, Koreans had to have their index finger printed. This fingerprint was attached to the Alien Registration Card, which also bears a photo of its rightful owner. Refusing to do this was the heart of the so-called fingerprint refusers campaign undertaken by the Koreans and their supporters. Now only short-stay foreigners have to be fingerprinted, but ethnic Koreans must still carry their cards with them at all times like other foreigners. Ethnic Koreans and Chinese can become Japanese citizens, but 'they are not encouraged to'. (Unlike Britain and the US where citizenship is a right of birth, people who are born in Japan are not automatically citizens, but are stateless and have to be made citizens of their parents' country.) Most Koreans choose not to partly because they are required (as is anyone who adopts Japanese citizenship) to change both their surname and forenames to Japanese names.

We live at the top of a steep hill in what is called a mansion, a small block of Western-style flats. Our living room overlooks the Shuto and the office blocks the other side of it, including that of the YKK company, the letters of which you will find on almost all your zips. Down below us is the Mitsuiyama, Mitsui's mountain, a complex of modern flats that are home to the staff of the US embassy. Mitsui is one of the most powerful conglomerates in the country, a reassembled *zaibatsu*, the family-owned groups which more or less ran the economy and government of pre-war Japan. In the twenties, Mitsui controlled one of the two main political parties and Mitsubishi the other. At the onset of the occupation, the Americans tried to break up the *zaibatsu*, which had been enthusiastic supporters of, and bankers to, the military. Some fifty thousand businessmen were purged during this time. However, this American infatuation for changing Japan did not outlast regional political realities. As a *quid pro quo* for Japan becoming a bulwark against communism in Asia – 'a floating aircraft carrier' for the Americans, as Nakasone put it later – the *zaibatsu* were allowed to regroup by the US which by 1948 had stopped all efforts to disband them: the political–bureaucracy–business triumvirate became more entrenched, glued together by ever thicker wads of cash, as every post-war 'money politics' scandal reveals.

In our neighbourhood, like every neighbourhood in Tokyo, everyone knows everyone else. And everyone knows your business, it's the way it is: village society writ large. The local policeman came and introduced himself when we moved in. Our names are on the map at the local *koban*. The policeman will come back next year. This annual visit is standard, something Westerners might find intrusive, too high a price to pay, too much surveillance even for a relatively crime-free environment. The fireman came once too, wearing full regalia, silver space hat and matching silver coat and trousers. He came to remind us to turn off the stove in case of an earthquake. It was the fires after the 1923 earthquake, which happened at a peak cooking hour, not the earthquake itself that caused the devastation of Tokyo and Yokohama. Most nights a volunteer walks our streets, slapping together two pieces of wood, making a click-clacking sound that at first I thought was the night cry of some extraordinary creature. It's a lovely sound but when you hear it you are supposed to rush around checking for fires, unturned off rings and gas leaks. Every summer on Earthquake Awareness Day, the city traipses off to the designated neighbourhood meeting points, the tiny open spaces where you are supposed to go in the event of a violent earthquake. Here you drill, practising throwing yourself under a kitchen table in the back of a specially designed earthquake lorry that shakes up nine points on the Richter scale. That the open spaces where Tokyo's millions are instructed to gather are nowhere near big enough to hold them is a moot point, as is the fact that you would never get out of this heavily congested city should such an earthquake occur. The drill is the thing.

When the policeman first came to the house where we originally lived it was to chide me for not registering with the Ward Office as an alien, as this was 'making things difficult'. He took off his shoes and left them by the door. He sat on the couch drinking tea. I sat on the floor cushion doing likewise. I knew I would have to give in eventually. I couldn't get a press card without the production of what was then an Alien Registration Book rather than the card it is now: 'a passbook' as the protesters called it, thereby evoking Apartheid. Moreover without the book or card you cannot leave the country because you cannot get a re-entry permit, which is to say you are free to leave but, without a permit in your passport, you cannot come back, even though you have a visa to live here. At the Ward Office, before they would give me my book, I was required to write a letter apologizing for not registering earlier and explaining my reasons for not doing so.

This house was in Jingumae, at the back of fashionable Omotesando dori. In the summer you can hear the prehistoric cries of the thick bean-green cicadas that cover the trees on Omotesando, an incongruous bleating, chirping sound beneath the grumbling traffic of central Tokyo. It is a tropical noise, insistent and magical, that fills up the night, increasing in volume as the mercury rises, invading your sleep. The house was built along the lines of an imaginary European house. There were three floors with one room on each, giving it the feel of a three-room flat tipped on to its side. Like a traditional Japanese house, it had small windows and (modern touch, central heating still being a rarity) the heat came from pipes under the floor where, in a traditional Japanese house, you would of course sit on cushions on *tatami*. Below-floor heat seemed odd with Western style wall to wall carpeting. I always hated that house, its stench of damp misery. It was closed in on itself, under siege, the way I often felt back then, wondering whether I was ever going to get to grips with this country which, once you are no longer a casual tourist, can seem harsh, forbidding, utterly disorienting; or perhaps more accurately, disoccidenting.

We were burgled there by a light-footed robber who came in the night. He prised open the kitchen window with a knife and climbed in. He took his shoes off and left them on the window ledge. The next morning, the police found the imprint of his shoes on the sill, but not on the sink or in the house. They dusted the ledge down with fine powder. The robber had left his shoes neatly together, sides touching, toes pointing out towards the moon, ready to step into them when he left. Why did he go out the same way he came in? Why didn't he use the door? I thought, my mind bolting off like a startled horse, gathering up the sort of irrelevant rubbish that accumulates at such times. He had taken everything out of the cupboards and drawers: papers, files, records, tapes, books, and receipts, all were piled neatly on the floor. When I staggered into the kitchen in the morning at first I didn't notice anything was wrong, until I saw my attaché case on the dining table, my telephone cards, press card, club card, credit cards, Alien Registration Book and *meishi* arranged like a game of solitaire beside it. Only money was gone, a pathetic amount of a couple of thousand yen that you can just about buy lunch with. He had sat in that chair looking at the various documents; he had sorted through my *meishi* box looking over all the people I had met. The police found his fingerprints plastered over every card and every piece of paper.

I looked out of the kitchen window, over the dusted outline of his shoes to the house behind, small and shuttered, surrounded by a high wall. There were *shoji* screens up against the windows. I looked at the thick wires leading to our house, trailing alongside of it. You could not see the oversized microphones from inside but you could see them from the street, one on either side of our house, pointing at our walls. The inspector called me downstairs. There were six pairs of policemen's shoes in the well by the door. Our tiny nameless street was blocked by four squad cars, as if I had said 'murder' not 'burglary'. The neighbours stood about with crossed arms and knowing looks as if they expected us to be arrested, and not before time. The inspector pointed at the microphones. He wanted to know what they were, which is to say he wanted to know why they were there. I told him about the neighbours at the back in the small house with the *shoji* screens on the windows. I told him about the *obaasan* and her middle-aged son who had laid the wires and affixed the microphones, angling them towards our house. I explained that we had complained, asking our landlord to intervene, but that he had said there was nothing to be done, that the *obaasan* had told him she wanted to ensure that we were not making too much noise. 'You would think that if she couldn't hear it without the microphones . . .' I heard myself start to say, then wondered what I was doing discussing it in these terms, as if they had a right to put microphones along the side of our house.

'Eh, eh, eh, eh,' the inspector grunted. He held his notebook close to his face and wrote this down. His face did not move. I wanted to say: when I first saw these microphones I felt unreal, as if everything was slipping through my fingers like dishwater, as if they could do anything they wanted to us.

The *obaasan* was in her late sixties. She wore the muted kimono of her age group, with the three-quarter-length butterfly sleeved jacket pulled tightly over it, winter and summer. She was fat, and the effect of these clothes wrapped around her in layers made her look like the cocoon of the cicada, bulging, ready to split open and release something green and blindly driven into the air. Once when I greeted her in the street, she looked at me with eyes dirty and unfocused with hatred. The inspector stared at her house, dragging his eyes over the high wall. I knew what he was thinking despite his blank mask, I could almost hear it. It had not occurred to me until then. Robberies of single dwelling houses rented by foreigners are common enough, ostensibly because foreigners keep a great deal of cash at hand, though not as much as the Japanese, who do a lot of banking under the bed. I saw the son sitting at the kitchen table carefully examining my papers, his eyes still and watchful in his shuttered face. It was a good way for them to chase us out. I wanted to go anyway. I wanted to leave the moment I arrived, to go off and live in another area which was less full of itself.

The inspector presented us with forms to be completed; the usual questions needed to be answered: 'Name, Occupation . . .' as if he didn't know. The inspector addressed all his questions to me, completely ignoring my husband. 'And what is his name, his occupation?' he said, nodding cursorily in his direction. We gave our fingerprints in order to identify those of the criminal. In the absence of a *hanko* (personal seal), which the Japanese use to sign legal documents, we had to use the thumbprint of our right hands to validate our statement. The police were dusting everything in a slow frenzy, if such a thing is possible, like men possessed by particularly demanding demons. When they had finished we accompanied them to the door. The policemen stood about by their cars. The inspector, who smiled a great deal, like a man who has just won the pools and doesn't know quite what to say, suddenly pointed upwards to the sky: 'Never fear! I will catch this robber!' he said in heavily accented English, a language he had previously shown no sign of knowing. Pleased with himself, he repeated his one phrase and closed the door behind him with a flourish.

He never did catch this robber (not that we were ever told) but the microphones were taken down that very day, confirming what I had always suspected, that we shouldn't have listened to the landlord's beseeching comments about not going to the police, we shouldn't have bought the line we were given about the way things were settled in Japan, extra legally, quietly; we should have made a fuss. The next time I saw the *obaasan*, she bowed slightly, a normal street greeting, and let loose what could pass for a smile. It was as if something had been settled.

Boy, *have things changed.* *Japan's got so rich, everything's* *so prim and proper*

SHIMADA MASAHIKO (1961–), MOMOTARO IN A CAPSULE

Comparatively speaking, surveillance by the police and neighbours does keep crime low. Only around half a dozen people are murdered each day in this country of 125 million people, the same number as in New York City alone, giving Japan one of the lowest per capita murder rates in the industrialized world. In metropolitan Tokyo, one of the biggest cities in the world, the murder rate is enviable: since 1951, when figures were first kept, the highest number of murders recorded was twenty-nine in 1966, the lowest was six in 1973. Japanese murders are Gothic. Three-quarters of all murders are committed within the family. According to the National Police Agency, the most common reasons a murderer kills are 'smouldering anger, hatred, resentment or jealousy'. The victims for the most part are killed in Victorian ways: poisoned, strangled, or stabbed; claustrophobic methods, which reflect claustrophobic lives as much as strict gun-control laws.

A man strangles his wife because she opposes his plans to go to Europe to study: divorce does not occur to him. Until late 1987 it was legally impossible for the 'guilty' party to obtain a divorce against the wishes of his or her spouse, no matter how long the couple had lived apart. Now it is just 'difficult'. This murderer was so obvious, lurking around the cemetery, 'playing at a husband in mourning,' the papers said later. He looked like a kabuki villain. The police thought so, too. He had, they said, 'overdone his playacting,' buying his murdered wife a box of cakes on his way home from work. The neighbours said that he never did that. The neighbours know what you do. The neighbours told the police they were sure that the man had never brought home cakes for his wife before, *ever*, they could swear to it.

Even to break off an unwanted engagement is so socially 'difficult' that murder or murder followed by suicide may seem preferable: a young nurse, for example, put paraquat in her fiancé's Coca-Cola rather than, as she said, 'face the shame' of breaking off the engagement. She had tried for several years, apparently unsuccessfully, to make his parents dislike her, so that they would break it off for her.

The papers are filled with these grimy stories of lives in which anything is preferable to social impropriety: 'Darling, I'll be coming to you soon. But I never thought in my wildest dreams that I would ever kill you. Let's try over again in that other world.' A woman left this note on the draining board in the kitchen of an apartment she shared with her lover, a man whom she has just stabbed to death with a carving knife. The lover was a has-been television mimic. He owed millions of yen in gambling debts from playing *mahjong*. The woman had been lending him money. They had known each other for less than a year. After she drowned herself, a friend of the couple said that it was the woman who had wanted to end the relationship, but she couldn't bring herself to do it. 'This is why she had killed him and then killed herself,' the friend explained. There is a lot of this. A fifty-seven-year-old unemployed man hired two hit men to kill his twenty-year-old daughter for her insurance. The girl had sensed what he was up to. She told a friend that she thought she would be killed for her insurance money, but still gave in to her father's pressure to take out the life policy, 'because she felt she could not refuse him'. A Todai graduate, a boy everyone seemed to want to marry, finally became betrothed. On the night before his wedding he stabbed his fiancée to death and then killed himself. He left a note explaining that he was sorry but that he just didn't want to get married.

Sometimes a madman grabs the headlines for beating to death an old person in the park with a baseball bat or for killing children. At the end of the eighties there was a series of murders, rapes and violent attacks on children in Tokyo's affluent suburbs. Over a period of months, two four-year-old girls were murdered, two others went missing presumed dead, and fifteen toddlers were stabbed and wounded by a knife-wielding assailant on a bicycle. Forty attempted abductions of children were also reported. Social scientists clogged up the television screens decrying 'the Americanization of Japanese society'. The police declared a 'state of emergency' and the editorialists went into overdrive, mostly blaming affluence, which the *Asahi* said was accompanied by 'some sort of distortion or imbalance in the minds of some people'. The editorial continued: 'These crimes represent the dark side of our society where irritation and dissatisfaction has no outlet.'

In that instant, the architecture of K's mazelife collapsed

KOBAYASHI KYOJI, *MAZELIFE*

'I cannot tell you how afraid I was,' Menda Sakae says. 'I am ashamed of this, but it is my honest feelings. When I heard the click from somebody else's cell door, I was just so thankful that it wasn't me.' I nod at him stupidly, thinking that I should tell him he shouldn't be ashamed, that shame couldn't possibly come into it. But it seems irrelevant. In 1983, Mr Menda became the first death-row prisoner ever to be acquitted in a retrial in post-war Japan. He had served almost thirty-two years on death row – he is in his sixties now. He doesn't hear very well and holds his hand up to his ear like a fan. He is very neat, except for his ruffled hair. He is talking about the prison routine on the mornings that hangings take place. 'When it is someone's time you can always tell,' he says. 'Prisoners are allowed to take a bath and there is no exercise. It happens shortly before ten in the morning, you can hear the guards marching towards the cell. And then they stop and the key goes into the lock. My heart would freeze when I heard that click.' He speaks very softly; there is no bitterness in his voice, just a preternatural calm. He reckons that over his three decades on death row he heard this click some seventy times. There were approximately 445 hangings at various prisons around the country during those thirty-two years.

'One of the prison officers will go inside the cell and inform the inmate that his time has come,' Mr Menda says. 'In most of the cases I have seen the condemned man will usually smile as he comes around to exchange a few polite words of farewell with every inmate. But prison officers once told me that for many, once they see the gallows, they refuse to get on to the scaffolding; they have to be dragged on to it.' Mr Menda, like his fellow prisoners who were later acquitted from death row, always claims that he was violently forced to confess to a murder he did not commit.

One of Japan's most famous civil rights lawyers, Igarashi Futaba, contends that forced confessions are more common in Japan than one might think. She attributes this in part to the 'substitute prison' system, in which a suspect is held in a police station cell or a detention centre as opposed to a prison. She says that '80 per cent of all those arrested, over 100,000 people annually, are detained in this way. In practice there are no trials without a confession of guilt from the suspect, so a confession has to be obtained by whatever means necessary. Judges believe confessions: 99.8 per cent of all people brought to trial in Japan are found guilty by the courts.'

There is no trial by jury in Japan. Prisoners are tried by a panel of judges. Recourse to the law is limited. The government restricts the numbers of lawyers allowed to practise: there are only six thousand lawyers in Tokyo, a city of over twelve million people; and under fourteen thousand lawyers in total for the whole country. There is no public defender and no legal aid. There are too few judges as well, under three thousand, exacerbating the treacle-like slowness of the judicial system.

In the late eighties, Ms Igarashi took her government to the United Nations Human Rights Commission over the abuses of prisoners which her group had documented. The government did not, and does not, take kindly to dissidents airing dirty linen in public. 'Our government representatives, members of the Japanese delegation, got us in the lift at the UN and threatened us – 'You are bringing shame on Japan,' they told me. They threatened me, physically and with the loss of my licence to practise law. Of course, it is the government who is bringing shame on Japan every time an innocent person is gaoled or hanged.' The human rights group comprises fifty lawyers, writers and scholars and operates from Tokyo under the unwieldy English language name 'The Civil Centre Campaigning Against the Proposed Two Bills on Detention and Demanding the Abolition of the System of Substitute Prisons'. At the UN they accused the Japanese government of 'a consistent pattern of gross violations of human rights'. Ms Igarashi had broken the primary rule: things are supposed to be settled within the family of Japan, even when this is clearly impossible, as if it is an engorged feudal household. Even the Federation of Bar Associations, who have spent more than thirty years of futile opposition to substitute prisons, thought that the human rights group's submission to the UN was 'inappropriate'.

Japanese government officials continue to try to undermine the campaign, writing to newspapers when articles or advertisements decrying substitute prisons appear. The government's technique is not to argue against the groups claims as such, but to elucidate the protection of human rights as provided for under Japanese law, which is not in dispute; *adherence* to the law is what the group is calling for. The government claims the Civil Centre's complaints are 'based on their own misunderstandings', which is something of a classic statement in Japan – one that will brook no contradiction.

According to the Tokyo Bar Association's study, which was part of the submission to the UN, twenty out of thirty prisoners who were recently forced to confess to crimes they did not commit testified they had been physically tortured; twenty-three reported lengthy interrogation sessions of fourteen or more hours a day; ten were held in police cells for more than one hundred days; and all said they were denied food, sleep and access to lawyers.

'In practice,' Ms Igarashi said, 'the interrogating officer is in charge of everything: when and if a prisoner can eat, when he or she can sleep or see a lawyer. Often the suspect is made to kneel in his cell for hours at a time; he or she is not allowed to lie down outside of sleeping hours, or even lean against the wall. When they are taken into the interrogation room, the suspects are made to sit bolt upright on a hard wooden chair without moving; sometimes they are strapped to that chair. Their families are not informed they are in police custody, and the suspect is often told that their lawyer, who is trying to gain access, is refusing to see them.'

Prisoners who were subsequently found to be innocent after serving many years in gaol accused the police of a litany of abuse: punching, kicking, strangling, poking them in the eyes, banging their heads against the wall, and making them squat on their heels for hours at a time on folded metal chairs or stone floors. (As a matter of admitted policy, prisoners are not allowed to lie down or stand in their cells but must sit or kneel on the floor.) Some claimed that the police made them lie down on the cell floor and then walked over them. Others said they confessed because they thought their lives were in danger. If they held out and did not confess, they claimed, the police threatened to prosecute them for a more serious crime, or to continue the interrogation indefinitely, or to circulate rumours of their supposed crimes within their neighbourhoods. Sometimes the police threatened to arrest parents, siblings or spouses, going as far as producing fake warrants, or said they would destroy the suspect's business.

'On average,' Ms Igarashi continues, 'we found that a suspect is allowed only one fifteen-minute meeting with his or her lawyer before being brought before a justice official, which legally must be done within seventy-two hours after the arrest. Of course, sometimes suspects are coerced into coming "voluntarily" to the station, in other words they are not arrested at that time, so the period of initial incarceration can be much longer than seventy-two hours. Once the prisoner has been "detained until indictment" by the judge, he or she is usually allowed to meet with a lawyer for fifteen minutes once during the first ten days, and for fifteen minutes once again within the next ten days, and so on. Access by lawyers to their clients is controlled by the police, and lawyers are prohibited from attending interrogation sessions. What we find over and over is that a lawyer is told that his or her client doesn't want to see him or her and vice versa.'

At any one time there are around twenty-five to forty prisoners on death row, with double that number awaiting confirmation of their death sentences. A prisoner's lawyers may keep appealing the case, subject to new evidence or information. Consequently, given the slowness of the legal system, as many as a fifth of all death-row inmates will have been there for over twenty-five years. Since 1977, according to figures released by the Justice Ministry, there have been between one and four hangings every year, a sharp decrease from the years 1945 to 1976, which averaged seventeen hangings annually. The government's reasoning for retaining the death penalty is that it reserves the right to execute dangerous murderers when and as it sees fit. Certainly, as hangings are carried out in utmost secrecy, it is difficult to see how they could be said to act as a deterrent. Despite the release over the last few years of five innocent people who had been convicted of murder, 66 per cent of the public continues to support capital punishment. Four of the released had spent most of their adult life on death row.

As Kurata Tetsuharu, Mr Menda's lawyer, points out, it is most probable that many innocent people have been hanged: 'Not one judge who had brought in a wrong verdict has reflected on his mistake, taken responsibility and resigned from his post. In the case of Menda's trials and retrial, altogether sixty-eight judges found him, a now proven innocent man, guilty and deserving of the death penalty. If the four death-row retrial cases are taken into consideration then two hundred judges have made this almost fatal error. For over a hundred years, lawyers and intellectuals in this country have been calling for an end to the death penalty. Given my experience with the system [Kurata represented another of the four death-row inmates freed at retrial], I have to wonder how many people have died on the gallows shouting their innocence.'

Up until seven a child lives with the gods

PROVERB

Our mansion block is managed by two elderly gentlemen who have a propensity to sit nodding and smiling from behind the desk of their raised station in the lobby. In demeanour they bear an uncanny resemblance to the Muppets, Waldorf and Astoria. From the window of what has become our office in the flat, we can see the forecourt where very often Astoria spends much of his days playing with our son (having extracted him from the babysitter), jiggling him between his hands like a pocketful of change, as he points out all the passing cars. Neighbours stop and pass the time of day with Astoria, clucking and cooing at the baby. Babies and children are excessively attended to here, indulged, coddled, talked to, admonished and cooed at by everyone. You can take babies or children anywhere, even to the cinema. It is assumed they will behave, and they usually do. If they start wandering around or crying in restaurants people will immediately come to your aid, talking to older children or mugging at babies until their mood improves. Children are the responsibility of everyone, you are not expected to cope bravely alone.

Children are not normally told off or smacked by their parents until they are around six or seven, but rather controlled psychologically by softly spoken constant admonishments, some such as 'Mummy doesn't love you any more,' producing considerable emotional anguish: that love is conditional is a lesson learnt early. Everyone I know can remember the first time they were smacked and the shock of it. It had never happened before and they had no idea that as much as a raised voice would ever be directed at them. For Akira it was when he walked into the house with his shoes on, quite literally on the day of his seventh birthday. Before that when he forgot his mother had just ticked him off and gently told him to remove his shoes. This time she smacked him, hard. 'I never forgot to take off my shoes again,' he said.

Mothers are constantly attending to their children in a way that would be considered neurotic in the West. Dependency on the mother is actively encouraged; independence discouraged. As a result Japanese children are much more docile than their Western counterparts. The playgrounds are fields of relative serenity, full of tidy children with clean overalls on top of their clothes, playing quietly with each other. There is little noise and hardly any fighting. Children stick close to their mothers, who keep up a constant banter, instructing them how to fill the bucket with sand, how to dig a hole, and how to sit while doing both.

For *gaijin* babies and infants, especially those with blue eyes and blond fuzz on their heads, life in Japan is paradisiacal. They are constantly the centre of rapt attention, so much so that by the time our son was eight months old and we went into a restaurant, he would actually shout if no one noticed his entrance. As has been carefully explained to me by many people, the Japanese like *gaijin* children so much 'because they are like dolls'. The idea that Westerners think the same about Japanese children invariably comes as somewhat of a surprise to these elucidators of the culture.

Astoria always rushes at you as if someone has shouted 'fire'. Both Waldorf and he run about like this in a permanent state of panic. They were both once *sarariman*, who retired at fifty-five. Twenty-five per cent of all retirees work, and it is quite common for former corporate warriors to take up jobs as caretakers, car park attendants and apartment house managers. I can never imagine Waldorf or Astoria as tight-faced *sarariman*. There is something too feminine about them which a blue suit of armour would have had to work hard to dispel. I asked them once whether they had enjoyed their previous jobs. They replied, simultaneously, that they had worked for a good company. I asked them if they had enjoyed the work itself. They looked puzzled and searched each other's faces for clues as to what this ignorant foreigner was trying to find out. Although there is considerable job snobbery in Japan, working for a good company – even as the gatekeeper – confers status, and there is no shame in doing manual work after you retire. As Waldorf and Astoria say, it is better than being at home. Wives, who have seen little of their husbands during their working life, are not well disposed to having them underfoot. Retired husbands who hang around the house all day are called *sodai gomi* (giant rubbish), the name for a broken stove or other difficult-to-dispose-of junk.

You could sit at home for a long time after retirement. The Japanese are the longest lived people in the world: a man, on average, can expect to live until just over seventy-six; a woman until she is eighty-two and a half, figures that despite the stress and bad habits continue to increase slightly year by year. The country is greying fast: by the year 2025, a quarter of the population will be over sixty-five, eligible to be honoured on Respect for the Aged Day in September, a public holiday and a tradition of recent vintage.

Astoria is excited, they have taught the baby a new trick. Waldorf clasps his hands together, holding them by his chin, beaming and rocking back and forth on his heels like a poodle trainer. They line the baby up behind his wagon. He pushes it off, marching with solid unbending legs from one end of the lobby to the other. When he reaches the far wall, he picks up the cart, pivots around, slams it down and marches back towards us. Waldorf claps and laughs. He is tall and thin, and sways like a bendy doll. Astoria is small and pudgy but his movements are jerky. '*Kawaii desu ne!*' he says (Isn't he sweet? or 'cute', as it is usually translated – English in Japan is American-English), the phrase always employed around babies and children. The words won't let you alone when you are with a baby or child, they flit down the street after you like a flock of technicolor birds in a Disney cartoon, twittering in your ear at bus stops and traffic lights.

Opposite our mansion block is a steep hill at the bottom of which is the nearest supermarket, a small noisy affair full of electronic announcements and perfectly formed fruit. As in most shops bigger than 'mom and pop stores' but smaller than the upmarket *depato* (both of which have people to welcome you), your foot sets off an electronic welcome message lurking under the rubber mat: 'Welcome, thank you very much for your custom,' it says, in a preternaturally high squeak, as every shoe, boot and *geta* stumbles over its tripping mechanism. The green apples are a uniform lime-green, four to a plastic-wrapped packet, all exactly the same big size. They are shaped like peppers. The red apples, two to a plastic-encased packet, are vermilion, bigger than croquet balls and, again, each one exactly the same size and shape – a tribute, you fear, to the agrichemical industry as much as tender loving care. Even the loose, supposedly less perfect, apples are unblemished. They look as if they are made of fine bone china; you can see your face in their flawless sheen.

Along one side of our neighbourhood streets are waist-high metal fences separating us from the traffic. One day when I came out of our flat a blue Mini roared up the hill, stopped, and then shot across the road and crashed into one of these metal barriers. The driver got out, looking perplexed. He walked off up the road in the general direction of Roppongi. The seats of the Mini were covered in the Burberry pattern. There was a cap in the back window, checked like the sort favoured by British yuppies playing at country squire. When I came home later that day the Mini was still there, its nose buried into the now bowed metal fence, its body at a rakish angle. I have no idea why or how the car crashed into the fence. The driver had stopped at the top of the hill, there was no traffic coming, he just seemed to drive at the barrier as if he thought it might get out of the way.

There are a lot of seemingly avoidable accidents here. Once I was sitting in a taxi at a crossroads when a car very slowly drove towards us. I looked at the driver. He was staring intently at the taxi as he drove straight into the back door. The taxi driver sighed and got out of the cab. The car driver was already out of his vehicle. Both men looked at each other. No one said anything. The passenger cannot open or shut the back door of a Japanese taxi, the driver does this from a mechanism in the front. As a result, to get out of the cab I either had to clamber over the front seat and leave by the driver's open door or wait for what promised to be an aeon as they sorted things out.

Outside I found the taxi driver and the other man inspecting the point of contact in silence. They appeared confused, as if they had no idea what to do, as if this was something they had never been drilled for. The taxi shouldn't have been in the box, he had got trapped there because he had misjudged the speed of the traffic in front of him. Cars are not supposed to be in the box. The other driver knows this. This breaking of the rules flummoxes him. He expects the taxi to move although it cannot because the light is against it. He goes on expecting this as he drives into the taxi.

Expecting something to happen because it should, and not being able to react when it doesn't, is also what appeared to have happened to the two delivery boys I saw biking towards each other on a more or less empty pavement; both were carrying a tower of sushi bowls. One bike went past me, the other was coming towards me. The boy coming towards me was looking straight at the other boy, not aggressively, or with any sort of bravado, he was just looking at him. Neither boy changed his path one iota, as if each expected the other would do so. They drove into one another, head on, swerving right at the last minute so that their bodies collided, but they managed to maintain a wobbly balance, right themselves and carry on without stopping. Neither said a word. As they went off both were looking around at the other, their faces full of bewilderment, as if the world as they had known it was no longer so.

At the end of our street was a series of old wooden shops, one selling food, one selling futon and floor cushions and one selling stationary. The lovely old futon shop has gone now, ripped out like a bad tooth in less than a day. To watch Japanese construction workers in action is like watching one of those game shows where the contestants have to build or destroy something in the shortest possible time. Dozens of these men, seemingly chosen for their small wiry physiques, swarmed all over the futon shop, ripping out the frame sometimes with their bare hands, balancing on the wooden structure like parrots, gripping hold of it with their feet encased in cloth boots. The boots, worn by all construction workers, are split at the toe and have some sort of super-grip sole in which you half expect them to be able to walk up the wall, like Spiderman. Sometimes you see these men quietly eating an *obento*, precariously perched on a wooden cross bar, but mostly all you see them doing is working at this frantic pace as if the city had been reduced to ashes once again and needed to be rebuilt quickly from scratch.

The futon shop was as instantaneously replaced by a chrome and glass dress shop. You can be too rich and too thin. Money of the Japanese magnitude makes everything the same. It sets and defines the taste. An everywhere and nowhere aesthetic: lots of mirrors, lots of glass, lots of chrome equals sleek; a white hole lacking atmosphere and presence to slip and slide over. The futon shop was dark, too peasanty to survive this yearning for chic blankness. It was lined with creaky old wooden shelves stuffed full of the paraphernalia of sleep: futon, duvet, under duvet, big long pillows, the thick pads that go between you and the futon. The floor cushions sat in alarmingly unbalanced heaps in the middle of the shop. An old lady and her son owned and ran the business. Winter and summer she sat in the back by a paraffin stove of the old type with three bent legs. She too must have been very old. Her face was like a screwed up five-pound note, her mouth was toothless. When she died her son sold out. If they owned the land on which the tiny shop sat he would have become a millionaire in anyone's money. But perhaps he had to sell; it is often the only way to pay off the inheritance taxes. I felt sad when they tore down the futon shop in such unseemly haste, not only because I loved the old wooden interior and the haphazard piles of bedding, but because of the old woman. She was always so relaxed and happy, full of sly humorous comments. I missed her. Now when I looked towards where she had sat warming her hands over the stove, all I saw was myself in the mirrored wall, trudging home with ungainly gait.

Opposite the shops is a school, where at the beginning of every school year you can watch that year's crop of five-year-olds in their yellow floppy hats walking with their mothers to their first day of school. All the mothers dress in their best full kimono to signify the special nature of the occasion. Across the road from the school is an up-market *yakitori* bar, all blond wood and *shoji* screens. Outside its door a mountain of fresh salt is placed daily for purposes of purification. Along the edge of the *yakitori* is a six-inch-wide rock garden on to which pours a steady stream of water; it's a lovely sound when you can hear it early in the morning or late at night when the traffic is sleepy. At the end of the street is the main road. Across this road is a building that looks like an ordinary office block but houses the Cavern Club, a replica of the Liverpool original, in which replica Beatles sing: 'Close your eyes and I'll kiss you . . .' Close your eyes and you are sure it is them, all nasal and young and freshly minted, period music, the music of my childhood, of a Britain of bulldozers and new aspirations; a vanished Britain that, in this way, was not unlike contemporary Japan.

The feeling fades away and vanishes in some distant, boundless place

BANANA YOSHIMOTO (1964 –), KITCHEN

You can take a bus to the top of Omotesando dori, 'the 'Champs-Élysées of Tokyo' as the Tokyoites to whom their city is the 'Paris of Asia', like to call it. (That is if you can figure out which bus to take. The underground, with its clear signs and decent map, is much easier to navigate than the Byzantine bus system.) However you arrive, go to the top of Omotesando, the wide tree-lined avenue that is the main thoroughfare of exuberant rich Tokyo. It sweeps down to Yoyogi Park and the Meiji shrine and is crammed with boutiques, fast-food outlets, galleries, pop stars' apartments and trendy cafés and restaurants. At this end of the avenue is the Hanae Mori building, home of the doyenne of Japanese fashion (and wife of the real estate magnate). Madame Mori, as she is known 'even in Paris,' has her fashion emporium housed in a fashion statement, a building designed by Tange Kenzo in semi-reflective glass, all the better to see yourself in. To the young of Omotesando, Madame Mori is passé. For those who can afford it, the designers are Miyake and Kenzo. No city's inhabitants look more chic than Tokyo's. Everyone is, in one way or another, dressed to the hilt. The average unmarried woman, who still lives at home with her parents, is said to spend half her income on clothes, and it shows. No one goes out of the door looking scruffy; no one is careless about the way they look. The boys are as carefully dressed as the girls, in their baggy pants and wide jackets, outgrowths of the kimono. There is nothing frivolous about appearances. The Japanese concur with Wilde that the man who doesn't judge by appearances is a fool.

On the weekends, and especially on Sundays, there are several distinct high fashion tribes promenading up and down Omotesando, checking their image in Madame Mori's window. Depending on current fashion you may see teenagers – looking as if they have been drawn by a cartoonist – with their little girl short skirts over knee socks, thick-soled shoes, American baseball jackets and hair in bunches; the twenty-something Sloane Rangers; the almost-and-just-twenty-something fashion victims in micro minis and macro hair; and the indeterminately aged renegades, the beautifully scrubbed kids carefully dressed up as postcard-perfect punks, with their gleaming safety pins, tidily ripped tartan pants and variegate hair.

There is a bar just off of Omotesando in the *ura dori* of Jingumae called O God! where many of these punks and their older brothers and sisters, the cord-clad members of the intelligentsia, like to congregate, read *manga* and watch old movies about extra-terrestrials. O God! is a 'movie bar' where they show all sorts of films you've never heard of and some you have but would never have paid to see. The bar itself is very studenty with wooden chipped chairs and tables, and is very dark, 'funky' as it might have been called in another time and place. The clientele and the atmosphere are an antidote to the relentless niceness of the area, and when we lived here we went there often to watch the kids try on attitude. Our yellow-haired waiter was choked with wonder over London, a city to him full of double-decker buses, punks and Dickensian backstreets. He'd read *Alice in Wonderland* and the Pooh books. He still loved the long defunct Sex Pistols and could do a perfect imitation, although he could not speak much English and had no idea what the lyrics were about. He thought England weird and wonderful beyond his wildest films; he couldn't wait to get there.

The *ura dori* off Omotesando are crooked and at times hilly, fairy-tale streets lined with tiny houses that are surrounded by high walls. Traditional Japanese houses with their dainty windows shrouded by *shoji* are dark inside. Light and air have always been kept at bay. This has as much to do with a climate of searing winters and sweltering summers that afflicts most of the country, as with the turned-in, private world aesthetic publicly exemplified in bars and restaurants. At night the *ura dori* glimmer in the moonlight like a stage set. Behind the high brick walls you can see the rolled up tops of the houses, one after the other.

On either side of a children's playground that doubles as a pedestrian thoroughfare are flats – corporate flats from the look of them – like army barracks or better kept council flats. Up until just before Tomo was born Akira and Junko lived in one of these company dormitories, as they are known. Akira had lived there first as a single man. The section of the flats for single *sarariman* have a cut-price cafeteria attached. When they married, in order to be able to save for their own flat, Junko and Akira moved into the 'barracks' as she puts it. The married quarters are cheaper than a comparable flat would be. As Junko worked she was 'thankfully out of the circles'. The circles are formed by the wives of higher ranking *sarariman* who invite the other wives to join them for *chanoyu*, lunch, English classes, cooking classes or whatever. Refusing to join such circles damages a husband's chance of promotion and many wives' participation is less than willing. Most *sarariman* manage to get out of the company flats by the time they are forty, even if they cannot afford to buy a place. To stay in these quarters after you are forty is really not done and many *sarariman* in this position will rent commercially to avoid it.

Akira and Junko knew that they had to get out before Tomo was born as Junko intended to go back to work. The pressures on them for her to stay at home and join a circle would have been too great to resist. Should they have resisted, in all probability Akira would not have been promoted.

These flats are exposed to public view, separated from the playground by pieces of chicken wire. The *shoji* on some of the windows are open. Inside one of the rooms the walls are covered with shelves packed full of knick-knacks: china animals, cats and dogs mostly, the usual display. The furniture is crammed into the tiny space: a red sofa nestles against a big Formica table with a television on top blaring out a game show. Two children, a boy and a girl, sit in front of the television, their heads bent over piles of textbooks, scribbling furiously. Their mother, who in her expensive blue dress is at odds with the room, stands with her arms folded, looking down at them. She glances at her watch and says something then edges sideways out of the room. The children nod their heads but they do not look up. The boy's hair is cropped close to his head, the girl's sits on her shoulders. The two don't speak to each other. He is about ten and she is about twelve. She turns and looks out of the window, her eyes cool and still, her face flat, without emotion. Her mind is lost in her books.

Further on there are houses again. Through the gaps in the gates you can see miniature gardens made up of a bush or two, a few flowers and sometimes a small tree. Like the British, the Japanese prefer houses to flats. Before the city was rebuilt in the twenties after the earthquake, there were no blocks of flats. Merchants and artisans were housed in subdivided row houses in the old Shitamachi, while the upper middle classes inhabited houses in the Yamanote. The low-rise Dojunkai Aoyama apartments on Omotesando dori, built in 1925, was one of the first blocks of flats specifically to house wealthy people.

At the end of Omotesando, to the right before the Meiji shrine, is Takeshita dori, the main street in Harajuku, the teenybopper heaven. Takeshita dori looks a bit like Carnaby Street does now, only with more adventurously named fashion and feeding emporiums: Itsutsu No Lemon, Romantic Game, Super Freaks, Shop My, Happy Call, Happy Again, Art Flower, Fashion in Bus Stop, Racing Queen, and Cute and Cute. Dotted among the boutiques and eateries are the fortune tellers. On the weekends, if you stand at the top of Takeshita dori looking back down the hill, you cannot see the road for the people, a swarm of heads bob towards you, a shoal of coal-black buoys. Japanese homogeneity is exaggerated by its politicians, who choose to ignore the ethnically different Hokkaidoans and Okinawans, the immigrant Koreans and Chinese, and the country's Sino, Korean, Mongolian and Polynesian origins, but to a Westerner brought up in a multinational society, Japan looks extraordinarily monoracial.

Many of these teenagers are heading to the Meiji shrine, a favourite of Tokyoites, or to Yoyogi Park which abuts it. To get to Meiji you drift up an expansive grey gravel roadway, flanked on either side by deep mute woods that fill you with a feeling of quietude, of being removed from the frazzled capital to a stiller, more collected time. This is one of the eminent shrines of Japan, and one of the most visited. On the most important festival days the roadway and grounds teem with people in full traditional dress. The sound of *zori* (wedged thronged sandals) on the gravel is quite different to that of shoes − softer, a long whispered hushing sigh.

On 15 January, Coming of Age Day, when that year's crop of twenty-year-olds are welcomed into society as adults, hundreds of thousands of young women and men shuffle towards the shrine. The women's kimonos are ornate, elaborate and expensive, blue and red mostly, vividly painted with flowers, trees and leaves − such a vehement contrast to the dark garb which continues to dominate everyday Western dress. The men wear samurai-type outfits; big wide-legged grey striped trousers, with a heavy black silk three-quarter-length coat over the top. In these clothes they swagger, swinging their legs around in wide arches, playing the part of the samurai as seen on TV and at the movies. The women wobble, totter, and shuffle, knees knocked together. Until Emperor Meiji was on the throne, kimono was loose, similar to traditional Korean female dress, something you could run and play in as Korean girls still can. There is nothing quite so uncomfortable as a modern kimono with its *obi*, thicker than a heavy drape, bound around the ribs, leaving you breathless. Modern kimono is debilitating, all artifice and distortion. The whole thing is tight, it binds the body, making it difficult to move. To sit in the traditional kneeling position on the floor for any period of time is to suffer excruciating backache; to walk is difficult, to stride impossible: the wearer is clipped, pruned, stunted and twisted into a human bonsai tree, but she looks exquisite, the embodiment of perfection.

The pathway to the shrine is as wide as a dream. The new adults drift down it, breaking like waves over the small humped bridge. The pathway leads to the past. When a Japanese dreams of the future he or she dreams of the past; the dreams are vibrant, full of meadows laden with flowers, and children in Tokugawa dress. Novels, films and stories are full of these Elysian fields, awash in the 'summer grass: where the warriors used to dream,' as Basho, the Tokugawa poet, wrote. Three hundred years after his death that summer grass still grows beneath the concrete streets of Tokyo, poking its green stubbly fingers through the cracks. The past is always with us here, but deep in the back of the mind, covered up by layers of modernism, wallpapered over with imported chic. The past is so much prettier than the present; the past is all-embracing, easy as a warm bath, an impeccable array of beautiful clothes, muttered confidences and courtly intrigue. The past doesn't shout, it whispers – like the *zori* on the gravel, it hisses and shushes, carrying you home again, rocking you at dawn. The past is an erotic dance. In the past no one is jammed on to a commuter train for two hours each way; no man is away from home eighteen hours a day; no woman atrophies over the kitchen sink, left to stretch out her days as she will, idling over the tomatoes and dreaming of romance. The past is moral, noble, full of good causes, of warriors and ladies, of gods and goddesses. The past is a once and future magic kingdom, always within sight, always slightly out of reach, like perfection itself.

Coming of Age Day is a post-war invention. No one can invent tradition as quickly as the Japanese, and no one can make it stick so fast and seem so ancient. In the Meiji era 15 January was once Women's New Year, a holiday from all the cooking and cleaning that had taken place during the big New Year celebrations. These celebrations only last until 5 January now, whereas then they lasted until 20 January, Bone New Year, so called because that was all that was left of the feasts prepared in the previous year. Then, the first dream of the New Year was thought to be prophetic, auguring good or ill for the year to come. To facilitate a good first dream, people slept with treasure boats under their pillows, paintings of sailing ships manned by the seven gods of good luck. Now first dreams float away unheeded, but everyone still comes to the shrines on New Year's Day, albeit usually in Western clobber, muffled in overcoats and scarves, crunching the gravel with their shoes and boots, and OLs return to their offices on the fifth in full kimono, momentarily turning the city back to its first days as the capital.

At the Meiji shrine on New Year's, a board on which is

painted that year's Chinese zodiac animal is hung on either side of the dark wooden structure; paintings of snakes, dragons, dogs, goats, et al. Around it is installed a huge trough to collect the money that will be thrown into it by the millions of visitors, the permanent wooden collection trough being too small for the expected quantities of donations. Granite-faced riot police stand in front of the wraparound money bins in the shape of horse troughs, their visors pulled down over their faces to stop them getting cut by misdirected coins; guarding the money, and guarding against the sort of trouble or accidents possible in such breathtakingly dense crowds. Money rains down in a broad arc, a fountain of coins from every part of the crowd, clanking and clinking, bouncing off the riot police's helmets, rattling against the money already in place, a loud jangling noise that drowns out speech. This is a metallic request for a year's worth of good luck, for blessings from the god whose rule was an accident of history.

On Sundays the main road that cuts through Yoyogi Park is closed to traffic, turned into a smorgasbord of pop culture. Every major international post-war period and style of pop music is represented: fifties rock, seventies punk rock, heavy metal, and all the styles of the sixties – from The Who to Gerry and the Pacemakers – compete for ear space along the jammed thoroughfare, a musical Speakers' Corner. Some of the kids sing through portable karaoke contraptions, but most are backed by fully equipped bands, amplified by huge speakers powered by generators. Interspersing the bands are dance teams, groups of between ten to twenty girls, identically dressed like American cheerleaders, in short pleated skirts and sweatshirts that have things like Harvard University written on them in English. Their routines are done on skates as well as feet and often involve leaping over several curled up bodies. To the sides of the main performers are the fringe acts: fat boys dressed up as white dolls, lone double bass players, and traditional drum players in karate-like costumes of white trousers and belted jackets, beating out with the flats of their hands a native music, a strong voluptuous sound from the bowels of the earth, disturbing the civilized façade with the urgency of its sweaty rhythms.

During the week the most music you will hear inside the park is a lone trumpeter or saxophonist practising under one of the pedestrian bridges, playing over and over the same melancholy few bars, serenading the small band of Tokyo's dispossessed who make Yoyogi their home. The homeless sleep under the bridges, in the long grass around the support pillars, hidden away from the even longer gaze of the law. All seem to have old Walkmans or transistor radios which they listen to while sitting on the park benches eating, with great decorum, something rescued from the rubbish bins. Some push their eclectic possessions around in diminutive supermarket trolleys. If you come here early in the morning, you will sometimes see the trolleys lined up by the drinking fountains and the homeless queuing up to wash. Afterwards they sit on the benches with their flannels over their heads, as you do when relaxing in a hot spring. Perhaps it reminds them of better times. The homeless are usually neat and clean here, much less obviously insane, and much less visible. It is quite unusual to see an unmistakably homeless person wandering around the centre of Tokyo, although the more gnarled and urine-soaked specimens squirrel themselves away in the main railway stations such as Shinjuku. If they cannot hide away in the parks or stations they are more or less confined to Sanyo, an entire district of day labourers, derelicts and alcoholics, who live in flop houses or on the streets.

All of Japan's major cities have areas such as Sanyo, secreted away, unthought of until there is trouble. These slum areas are overrun by *yakuza*-operated gambling joints, extortion schemes and semi-legitimate businesses that supply day labourers to the construction companies in which the *yakuza* syndicates have more than a passing interest. The police, some of whom are in the pay of *yakuza*, leave the gangsters to get on with their businesses unimpeded, but jump on the homeless for any minor infraction. Cameras are installed on some of the streets and monitored at the local police station, giving these ghettos the feel of the open prison they really are. Sometimes there are riots, as there were in Osaka's Airin district in the early nineties, triggered by the police breaking up a gathering on the street. The crowd had come to listen to a man condemn Akihito's *daijo sai*, a point of view the police considered not to be in the national interest.

Mr Nagano showed me Sanyo. He had lived there for a time after falling down on his luck. He had lost his job, run out of money, been forced to give up his flat and, as he had no family to help him, had ended up in Sanyo. I met Mr Nagano at the Asahi Beer Hall, which sadly no longer exists, or rather has been replaced: the new Asahi Beer Hall, built by Philippe Starck, is another pleasure dome for the young and wealthy, complete with Olympic flame windows and illuminated steps. A gaudy bauble in the midst of Asakusa's ramshackle streets of tiny wooden shops and down-at-heel buildings. Asahi beer is still drunk, but with French food now.

When I frequented the beer hall it was a big smoky barn of a place, dotted with hot open braziers around which you sat and cooked the raw food you had ordered. You drank beer out of long pint-and-a-half mugs and in the season you watched the sumo on television. I found it by chance, wandering along the Sumida river in the rain. The sumo was on the television. It was warm and steamy inside from the heat of the braziers and the wet clothes. The women favoured tight leopard-skin dresses and lots of candyfloss-style hair. They sat around the edges of the room at the tables without braziers, those earmarked for two and for drinking. The men they were with wore badly fitting polyester suits, in light blues and light greys. They favoured plastic white or grey shoes. The atmosphere was noisy – not the noisy of late-night drunkenness, but noisy with conversation and laughter. Many of the couples were holding hands and looking at each other, speaking volubly as if they were enjoying being together, which, with the exception of the young who are enjoying a fling before the serious business of finding a mate, is so unusual to see in a public place. Most couples do not speak much, never mind touch. And there was something else. There was no tension: not at the tables, nor at the bar, nor at the braziers. No one was sitting perpendicular, nodding an agitated assent to what someone else was saying. No one had a stiff smile painted on his or her face, and a neck visibly creaking with anxiety.

Around one brazier, half watching the sumo and half talking, sat three men. They smiled and nodded shyly when we plopped down. They wore the construction worker's one-toed cloth boots.

When their food came – a whole fish on a stick, one for each of them, and a selection of potatoes and peppers, each on a separate stick – they carefully painted them with soy sauce, using a brush and a technique that looked as if it was employed in calligraphy. They then placed the food on the square brazier in perfect formation. They watched us, heads on one side like budgies on a perch, as we attempted to do the same. A short time later one of the men put down his plate and picked up our food, turning it over. 'You have to turn it now,' he explained, 'or else it will burn and not cook in the inside.'

Mr Nagano then took over the cooking of our meal. He had once been a *yakitori* cook, he told us, repainting the food. He had been born a couple of miles away in Ueno: 'The park is famous for cherry blossoms, have you seen it?' We had and we had also seen the big outdoor market, which impressed him more as it was, to his mind, off the beaten track. The *shitamachi* was the font of Edo culture, the artistic and bawdy side of town, where the *ukiyo-e* was born. Now Kappabashi Street is where you go to buy the *purasuchiku fudo* (plastic food) that adorns almost every restaurant window: plastic pieces of sushi, plastic spaghetti bolognese, risen up from the dish in a state of rigor mortis and wrapped around the fork, plastic tempura, plastic fried eggs, doughnuts, steak, carrots, anything. Kappabashi, where you can also buy every conceivable kitchen item, is signposted on top of a building by a forty-foot chef's head, modelled on the founder of a tableware company.

On Omotesando dori some restaurants, in addition to the plastic food in their restaurant windows, put a real steaming example of their lunch or dinner *seto* (set specials) outside the door on a little table, complete with place mat, cutlery, napkin, and glass of something. Mr Nagano laughed when I told him this. He seemed to think that such an arrangement wouldn't last very long outside a restaurant around here, that someone quite sensibly would eat it.

I saw quite a lot of Mr Nagano after our first meeting. He was a regular at the Asahi, coming in for his dinner and companionship almost every evening. He took me to the *pachinko* parlour he frequented in Ueno and taught me to play. Seventy per cent of men and 30 per cent of women play *pachinko* regularly. Like Mr Nagano, they find it relaxing. The noise of hundreds of thousands of steel pinballs wildly clattering around these machines is stupefying, and to me nerve-racking. The faces of the machines with their sickly red, greens and blues, are the colours of a headache. The overhead lighting is as white as a shriek. It was not a passion I could share.

Throughout the country *pachinko* parlours adorn most shopping streets and arcades, often announcing their presence with giant pink and red plastic bouquets outside the plate-glass shop front, propped up on frames, funereal style. Inside sit rows and rows of people on red bucket seats, intently working the electronic flipper. The game is easy to learn – you just pay your money and flip the flipper. What was once a pre-electronic game of skill is now a game of luck. When you win, a landslide of tiny balls pound into the dishes. The prizes received in exchange for the balls are meagre: chocolates and cigarettes, or tins of peaches. There are sometimes kiosks next door where you can cash in these goods, often run by the *pachinko* parlour owner, a subversion of the law forbidding cash prizes for this sort of gambling.

Mr Nagano plays two or three times a week, for two or three hours each session. He tells me that the housewives are 'the most dedicated players', sometimes playing for six hours or more a day. You see them during the day, women with withered skin, macabre under the strip lighting, propping up small squealing children on their laps, blind and deaf to any want but that of the machines. It is estimated that about twelve billion pounds passes through these machines every year, making their predominately Japanese-born Korean owners very wealthy (no one really knows the true figure as the parlours are adept at hiding their revenues from the tax man).

Mr Nagano showed me the block of flats where he lived on the top floor. I could see into one of the rooms on the ground floor, a six-mat box of clutter, stuffed with porcelain animals, and serviced by a couple of gas rings. At the back of the house ran balconies, covered with futons airing in the sun. Outside many of the doors were washing machines in pastel hues, a common sight even in the ritzier parts of town, where there isn't sufficient room inside the flats for even basic gadgets. Mr Nagano told me his flat was the standard six-mat room, 'Plenty big enough for someone on their own.' Even the more up-market houses and flats to which I have been invited have tiny rooms. The Japanese gladly invite you to their house or flat for lunch, drinks, dinners or parties, if it is big enough not to cause them embarrassment. Often it isn't, and so, like Mr Nagano, they do not.

Mr Nagano left school at fourteen, the year the war ended. He had stayed in the city all through the war. His family's flat had burned to the ground and he and his mother were rehoused, 'up in the Yamanote' in an upper-middle-class house, the likes of which he had never seen before. It was policy for wealthy Tokyo families to open their homes, free of charge, to those made homeless by the bombing. Although the way the middle and upper middle class lived was fairly modest by today's standards, to the city's poor it was unbelievable. Seeing that the sacrifices of some were greater than those of others, many 'went crazy and began looting and rioting in the streets'. Not Mr Nagano and his mother, however, although they were removed from the house they were billeted in, along with the rebellious dispossessed. The government had by then requisitioned schools and temples and public buildings in which to rehouse them.

Tokyo, like everywhere, was made mostly of wood. No more than 8, maybe 10, per cent of the structures were built of less flammable materials. Fire lanes to stop the spread of the fires were not constructed until after the first series of firebombings in March 1945. There were no air-raid shelters because the government decreed that Japan would never be bombed. Tokyoites could not shelter in the underground because, unlike the one in London, it was too shallow. Mr Nagano saw people on fire jumping into the Sumida river. Thousands of corpses were washed up on the banks of that river the mornings after the firebombings. In one night over 100,000 people were burnt to death, over a quarter of a million houses were destroyed and a million people made homeless.

Mr Nagano's two older brothers and his father were killed in combat. He sought such work as he could to help his mother, finally finding a job he enjoyed in a *yakitori* bar where he stayed until the bar closed in the mid-eighties. The owner sold it to a developer because he had racked up debts: gambling debts from playing *mahjong*, debts on the horses, entertainment debts from the swank night-clubs where he took his mistress, shop debts from the clothes he bought them both to wear, school debts from his children's education, mortgage debts on his extravagant house.

Mr Nagano's litany of this man's debt-ridden life was amused and admiring. He spoke of his former boss as one who 'knows how to live,' his voice brimming with warmth and affection for this man who had, after all, been the source of his downfall. Mr Nagano sees in his boss what he would have liked to have been. He thinks of himself as a person who doesn't know how to live. He never married. 'Women of my generation wanted something better, someone with more prospects,' he says without any obvious bitterness. His sadness comes through, though, when he talks about not having had children, of being cut out of the continuity of life. 'When I die there will be no one to tend my grave,' he tells me, and no one to tend his family's grave either. At the time he lost his job his mother was dying: 'It was convenient because I could look after her full-time.' But it made him despondent. It wasn't just the loss of his mother but the sudden awareness that his own life had been lost too, that it had failed to thrive. He knew that once she had gone he would have no one. 'I thought about dying when she did,' he says. Towards the end of his mother's life he started to look for another job, realizing that, unless he really was going to kill himself, he needed to earn money, and quickly. He was in his early fifties and thought it would be easy enough to get another job in a *yakitori* bar. It wasn't, and he didn't. He doesn't know why: 'Perhaps I didn't try hard enough . . .' By the time his mother died, the only money he had left was to pay for the funeral. He could no longer cover the rent and was evicted from the flat he had lived in since he was sixteen. 'That's how I ended up in construction,' he told me, leaving Sanyo unspoken.

After I had known him for a while he took me to Sanyo to visit an old friend of his, a Christian missionary. A slum is a slum the world over. This one isn't particularly dangerous, just depressing. The decaying buildings and filthy streets, the acrid smell of urine and cheap booze, the sight of all these hopeless people –

many of them drunk, others not quite sane, more in despair – brought Mr Nagano to tears before we even reached his friend's house, which functioned as a drop-in centre. Mr Nagano had brought him a present, something he has done every year on the anniversary of the day he left Sanyo to move into his little room in Ueno. The missionary looked overburdened. He was less interested in his gift than in telling Mr Nagano how sorry he was that he had 'not saved him'. He told him that he regarded this as a personal failure. Mr Nagano sat on the chair examining the floor, nodding and agreeing, saying, '*Hai, hai, hai, wakarimashita, wakarimashita.*' The missionary went on to harangue him about God and 'Christ the one true saviour,' as irritating with his righteous certainties as a speck of grit in the eye.

Afterwards, Mr Nagano, usually so chatty, was quiet as we walked around the streets. There was something about the Christian message that he found inimical to his way of thinking, something he was unable to put into words. He couldn't get to grips with this idea of being saved by someone, even the Son of God. Buddha doesn't save you, enlightenment does. The emperor doesn't save you, the emperor embodies you as a Japanese; the emperor is a god, you die to save the emperor. Mr Nagano doesn't especially embrace either Buddhism or Shintoism but understands their beliefs in a way you can only if you are brought up with something: corporeally, as a given.

I watched him looking at the faces that surrounded us, looking into the sunken eyes that stopped before they got started. He wanted to go to Kannon temple in Asakusa. He wanted to forget this place. After a while we reached Nakamise dori, the street leading to Kannon temple, the downtown version of Omotesando. Here in the tiny quaint shops you can buy things you cannot buy elsewhere in Tokyo: a geisha lip brush, for instance, a special tool with which to achieve the precise rosebud mouth. Nakamise is stuffed with such specialist shops selling the trappings of the old way of life: seaweed shops, spice shops, kimono shops, kimono accessory shops, rice cracker shops, bean-paste sweet shops, shops selling hundreds of different kinds of hair ornament, fans, folk art, wooden toys, etc. After Sanyo, this is what Mr Nagano wanted to see, to take time to explain, these lovely precise things that have come out of his country, these touchstones which make him feel connected, backwards and forwards, side to side, the physical manifestations of his culture.

We went into Kannon's grounds, which were full of the sickly smell of incense emanating from a pyre in front of the temple. Mr Nagano lit another stick, and, as everyone was doing, waved his hands through the smoke it released into the air. He stood before the temple, clapped his hands, summoning Kannon, the Buddhist goddess of mercy. He stood there for a long time, holding his hands together, his head bowed. He believes that when you die you become an ancestor, a spirit, and it worries him greatly that he has no descendants to visit, no descendants who will care for him, look after his memory and tend his grave, no descendants who will honour him. He feels that he will, in effect, become homeless again, condemned to wander around the spirit world's equivalent of Sanyo, cast out, unwanted by, and unconnected to, the Japanese race.

EPILOGUE

EPILOGUE

'What shuts you out, shuts us in.'

Unwanted by, and unconnected to, the Japanese race: a horrible prospect for the average Japanese. More than any other first-world country, Japan can still claim to be a nation state, with one language, one culture, made up, for all intents and purposes, of one race. The Ainu, with their Caucasian and Asian antecedents, were long since quelled, pushed back into Hokkaido in the ninth century; and the descendants of the Korean and Chinese forced labourers (who comprise less than 0.1 per cent of the population) blend racially, if not socially, into the country's ancient melting pot of the Chinese, Korean, Mongolian and Polynesian peoples that all make up the modern Japanese race.

Yet Japan, a country 99.9 per cent Japanese, is peculiarly uncertain about its nationhood. From the prestigious institute in Kyoto, whose sole function is to define Japaneseness, to the re-education institutions that have sprung up to help reintegrate the so-called returnees, the Japanese are positively neurotic about what makes them *them*. They are terrified of being changed or polluted by outsiders. As a matter of policy Japan does not accept immigrants, except in a very special 'case-by-case' way that involves only a small number of people.

During periods of acute labour shortages Japan will, to a certain extent, turn a blind eye to illegal third-world labour. When Japanese sex tours of Asia were roundly condemned (by Japanese feminists as well as the Asian recipients of the more boorish examples of Japanese manhood), an equally blind eye was turned towards the influx of Asian prostitutes brought in by the *yakuza* to service the home-based sex industry. But the number of illegal workers is kept at between 200,000 and 300,000. The laws that they are allowed to circumvent temporarily are draconian, and illegal workers are periodically rounded up and deported.

In 1990, in an attempt to get around its labour shortage, while not polluting its racial pool, the government passed a law that specifically allowed people of Japanese descent three-year work visas. These children and grandchildren of Japanese emigrants mostly come from Brazil, which has over a million ethnic Japanese, the biggest number outside of Japan. Being culturally Brazilian, their reviews of Japan are decidedly mixed. Not being 'proper Japanese' they, like Japanese-Americans and other hyphenated ethnic Japanese, are not a fit; finally, they too are outside people.

Foreigners and returnees are, on one level, a threat to the flimsy sense of Japanese racial identity; but most importantly they are, as they were in the sixteenth century, a threat to social control, to the continuance of the established ruling élites. Outsiders, and those tainted by the outside world, do not automatically adhere to the rote-taught codes of conduct and behaviour that ensure the continuance of the status quo. As we have seen, children are constantly tutored in the art of being a 'good Japanese', something that clearly does not come easily or naturally.

Like the distrust of outsiders, censorship is broad and deep in Japan; as an instrument of social control it has a long history. Writers, historians and scholars routinely have their work censored. Imported books are translated without their 'subversive' ideas. Even a book of harmless pop feminism such as *The Cinderella Complex* was censored during translation to remove any destabilizing alien notions of women's equality. What is and is not acceptable thought is so ingrained that most censorship is carried out unthinkingly without constant intervention by the government. Routinely, publishers will not include or translate ideas that are counter to the prevailing orthodoxy.

A British photographer who has lived and worked successfully in Japan for many years found herself up all night with the publishers of one of her books fighting to retain some of the captions and biographies of Japanese personalities that the publishers had altered. This included one innocuous caption I had written about Doi Takako, the socialist leader. While the photo was being taken, Ms Doi was telling her audience that Hirohito should bear responsibility for the war, a fact I included in the caption. Although by the time the book was put together the content of Ms Doi's speech, and the subsequent death threats against her, were a matter of public knowledge, the publishers did not want this in print. My friend won her battle to keep the book as it had been written, something that would have been much more difficult had she been Japanese.

Like the Tokugawa prohibition that forbade the Japanese to leave Japan, as well as foreigners to enter it, the government assiduously tries to control what the world reads and thinks about Japan, and expects its citizens to follow suit. The lawyers who attracted international attention by bringing to the UN a case of human rights abuse against Japan for its treatment of prisoners were threatened by government officials because by airing the country's problems in public they had brought 'shame on Japan'.

A Japanese colleague, who was about to take a job in Japan on one of the British dailies, was approached by officials from the Japanese embassy in London and told that as a good Japanese it was expected that they would be loyal to Japan and not write the sort of disparaging reports currently being written by the British correspondent. This person (who as a student in Britain was a member of the Young Conservatives, and hardly a radical) was then informed that the embassy was well aware of what he had been doing while resident in Britain. 'In a way that was menacing, because they knew everything about me. They made it clear I had been carefully watched.' This sort of thing, like the death threats from the *uyoku*, is simply part of the fabric of Japanese life; part of the way of keeping control.

So accustomed are Japanese officials to behaving in this way that they unthinkingly apply similar strong-arm tactics on foreigners who are seen as being critical. Catherine Muzik, an American marine biologist working in Japan, was told by the Japanese delegation at a meeting of the International Union for Conservation of Nature (IUCN), 'If you want to come back to Okinawa to teach you will withdraw that resolution.' The resolution was one that called for a halt to the destruction of Shiraho, an eight-thousand-year-old blue coral reef in Okinawa that had been chosen as the site for a proposed airport. Subsequently, having failed to convince her colleagues in Japan, and the then Crown

Prince Akihito (himself a marine biologist) to help save the reef, Professor Muzik brought the matter to the attention of the next IUCN meeting. (Professor Muzik says that Akihito's response to her face-to-face plea for the reef was *shikatta ga nai*, what can you do?)

What can you do when you are taught that change is undesirable, unJapanese and impossible? You can, as we have seen, become an extremist, or you can, like Professor Ienaga and countless other rebels, give your life to a cause you are certain to lose. But when confronted by the ineffable, the most common response is to blame the outside world. In the late eighties a curious event occurred in Japan: a gaggle of anti-Semitic books became bestsellers. At lunches, cocktail parties, meetings and dinners, it suddenly seemed that everyone, including top bureaucrats, had uncovered the existence of a 'Jewish plot to destroy Japan'. These books are still widely read and some of their authors, most notably Uno Masami, have become veritable factories, producing one or two anti-Jewish volumes every year. Mr Uno and his fellow authors are not members of a lunatic fringe but mainstream players; people such as Fujita Den, the flamboyant half owner of Makudonarudo (the American parent company owns the other half) and Eizaburo Saito, an LDP MP.

Most Japanese have never met a Jewish person; nor would they know if they had. There are no Japanese Jews. At any one time there are only about two hundred Jewish families in Japan, mostly American expatriates on a tour of duty in Tokyo. However, there has always been a fascination and, to a certain extent, an identification with the Jews, defined as an oppressed people who have achieved a great deal through intellectual and cultural superiority. This is how the Japanese often see themselves, as a tribe – despised and cast out because of their intellectual and cultural superiority.

Books about Jews have always been popular in modern Japan. In the early nineties over one hundred new books with Jewish themes were published yearly, adding to the hundreds already on sale. Most are about the culture and history of the Jews. The anti-Semitic tracts account for only some twenty to thirty of these books, but their influence, and the respect accorded to them and their authors, has made their message pervasive.

It seems that the public cannot get enough. Uno, like many of the other authors, is a fixture on the lecture circuit. Yet the contents of these books are as similar as their titles: Uno's *The World with an Understanding of Jewish Power: A Script for the Ultimate Economic War in the 1990s*; *Japan with an Understanding of Jewish Power* or *Understand the Jews and the Epoch Comes Into View* are really one book which trots out the same themes and theories, echoed by other apparently disparate authors such as well-known psychoanalyst Kawajiri Toru in *Scenario for Annihilation*, or Yamakage Motohisa in *The Jewish Plan to Conquer the World*.

'America is a Jewish nation and American Jews have begun a targeted bashing of Japan . . .' as Uno writes, so write the others. In most of these books there is the 'Jewish power' which 'controls the US' in every conceivable field; and Japan's current economic problems were 'designed by this secret power'. The more books that are written, the older this 'Jewish plot' becomes. Thus the Japanese reader discovers that most senior staff at GHQ during the occupation were Jewish; that the Lockheed corruption scandal was part of post-war Jewish strategy aimed at destroying the imperial government and the Japanese patriotic and racial spirit. Uno and others conclude that Japan must now confront the same 'Jewish problem that existed in Europe' before the Final Solution. Typically, the Holocaust is either denied outright or played down.

These books sell in the millions, though mainstream publishers have become coy about how successful their anti-Semitic lists are. Under pressure from the US, the Gaimusho approached the Japan Book Publishers Association to ask it to send members a copy of its statement that, in part, told publishers to be 'more sensitive' as 'the Government of Japan regrets to see that the label of "Japanese anti-Semitism" has taken root among American Jews.' The Association refused to circulate the memo, because, it said, it did not want to encourage censorship among its members.

Most of the bestsellers expend their contemporary vitriol on

American Jews. As you read one depressingly banal tome after the other it becomes clear that 'Jew' is a synonym for 'American' and 'American' a synonym for 'Western'. What these books really are is a manifestation of *bubei*, a visceral turning against the United States, and by extension the West.

This is an old story. Extreme immersion in, and absorption of, things and ways foreign has historically always been followed by a rampant xenophobia, each phase tumbling after the other down the ages in a reckless game of point and counter-point. This war against foreignness and its apparent overwhelming seductive qualities is a constant. Foreign things are brought in and frantically gobbled up in an all-consuming binge; there is no caution, no picking and choosing and shifting things around on the plate. This is as it was at its most extreme, first with the Chinese, then the Europeans a thousand years later, then with the Americans and Europeans in the nineteenth century, and, of course, today, in post-occupation Japan. Such times in the past have always been followed by abstinence, a time of revulsion against all things foreign, a time of insularity and nationalism, the edges of which are once again drawing closer to the centre today. In surveys, half of all Tokyoites say that they want no contact with foreigners whatsoever. Most are likely to get their wish. Out of a population of over 125 million, there are only a million or so classified foreigners. Three-quarters of whom are the third- and fourth-generation Japanese-born Korean and Chinese descendants of forced labourers. The number of real foreigners, the majority of whom are here for not more than five years, is several hundred thousand.

Much of the world is currently confronting the question of race, of co-existence of different races, cultures and religions within a state's borders. Not so Japan, which is operating within an updated version of Tokugawa isolationism. But it isn't averse to calling the West racist, often in highly creative table-turning. In the early nineties, after Kajiyama Seiroku, the justice minister, had incurred the wrath of Washington for comparing foreign prostitutes in Japan to American blacks moving into white neighbourhoods, forcing whites out and 'ruining the atmosphere', the Gaimusho spokesman Watanabe Taizo said, po-faced, that Congress was being racist in attacking Japan over the minister's comments: 'I hate to use the word racist,' he said, 'but . . .'

Kajiyama was hardly the first minister to spout unthinkingly a racist line. 'Since there are black people, Puerto Ricans and Mexicans in the United States, its level of knowledge and intelligence is on average far lower than the high level of knowledge and intelligence in Japan,' the then prime minister Nakasone said. He was addressing a meeting of the party faithful in the late eighties. It seems not to have occurred to him that these remarks would be reported by a Japanese journalist (foreign journalists were, as usual, kept out).

'That's not what I meant,' he said later to cries of racism from black Americans. 'What I was saying was that the US has made great achievements in the Apollo programme and SDI, but there are things the Americans have not been able to reach because of the multiple nationalities there. On the contrary, things are easier in Japan because we are a homogeneous society.'

A couple of years after Nakasone's remarks were still reverberating around Washington, Watanabe Michio, the current foreign minister and would-be prime minister, said, 'Americans use credit cards a lot. They have no savings so they go bankrupt. If Japanese go bankrupt they would think it serious enough to flee into the night or commit family suicide, but among Americans, there are a lot of blacks and so on who would think without concern – we're bankrupt, now we don't have to pay anything back.' At least Watanabe, who enjoys his reputation as a scrappy street fighter, refused to try to explain away what he meant.

Japanese politicians will learn to temper their public comments, if not their private feelings, but Japan will continue to go on its way, a nation state in an almost quaint fashion, perhaps even envied by other countries for its lack of racial division, but once again outside of the mainstream of history. As Junko told me, 'What shuts you out, shuts us in.' *Minzoku*, the word used and translated as 'people' in these speeches and conversations, also means 'nation' and 'race'. It is all of a piece in Japan, its *kokoro*: heart/soul/mind.

Chronology

The Age of the Gods	The archipelago of Japan was formed by the god Izanagi and the goddess Izanami. After Izanami descends into the Underworld, Izanagi gives birth through his nose to Amaterasu, the Sun Goddess, from whom the emperors of Japan are said to descend. Amaterasu sends her grandson Ninigi to rule over the islands.
660 BC	The ascension of the legendary first human emperor, Jimmu, Ninigi's grandson.
AD 552	First introduction of Buddhism to the Yamato court from Korea. Buddhism is the conduit through which Chinese culture was absorbed into Japan.
587	The Soga family takes controls of the Yamato court. In the convoluted power structure that prevails the Sogas are sometimes the power behind the regent, as in the case of Prince Shotoku who was regent for the reigning empress, Suiko. Suiko was put on the throne by her uncle, Soga Umako, after he had murdered the then reigning emperor, Sushun, who was his nephew. This pattern of actual rule being once, twice or thrice removed is common in Japanese history.
645	Taika *coup d'état* which destroys the Soga family. One of the leaders of the coup is Nakatomi Kamatari who will become the first of the Fujiwara clan.

NARA PERIOD (710–94)

710	Founding of Heijo, contemporary Nara, the first permanent capital, built in the style of the Chinese capital of Ch'ang-an.
712	The Kojiki, Record of Ancient Matters, the first book of the legends, is set down from an oral record.

720   The Nihongi, Chronicles of Japan, is also written down. Together, the Kojiki and the Nihongi are the seminal works of Japanese mythology and the basis of Shinto (the Way of the Gods), the native religion.

HEIAN PERIOD (794–1185)

794   The capital is moved to Heian, contemporary Kyoto.

805   Introduction of the Tendai sect by Dengyo Daishi.

806   Introduction of the Shingon sect by Kobo Daishi. Through the Tendai and Shingon sects Buddhism was spread to the ordinary Japanese people.

858   Fujiwara Yoshifusa becomes the first regent not of the Imperial Family. He ruled for a child emperor, the son of one of his daughters. This was the beginning of the Fujiwara clan's control of the court, which continued until 1868.

1002   Sei Shonagon, a lady-in-waiting to the Empress Sadako, writes *The Pillow Book*.

1020   Murasaki Shikibu writes *The Tale of Genji*, often regarded as the world's first novel. These two court ladies are now the most famous writers from a period known as the Golden Age of Japanese Literature, a literature largely created by the women of the court at Heian-kyo.

1051–62   Nine Years' War in which the Abe family was destroyed by the Minamoto clan.

1069   The Insei (rule by abdicated emperors) is established. From this date until the thirteenth century the Insei wrested back some control of the court from the Fujiwaras.

1083–7   Three Years' War. Destruction of the Kiyowara clan by the Minamoto.

1156   Hogen War. Most leading Minamoto are killed.

1159–60   Heiji War between the Minamoto and the Taira.

1180–5   Gempei War between the Minamoto and the Taira.

KAMAKURA PERIOD (1185–1333)

1189   Destruction of a branch of the Fujiwara clan.

1219   Assassination of the last of the Minamoto shogun, Sanetomo, by his nephew.

1274   First Mongol invasion.

1281   Second Mongol invasion.

YOSHINO PERIOD: THE TIME OF THE NORTHERN AND SOUTHERN COURTS (1333–92)

1333   The Emperor Go-Daigo attempts to restore imperial power and displace the shogun. The various warrior families take sides and the Hojo clan is wiped out at Kamakura. The Emperor sets himself up in a new court, called the Southern Court, in Yoshino outside of Kyoto. General Ashikaga Takauji, who had fought for the Emperor, now formed his own power base and installed a rival emperor on the throne of the so-called Northern Court in Kyoto itself. This period was one of incessant warfare.

1338   Takauji takes the title of shogun.

1392   Reunion of the Northern and Southern Courts.

ASHIKAGA PERIOD (1392–1568)

1467–77   Onin Wars. These wars, which embroiled the whole country, smashed any vestige of central control that had been put in place by the shogunate. The *daimyo*, provincial warlords, who were, militarily, a match for both shogunal and imperial power, began wars with each other that continued until the end of the Ashikaga period. Peasants during this period fought with the *daimyo*, forcing them to cancel the peasants' debts. During this time a completely feudal society emerged in Japan.

1543   The Portuguese, the first Westerners to reach Japan, land in Kyushu, bringing in their wake firearms to a country that hitherto fought its long bloody battles with swords and variations thereof. The introduction of muskets and the cannon enabled the stronger richer *daimyo* to devour their rivals at a far quicker pace.

1549 St Francis Xavier lands in Kyushu. The Jesuits begin missionary work.

PERIOD OF NATIONAL REUNIFICATION (1568—1603)

1568 Oda Nobunaga, a powerful *daimyo*, seizes the capital Kyoto and starts to take the whole of central Japan under his control.

1571 Nagasaki becomes the main port of foreign trade.

1573 Nobunaga disposes the Ashikaga shogunate.

1580 After a decade-long battle Nobunaga takes Osaka castle.

1582 Assassination of Nobunaga by one of his vassals. His most formidable general, Hideyoshi, a peasant by birth, continues the job of reunifying the country.

1587 Hideyoshi wins control over Satsuma in southern Kyushu and all of Western Japan. Christianity is outlawed.

1588 Hideyoshi's army conducts a 'sword hunt' and disarms the peasants.

1590 The *daimyo* of Eastern and Northern Japan submit to Hideyoshi. The Hojo clan is destroyed. After centuries of warfare Japan is reunited.

1592 Hideyoshi sends an army to conquer Korea. It is unsuccessful.

1597 A second invasion of Korea is attempted, but the expedition is withdrawn upon his death.

1598 Hideyoshi dies. He left his baby son to the care of his five chief vassals who were supposed to govern as a council in the child's name. One, Tokugawa Ieyasu, who Hideyoshi had given a large fief at Edo, contemporary Tokyo, takes power for himself.

TOKUGAWA PERIOD (1603—1868)

1603   Ieyasu takes the title of shogun, ushering in the period of the Tokugawa shogunate, sometimes called the Edo period.

1616   Ieyasu dies. Foreign traders are restricted to Nagasaki and Hirado. Japan is beginning to close its doors to foreigners.

1623   The English voluntarily close Hirado and leave the country.

1624   The Spanish are expelled.

1636   Japanese are forbidden to travel abroad. Those already abroad were forbidden to return. Ships large enough to sail abroad were destroyed and all further construction banned.

1637—8   Shimabara rebellion. Around twenty thousand Christian peasants were annihilated after they had taken over Shimabara castle in Kyushu to protest against religious persecution and the poverty of the peasants. Christianity went underground from this point but peasant rebellions continued apace throughout the Tokugawa period.

1639   The Portuguese are expelled leaving only a small contingent of Dutch traders now confined to Deshima, a tiny island in Nagasaki. Some trade with the Chinese also continued. These traders were prohibited from any contact whatsoever with the native population.

1853   Arrival of Commodore Matthew C. Perry and the US 'Black-ships'. This was the beginning of the end of Japan's isolation. Threatened by the technical and military superiority of the West, the Japanese saw that they had little choice but to allow foreign contacts once again.

MEIJI ERA (1868—1912)

1868   After an uprising by some samurai and lesser court nobles there is a short civil war that restores the emperor's power as an absolute and divine ruler. Mutsuhito, fourteen years old, is put on the throne. The palace is relocated from Kyoto to the shogun's palace in Edo, now renamed Tokyo.

1871   The seven-tiered caste system is abandoned.

1873   The Gregorian calendar is adopted as part of the general 'Westernization' that is occurring.

1876   The right of samurai to wear swords is revoked. This is followed by samurai uprisings around the country.

1894—5   Sino-Japanese war.

1902   Anglo-Japanese Alliance is signed.

1904—5   Russo-Japanese war.

TAISHO ERA (1912—26)

1912   Mutsuhito dies. In the imperial tradition he is posthumously known after his era as Meiji. He is succeeded by his son Yoshihito, who is mentally deranged.

1914   Japan, operating under the guise of Britain's ally, declares war on Germany and proceeds to take that country's Asian domains.

1918   Hunger produces rice riots. The riots, involving 'mobs' a million strong, sweep the country.

1921   Crown Prince Hirohito tours Europe. On 25 November, a month after his return, he becomes regent, taking the reigns of power from Yoshihito, his increasingly mentally incapacitated father.

1923   The Great Kanto Earthquake destroys much of Tokyo and Yokohama.

SHOWA ERA (1926—89)

1926   With Emperor Taisho's death Hirohito ascends the throne.

1928   Mass arrests of communists and other dissidents begin. Three proletarian parties are outlawed. First general election under universal manhood suffrage.

1931	Manchurian Incident. Japanese Imperial troops stage a sabotage attack in Manchurian as an excuse for invasion. Manchuria is deemed to be 'separated' from China.
1932	The Japanese state of Manchuko is set up under the puppet rule of China's last emperor. At home the Japanese public is swept up in nationalistic euphoria at the colonization of Manchuko, a 'country' much bigger than Japan.
1940	Tripartite Alliance with Germany and Italy is signed.
1941	Japan attacks Pearl Harbor. The Pacific War begins.
1945	Japan surrenders. The American occupation begins.
1946	Hirohito is forced to take to the radio to deny his divinity.
1947	The Americans outlaw an impending general strike. The American-writ constitution comes into force. Japanese women are given the right to vote.
1952	The occupation ends.
1971	The government begins to reclaim land from the farmers for the building of Narita airport outside of Tokyo.
1978	Narita airport opens. Fourteen Class-A war criminals are enshrined at Yasukuni in Tokyo.
1988	Recruit shares-for-favours scandal breaks, implicating the then present and former prime ministers as well as cabinet ministers. Hirohito falls ill.

HEISEI ERA (1989 –)

1989	Hirohito dies and Akihito ascends the throne. Takeshita Noboru, the prime minister, is forced to resign over the Recuit scandal. The LDP loses its majority in the upper house.
1990	Emperor Akihito is enthroned. Ten days later the *daijo sai*, a private ceremony during which Akihito becomes a living god, takes place at the palace in Tokyo.

1990—1 The Tokyo stock market begins a serious decline, losing half its value from the 1989 peak in the Heisei crash. Despite prior predictions from some Western economists that Japan would start the next world-wide crash, the Heisei crash has little effect on the London and New York exchanges. It remains to be seen how or if it will affect Japan as an economic world power.

1991 After much public angst and shenanigans in parliament, Japan's ruling party manages to get approval for monies to support the publicly despised Gulf War.

1992 The ruling party forces through a bill (at the behest of the Americans) which will allow Japanese troops to be sent abroad, albeit only in a peace-keeping function, for the first time since the Second World War.

Glossary

abunai	'dangerous'
Ainu	Indigenous peoples of Hokkaido, Japan's most northerly island. They are racially different from other Japanese, having both European and Asian antecedents
akusha	mourning marquee
Amaterasu	The Sun Goddess, the premier Shinto deity
ando	'relief that difficulties have been triumphed over'
banzai	'May you live ten thousand years!' The salutation to the emperor, which was also the battle cry during the Second World War
besuboru	baseball
bishonen	beautiful androgynous young heroes
Boei-cho	Defence Agency
bonsai	miniature potted tree
boomu	'boom/fashion/fad'
bosozoku	teenage motorcycle gangs whence the *yakuza* recruit their apprentices
bubei	contempt for America
bujutsu	martial arts
burakumin	'hamlet people' – Japan's untouchables, descendants of the *eta*. They are relegated to 'unclean' professions such as butchering and undertaking
burikko	'pretending to be children' – adult women who act like pubescent girls
bushi	samurai
bushido	'The Way of the Warrior'. The samurai code of ethics, sometimes dubbed 'the road to death'
chanoyu	the tea ceremony
chikan	'foolish men' – gropers and molesters
chugen	mid-year gift-giving season
Chukuka ha	The Middle Core Faction. A terrorist group which grew out of a 1960s Marxist-Leninist cell
chuo	'centre/middle/heart' – almost every city and town has a *chuo* street

daijo sai	The Great New Food Festival, the ceremony in which the newly consecrated emperor becomes a god
daimyo	provincial warlord
depato	department stores
dohyo	sumo wrestling ring
Eikoku	England, literally 'civilized country'
enka	sentimental popular ballad
eta	'the filth', the second lowest class of people in the Tokugawa period. They were relegated to 'unclean' professions such as butchering and undertaking. Their descendants, who still suffer from discrimination, are euphemistically known as *burakumin*, 'hamlet people'
Fuji-san	the reverential name for Mount Fuji
furusato	hometown
gaijin	foreigner, literally an 'outside person'
Gaimusho	Foreign Ministry
gambatte	'persevere/hold out/stand firm'
geta	traditional thronged wooden sandals with an oblong 'heel' on the front and the back
giri	webs of obligation
haisen	'defeat in the war' – this accurate phrase describing the end of the Second World War was never employed, instead *shusen* was used
hajimaki	cloth headband, usually with an inspirational phrase painted on it
hanbei	anti-Americanism
hanko	personal seal
Hantai Domei	The Farmers' League Against the New Tokyo Airport
haragei	perfect concentration, a state of being centred
Heisei	'Achievement of Universal Peace'. The name of the current imperial era
hena-jap	slang for strange Japanese person – one who is not considered a proper Japanese, often a person seen to be tainted by foreign ways
hibakusha	victims of the A-bomb
higai-sha ishiki	victim consciousness
hinkaku	noble Japanese spirit
hinin	non-humans, the lowest class of people in the Tokugawa period. The first *hinin* were convicted of taking part in a treasonous plot against the emperor
hiragana	one of the two Japanese syllabries

hondo kessen	last and decisive battle on the main island
honne	the way things really are, real intentions. That which lies behind *tatemae*
hoteru	hotel. *Hoteru* usually have a mixture of Western and Japanese rooms and styles
ijime	systematic bullying by his or her peers of a schoolchild perceived to be different
ikebana	flower arranging
ikki	popular/peasant uprisings
inanfu	'comfort women' – mostly Korean women who were forced into prostitution by the Japanese Imperial Army
Ise	central Shinto shrine
Japanist	pre-war term, still best used to describe the intellectual ultra nationalists who regard Japan as a religion and being Japanese its practice
Japlish	nonsensical English phrases used as advertising slogans or written on clothing and accessories
jieitai	troops of the so-called Self Defence Forces
jigai	ritual suicide 'allowed' for women of samurai families, the female method of *seppuku*
Jimmu	first legendary emperor
jinja	Shinto shrine
jinrikusha	rickshaw
jisshuku	self-restraint
juku	cram school
junshi	suicide at the death of one's lord
kaiseki	Japan's *haute cuisine*
kami	divinity or spirit
kamikaze	'divine wind' – the appellation given to the suicide pilots of the Second World War
kanji	Chinese ideographs
karaoke	'empty orchestra' – a sing-along machine
karyukai	Society of Flowers and Willows, in which the courtesans were the flowers, the geisha the willows
katakana	one of the two Japanese syllabries
Kawaii desu ne!	'Isn't he/she/it cute!'
keigo	ultra polite Japanese
keki	cake
keloid	distinctive scarring of welts and ridges most often seen on those who were severely burnt by the atomic bombs
kenbei	dislike of America

kikiku shijo	'returnees' – people, more usually children, who have lived abroad for periods of their lives
kirishitan	Christian
Kisha Kurabu	'press club' – organizations of specially accredited reporters attached to ministries, companies, sporting groups et al
koban	the prevalent mini police stations, resembling oversized gazebos
kohai	junior/apprentice. The socially inferior half of the *sempai–kohai* relationship, but one who is entitled to protection from the *sempai*
Kojiki	Record of Ancient Matters. The first book of the legends
kokoro	'heart/soul/mind'
kokujin	black person
kokusaika	internationalization
koseki	household register of families
kotatsu	often brightly coloured, electrically heated quilt
Kunaicho	Imperial Household Agency, an archaic and arcane bureaucracy of geriatric royal retainers, who run palace life
kurisumasu	Christmas
kuroi ame	black rain
kyaria wuman	career woman
kyoiku mama	'education mother' – a mother who aggressively pushes her child to succeed academically
LDP	Liberal Democratic Party, the English name for Japan's ruling party
Makudonarudo	McDonald's
mama-san	the chief hostess, manager or owner of a bar
mammon	funeral curtain
manga	thick comic book
mazakon	mother complex
meishi	business card
Mi tama shizume no matsuri	Pacification of the Soul ceremony
miko	Temple Maiden, a Shinto shamaness
minshuku	relatively inexpensive bed-and-breakfast style accommodation
minzoku	'people/nation/race'
mizugo	'water baby/unseeing baby' – an aborted fetus
mizuwari	whisky and water
Mombusho	Ministry of Education
mompei	baggy work trousers
muko	'over there/the other side/abroad'

natto	fermented soy beans
Nihon Shakaito	The Japan Socialist Party
Nihongi	Chronicles of Japan. The second book of the legends
Ninigi	first legendary ruler of Japan
niinamesai	Festival of New Food, a Harvest Festival type ceremony performed annually by the emperor
nokyo	farm co-operative
obaasan	'Granny' – the generic term for an old woman
obasan	'Little mother' – the generic term for middle-aged women
obento	a meal in a box, usually lunch
obi	wide, thick cloth that is wrapped around the waist when wearing kimono
Obon	Festival of the Dead
O-cha	'honourable tea'. Bitter green tea
ofuro	communal hot bath
okasan	mother
oku	depths within the house
okusama	Mrs/Madame, but literally more akin to 'her indoors'
OL	Office ladies. Clerks or secretaries, the majority of women office workers
omiai	'honourable meeting'. A formal introduction to a potential spouse
omote	surface or façade
omote dori	main thoroughfares
onnagata	actors who play female roles
osei fukko	imperial rule as it was in ancient times
oshiya	'honourable pushers-in' – workers on the underground whose job is just that
otokoyaku	actresses who play male roles
ozeki	champion sumo wrestler
poketto beru	pocket beeper
puribashi	privacy
rikishi	sumo wrestlers
romanji	Roman letters
ronin	leader-less samurai
rorikon	Lolita complex
ryokan	traditional inn
sake	rice wine
sakura	cherry blossom
samurai	warrior, a member of the old military caste
sarariman	white collar worker

seibo	end of the year gift-giving season
seiitaishogun	Commander in Chief against the Barbarians
seishin	spirit/mind/soul training
seku hara	sexual harassment
sempai	senior, mentor. Social superiors in the *sempai–kohai* relationship, but also benefactors and protectors of the *kohai*
sensei	teacher or master
seppuku	act of suicide by ritual disembowelment, which is sometimes called hara-kiri (belly slitting) in the West
Seto naikai	Inland sea
shamisen	ancient stringed instrument
shikatta ga nai	This is a recurrent phrase in Japanese conversation and is used, often with a shrug, to mean 'What could/can you do? There was nothing to be done.' The implication is that the subject under discussion – and finally everything – was or is fate
shiken jigoku	examination hell
shimbun	newspaper
shinda tsumori	imagined death
shinjinrui	'new human beings' – a somewhat derogatory term used to describe fashionable and supposedly fickle young people
shinju	'inside the heart', with the nuance of revealing the heart. A lovers' double suicide
shinkansen	sometimes called the bullet train, Japan's high-speed trains
Shinto	Way of the Gods. The native religion
shogun	military dictator. The title is derived from *seiitaishogun*
shitamachi	'Low city'. The downtown area of Tokyo
shoji	wooden screens covered, or partly covered, in white paper
Showa	'Enlightened Peace'. The name of Hirohito's era, and by which he is posthumously known in Japan
shusen	'end of the war' – the phrase always used to describe the end of the Second World War instead of the more accurate *haisen*
sodai gomi	large pieces of hard-to-dispose-of junk. What wives call retired husbands who hang around the house all day
Sonno joi!	Revere the Emperor, expel the foreign Barbarian!
soto	outside
sumo	Japanese wrestling
Susano-o	Amaterasu's brother
suki den	one of the two sacred halls built specially for the emperor's *daijo sai*
sushi	slices of raw fish served in hand-rolled wedges of cold rice
takarazienne	an actress in the *takarazuka*
takarazuka	contemporary all-female theatre
tatami	rice straw traditionally used as a floor covering

Tatenokai	Shield Society. Novelist Mishima Yukio's private army
tatemae	'face, pretence' – the way things are said to be, behind which *honne* is concealed
tenko	a seemingly real conversion that takes place under the pressure of state power
Tenno Heika	'Celestial Emperor' – the respectful way of talking about the emperor
Todai	Tokyo University
tokonoma	alcove. A fixture in all traditional inns and private rooms in elegant Japanese restaurants
tori	sacred gate of a Shinto shrine
tsukin jigoku	commuter hell
uchi	inside
ukiyo-e	paintings of the 'Floating World', the *demi-monde* of courtesans, geisha, kabuki players et al
ura	back or reverse
ura dori	backstreets
uyoku	violent ultra nationalist groups
wa	harmony
yakitori	grilled food served on a skewer
yakuza	Japan's gangster syndicate
yamanote	'High city'. The uptown area of Tokyo
yen	currency unit
yokozuna	Grand Champion sumo wrestler
yoshiwara	'Nightless City'. The old pleasure quarters of Tokyo
yukata	cotton indoor kimono
yuki den	one of the two sacred halls built specially for the emperor's *daijo sai*
Zenchu	farmers' union
zori	wedged thronged sandals